S/A50P

D1421254

TRUE BRITS

TRUE BRITS

INSIDE THE FOREIGN OFFICE

Ruth Dudley Edwards

Photographs by David Secombe

BBC BOOKS

FRONTISPIECE Receptionist at the British Embassy in Moscow

The photographs on pages 106–7, 108, 136–7, 156, 172, 178–9
are by Stephen Lambert

This book is published to accompany the
television series entitled *True Brits*
which was first broadcast in Spring 1994

Published by BBC Books,
a division of BBC Enterprises Limited,
Woodlands, 80 Wood Lane
London W12 0TT

First published 1994

© Ruth Dudley Edwards 1994

The moral right of the author has been asserted

ISBN 0 563 36955 8

Set in Baskerville by
Ace Filmsetting Ltd, Frome, Somerset
Printed in England by Clays Ltd, St Ives plc
Jacket printed by Belmont Press Ltd, Northampton

CONTENTS

To the memory of my dear friend
LIAM HOURICAN
who was taking a keen and critical interest
in this book when he died suddenly
in August 1993;
and to Pat, Michael, Emily, Bridget, Francis,
Martha and Myles Hourican in solidarity
and with much love.

PREFACE

Of all British civil service departments, the Foreign Office has the most negative public image. It is variously attacked by Parliament, the press and the British public as a secretive institution peopled by 'stuffed-shirt' diplomats who, instead of fighting for British interests abroad, are often the first to sell Britain down the river. As the *Daily Mail* put it: 'They seem to think that the Foreign Office's job is to look after foreigners.'

As diplomats are required by their trade publicly to subsume their own personalities and speak through politicians, they tend to have a distant, remote and off-putting image and to be bad at public relations. No country loves its diplomats, but British criticism of its foreign service is brutal by any standards. The purpose of this book, which accompanies the television series, is to look at what the Foreign Office actually does and consider whether the criticism it attracts is justified. I have tried to present a fair snapshot of an institution and its people at a critical time in its history.

The BBC approached the Foreign Office about making such a series in 1983, and the associate producer of the series, Roger Courtiour, and the head of documentaries, Paul Hamann, began negotiating in 1987. The Foreign Office finally agreed to give the BBC the access they wanted and filming began in 1992. This was at a time when the Foreign Office felt under attack from all sides and virtually friendless in the run-up to one of the most savage rounds of public expenditure cuts for many years. It coincided with a big increase in their workload as the Soviet Union disintegrated into fifteen separate republics, Yugoslavia fell into anarchy and the United Nations, on whose Security Council Britain and four other countries have permanent seats, was flooded with demands to sort out the new world order. The Foreign Office reached the conclusion that a television series and a book seeking to represent it fairly must be in its interests. The documentary team and I hope that we have made it possible for the people of the Foreign Office to project themselves to an audience who are curious about what diplomats really do and who have never before had access to inside information about them and the way they work.

Most of my research was done abroad – looking at diplomats in the unnatural habitats in which they spend a large part of their working life. I saw them operating in temperatures from 32F to 108F, in posts that ranged in size from a horrible hotel room in Belarus to a vast but equally horrible block in Washington. I visited homes that ranged from the grandeur of the Paris residence to standardised and claustrophobic flats in the Delhi compound. In all I went to twenty-one posts (including the delegations to the European Community, NATO and the UN) in sixteen countries: Belgium, Belarus, China, France, Hong Kong, India, Israel, Italy, Japan, Lebanon, Malaysia, Russia, Saudi Arabia, Syria, Thailand and the United States. This is not a book about the places I went to briefly and where I spent almost every waking hour with embassy staff: it is about the individuals I met and the institution for which they work.

Although the Foreign Office culture is extremely polite, and often, to an outsider, seems strangely formal, it is very open. People do not look over their shoulders when expressing opinions not held by their bosses. I cannot count the number of times whoever was in charge of my programme would say: 'You must talk to X. You will find he/she has very strong views,' and I would be taken to an angry clerk, a frustrated executive officer or an iconoclastic high flyer.

While I did offer confidentiality, almost never did anyone worry that being openly critical would have a bad effect on their career. The spectrum of opinion I came across ranged from people who want no change whatsoever to those who would virtually close the Foreign Office down and run it single-handed with a couple of fax machines. From top to bottom people were self-critical and anxious for honest criticism. 'Don't whitewash us,' said an experienced diplomat who is well on his way to the top.

'What did your friends think when you joined the Foreign Office?' I asked an extrovert, funny young clerk in Peking. 'They didn't believe me,' she said. 'As far as they're concerned, the Foreign Office wouldn't have someone like me, so I can't be in it.'

Well, she *is* in it. And so are a large number of unexpected people from unexpected backgrounds with unexpected accents. They come from Glasgow, Newcastle, Glamorgan and Antrim as well as the Home Counties and I calculate that along the way I listened to around 400 of them as well as to many diplomats from other countries.

I have tried to find out the answers to most of the questions that outsiders seem curious about, but I have to admit to virtually giving up on spies. I have absolutely no idea how many diplomats are spooks and I did not have the time to try to find out. What I do know is that most of them are not spies and they get fed up when people they meet socially assume they are. Most of them are quite busy enough without adding spying to their portfolio of responsibilities. Nor have I had the time or the space to do more than allude in passing to the British Council or the Overseas Development Administration (ODA). This is a book about the people of the Diplomatic Service and the work they do for that Service.

This book has been written for BBC Publications. The arrangement with the Foreign Office is that in exchange for open access to people and information:

The FCO would expect to have sufficient time before publication to review the manuscript for factual accuracy and sensitivity. The FCO would insist upon the exclusion of material which seriously damaged the work of the department domestically or in its relations with foreign states or would prejudice national security. The FCO for its part would undertake not to intervene for spurious or petty reasons.

When the Foreign Office saw the manuscript, the only changes they requested concerned the correction of matters of fact.

BBC Documentaries paid for part of my travels. The Foreign Office provided me with an economy ticket for the tour of the Middle East and the Far East and various members of its staff put me up when I went to locations where I had no friends to stay with. My hosts, like the members of staff I met everywhere, were considerate, hospitable and extremely open about their views of the Office.

In the course of this book I quote extensively from transcripts of BBC interviews conducted by Stephen Lambert, the series producer, with named individuals. In the case of the people I interviewed, few of them are named. People are more frank off the record and I thought it better to leave them unnamed for the sake of having their words unexpurgated.

I cannot list all the people in the Foreign Office who helped me, but I must single out Sir David Gillmore, who took the risk and gave the BBC and me whole-hearted support; Michael Horne, who organised my run-around the Middle and Far East and Glyn Davies of the Information Department, who extracted answers to my innumerable questions from all over the Office over many weeks. He was imperturbable and good-humoured throughout, even during the period where every day he received a fax with ten questions like: 'How many swimming pools and where are they?' and he was relentless in pursuit of any backsliding colleagues (of whom there were very few, for the Foreign Office is an efficient machine). Susan Grimes, his secretary, was on occasion his enthusiastic and effective stand-in. I cannot list all my hosts, but I am grateful to them all. I know I was an encumbrance and I drank their duty free.

I travelled a little and talked Foreign Office a great deal with Roger Courtiour and Stephen Lambert. Most of the time we agreed though we had our arguments at times over the text. Both of them were hugely generous with their resources and their time and to Roger, in particular, for the immense amount of intelligent work he put into turning the transcripts of filmed interviews into a usable source, I am very grateful. Though the views I express in this book are my own, I have gained a great deal from talking so much through with Roger and Stephen. I also owe thanks to Sarah Neale and Sally Francis at the BBC for innumerable favours and to Sheila Ableman and Martha Caute of BBC Enterprises.

My editor, Angela Mackworth-Young, performed miracles in reconciling differences of opinion between the BBC and me over the book and was at all times delightful to work with. My dear friend Gordon Lee, who is the unofficial editor of all my books, was as wise, supportive and loving as ever. Felicity Bryan, as befits a marvellous agent, was kind to me and tough with everyone else.

As usual, through her unremitting patience and helpfulness, Carol Scott enabled me to get an impossible job done and along with Pippa Allen and Evelyn Denyer converted yards of tape into reams of paper.

Others rendering specific help were Debbie Broxton, Paul Le Druillenec, Ronan Fanning, Michael Forbes, Kuku and Aruna Khanna, Helen Mann, Peter Moulson, Pat and Patricia O'Connor, and Jenni Russell. Liam Hourican, to whom the book is dedicated, gave me an enormous amount of help in getting to grips with Brussels.

My friends, as ever, kept me sane. Gold stars this time to Alva and Colm de Barra, Máirín Carter, Nina Clarke, Niall Crowley, Barbara Sweetman Fitzgerald, Alison

Hawkes, Neasa MacErlean, James McGuire, Jill Neville, and Una O'Donoghue and to the friend who has to remain anonymous who talked many of the issues through with me, read the text and gave me tremendous heart.

Most inconsiderately, the European Community renamed itself the European Union while I was finishing the book. Since many quotations refer to the European Community, I decided to stick with that rather than confuse everybody further. I also had to decide whether to refer to the central character as the 'Diplomatic Service', the 'Foreign and Commonwealth Office', the 'Foreign Office', the 'FO' or the 'FCO'. Internally it is known as the 'FCO', but I opted for the 'Foreign Office', as that is how it is most usually referred to publicly.

Like the Foreign Office, I am a conservative about style. So throughout this book, please assume that, where appropriate, 'he' embraces 'she'.

R.D.E. October 1993

THE BEGINNING

Minsk

The BBC was in Minsk, Belarus, looking for a suitable place to film the last of their series on the Foreign Office. I was with them, on my first expedition to watch what the Foreign Office did abroad.

There was a cautious optimism in the air. We knew that John and Heather Everard, the British chargé d'affaires and his wife, were driving across Eastern Europe towards Minsk in a car laden with Western essentials: things that they knew they would not be able to buy in their new post. John and Heather were about to become the UK's first diplomatic representatives to the new republic of Belarus. And we also knew that Cable and Wireless had transformed an old jamming station into a satellite station: swords into ploughshares 1993 style. There was to be a celebration later in the day.

The Germans, French, Americans and Italians had already established diplomatic presences in Minsk. The British were latecomers and had few resources. Whereas the Germans occupied the premises of the old East German Embassy and had fourteen staff headed by an ambassador, the British presence was to consist simply of John and Heather Everard. Heather would be trained to be what she described as 'Mrs Consular and Visa'. The Mission would be housed in a back room in the German Embassy: the Foreign Office is so short of financial and human resources that it has so far only managed to open up small missions in eight out of the fifteen new republics that emerged from the disintegration of the former Soviet Union.

The British Embassy in Moscow has been overworked for a long time trying to deal satisfactorily with the new republics instead of the old Soviet Union monolith. It is a very different job. As Sir Brian Fall, the British ambassador, explained:

In the past it was difficult to get out of Moscow because there is a huge amount that you find that you have to do in the capital city or you offend the government to which you're accredited. Some of the things are political, some of them are protocol, some of them are social, some of them are commercial, but you have to be there, and if you're not, you lose out.

ABOVE Sir Brian Fall, British ambassador to the Russian Federation,
dictating letters in his office in the Moscow Embassy.
PREVIOUS PAGES Russian guards outside the British Embassy in Moscow.

It used to be the case that 90 per cent of the working year was spent in Moscow. Since the formation of the new republics there has been great pressure on Sir Brian to visit all the new capitals – and more than once. In the first five months of 1993 he visited Armenia, Georgia and Uzbekistan three times, and Azerbaijan five times. Azerbaijan is particularly important because British Petroleum has huge interests there. Others from the Moscow Embassy who had also been making and developing contacts in the new republics included David Gowan, the commercial counsellor, and two young second secretaries – Tim Barrow, who had been rushing round the new republics at dizzying speed keeping in touch with political developments and Charlotte Harford, who had been assessing projects and identifying candidates who qualified for assistance from the British Know-How Fund (the Foreign Office's technical assistance fund for ex-Communist countries).

We had travelled down from Moscow overnight. David Gowan, a man of long experience who had served in Moscow in the bad old days, travelled with us. He speaks fluent Russian, has many Russian friends and is immensely dedicated. On arrival after an eight-hour train journey we checked in at the Belarus Hotel, where David rapidly changed his shirt before starting on a day of political and commercial appointments.

The BBC series producer, Stephen Lambert, and I went with David Gowan to the Foreign Ministry and sat on the sidelines of his meetings. The Belarus spokesman was delighted that the British chargé was on his way at last and was understanding about the financial and manpower constraints that had held things up for so long. Despite its shortage of hard currency, Belarus had found the money to appoint a chargé to London, someone whose English was good and whose diplomatic skills had been honed at Leeds University, where under the British Know-How Fund courses are held for young diplomats from Eastern Europe to teach them some of the basic skills for which there had been little call in previous years.

David Gowan proceeded on to further appointments and we went back to the hotel, where accidentally we ran into Simon Ingram-Hill and Ann Rossiter from the British Council, who had arrived five days earlier to set up an English-teaching institution: a vehicle for promoting British culture and values to a highly receptive audience. Funded by the Foreign Office, Simon and Ann were the best of their kind, idealistic yet realistic, veterans of tough postings in Africa, cheerfully living in a hideous hotel run along good old Soviet lines, where the food was unspeakable, everything was inefficient and uncomfortable and a bathroom in which simultaneously the electricity worked, the lavatory flushed and there was also soap and paper, was a cause for incredulous rejoicing.

By the time we went to the Cable and Wireless grand opening there was a heady sense of excitement and pride. In this corner of the world, judging by the enthusiastic reception David Gowan had received from the Belarussian officials, Britain seemed to matter far more than we had expected. And even though the post was being set up on a shoestring it was very much welcomed by the Government of the fledgling republic.

Cable and Wireless were celebrating their opening enthusiastically. A private jet had arrived from London bearing Dr Janet Morgan, a member of the main board, who was to be the speaker at the reception later in the evening, and a former home secretary, Kenneth Baker, was also there as a special adviser to his old Cabinet colleague Lord Young, the chairman of Cable and Wireless. Kenneth Baker and the Belarussian prime minister were to perform the opening ceremony that afternoon.

As one would expect of such an old pro, Baker carried out the job with élan, and the press and television cameras got their money's worth. The reception was devised with cultural sensitivity. The food on offer was that which is always on offer in Belarus, cold meats and orange caviar – a diet which is agreeable for the first few days, but whose monotony gets you down pretty quickly. The satellite was toasted with the only local alcoholic drinks, champagne, cognac and vodka, and the atmosphere was very cheery.

The American ambassador, on hearing that the British chargé was arriving that evening, said 'at last' and the substantial British expatriate community working at the satellite station was delighted with the news.

Towards the end of the proceedings I was in a room with perhaps ten people, most of them Cable and Wireless, mainly British but some American, when the series producer went up to Kenneth Baker and said, 'Hello, my name is Stephen Lambert. I'm from the BBC, and we're making a series about the Foreign Office.' Genially, and with an expansive gesture, Baker responded instantly with 'Oh why are you making a film about failure, when you could make it about a success like this?' It was just a knee-jerk response to the words 'Foreign Office', made, one sensed, with neither thought nor malice.

· 2 ·

PERSONAL RELATIONSHIPS

Ministers and Officials

Civil servants are accustomed to being abused by politicians, the public and the media. What hurts is to be publicly attacked or ridiculed by those who owe them loyalty – their own employers, the Government. When ministers announce cuts in the number of civil servants, they do so in the tones of triumphant rat-catchers. When Kenneth Baker, who has held one of the great offices of state, thoughtlessly denigrated the Foreign Office in a foreign country, he demonstrated graphically two things: the contemporary British passion for disparagement of its institutions and the frequent failure of ministers to realise that public servants are human beings too. Indeed, the foreign secretary, Douglas Hurd, himself an ex-diplomat, raised eyebrows at the Conservative Party Conference in October 1993 when he warned the party against being 'driven by ideology to question every function of the state, to make impossible the life of our public servants, or to depreciate the worth and quality of the different public services'.

Diplomats come off particularly badly. They are rarely popular at home, being resented for their internationalism, their perceived style of life and their suspect intimacy with foreigners. American critics dismiss them as 'cookie pushers'; the Irish laugh about their 'dining for Ireland'. Yet it is inconceivable to imagine, for instance, a retired French minister knocking the Quai d'Orsay (the French foreign service) abroad.

British diplomats, regarded by their foreign colleagues as among the best in the world, attract little loyalty from the governments they serve. Mrs Thatcher, whose guts and determination they admired even as they winced at her manner, treated them as the enemy within. In Parliament they have few friends. Most ministers who have done time at the Foreign Office give it at least a passive loyalty; they will not join the persecutors. But there are no votes in defending the unpopular, so it is rarely until ministers have retired from office that any of them say much about the Foreign Office's virtues.

LEFT The foreign secretary, Douglas Hurd, at his
desk in the Foreign Office.

19

'I admired the men and women of the Foreign Office', wrote Lord Carrington (foreign secretary, 1979–82) in his memoirs, 'and felt it a privilege to work with them – they were outstanding, and in my experience their quality exceeds that of any other Department – and any other Foreign Office.' And even Lord George Brown (foreign secretary, 1966–8), who treated his officials abominably, wrote of them shortly after leaving: 'My first impression of the Foreign Office, and my very last, was of its quite extraordinary professionalism.' These days they have a defender in Tristan Garel-Jones, ex-minister of state, but he is one of the few MPs who dares, or bothers, to defend them publicly.

'I think the most difficult thing for the public to see is the sheer mental and physical skill of Foreign Office officials,' he observed. 'The detail and the complexity of [European] Community business these days is daunting'. 'Sometimes', he recalled, talking of Michael Arthur, the Grade 4 diplomat assisting with negotiations during the British presidency of the European Community,

when I'm going along in a car with him, simply to tease him, I will just say, 'You know, Michael, I'm still worried about Article 122,' and he just goes, 'Well, you're quite right, Minister, because if you look at the third tiret [point], you'll find that the first five words . . .' and off he goes. I mean they just know this stuff backwards.

Foreign Office people are privately as grateful to the few politicians who speak up for them as they are bitter about the attacks or neglect from many more. A thoughtful first secretary in the Far East helped me to fashion the appropriate metaphor: the Foreign Office is a splendid Rolls Royce, whose owner keeps telling it to go faster, while cutting down on the fuel. Pride ensures that appearances are kept up: the chrome is as highly polished as ever and the exterior is kept perfect. But from time to time, although the owner needs the Rolls for professional purposes, he gets embarrassed at owning such a status symbol, administers an almighty kick to the bodywork and tells them in the pub that he is thinking of scrapping it or swapping it for a Ford Cortina.

In some respects the Foreign Office is its own worst enemy. It can be slow to change, it can be too perfectionist, it overvalues the rarefied intellectual and undervalues practical intelligence, and pride keeps it from hitting its owner where it hurts. Whatever cuts are imposed on the Foreign Office, however deep they bite, however many people are exploited by an *esprit de corps* that requires everyone always to work as hard and as long as the job demands, there is no reduction in standards of service to the five ministers.

The day a permanent under secretary tells a secretary of state that five ministers are too many and that their number must be reduced or their Private Offices cut, or that briefing will not be available for a particular event because of staff shortages, the battle for the necessary resources to help with the refashioning of an unstable world may be waged more enthusiastically. 'Our people at the top are far too deferential to ministers,' observed one young man who thought the level of briefing far too great. 'But I'm not yet quite broken to the wheel. In a few years, I may well think like my elders do now.' But the Foreign Office ethos is imbued with service. 'They [private secretaries] anticipate your every wish,' said Tristan Garel-Jones of his private secretary, Tim Hitchens. 'For instance I'm a chain smoker and Hitchens is a health-freak, but he's never without at least two packets of Benson and Hedges. They not only tend to your technical needs, but to all your physical absurdities as well.'

The Foreign Office is ridiculed for being stuffy, elitist and out-of-touch ('toffee-nosed twerps in plumed helmets', 'a cosy club for creepers and crawlers' are two recent tabloid descriptions). The irony is that it is its limpet-like adhesion to old values like patriotism, public service, excellence and stiff-upper-lippery that has kept it operating to a standard which foreign governments envy.

The quickest way to understand the heart and soul of the Foreign Office is to study its relationship with its ministers. Ministers decide the policy which diplomats implement. Ex-permanent under secretary, Sir Paul Gore-Booth, explained the relationship well:

Foreign policy is what you do; diplomacy is how you do it. Of course the two get mixed up especially when a diplomat is advising on policy or a member of the Government normally engaged in policy decision takes over a diplomatic operation which seems to merit top level or summit discussion. But generally speaking the task of a government is to decide and the task of a diplomat at any level is to try to make the decisions work.

The distinctions are rather more blurred than when he wrote twenty years ago. The world is nowadays fiendishly complicated and ministers rely on officials to give them clear options and recommendations on every area of foreign policy, but the choices are theirs. 'There ought always to be, I think', said Garel-Jones, 'an element of tension between the professional civil servant, who is here today *and* here tomorrow, and the politician, speaking for his constituents.' The minister should play devil's advocate, asking 'what may sometimes seem – to the professional – silly questions.'

What ministers want are loyal servants who will do their bidding with speed and efficiency, save them from embarrassments, protect them from petty cares and ensure that when they appear in public, they are primed to do the best job of which they are capable. In return, the diplomats want their political masters to have a clear view of what they want, to be intelligent and decisive, capable of arguing back and, if necessary, convince the diplomats that they are wrong, be courageous in sticking to an unpopular policy and strong in fighting political battles. If, in addition, the ministers give them respect, loyalty and affection, it will be repaid one hundredfold.

Tim Hitchens, who became Garel-Jones's private secretary in May 1991 at twenty-nine, talked about how a politician and diplomat can together be greater than the sum of their parts. He enjoyed his relationship with his particular master, finding him 'an

---

OVERLEAF The outer office of the minister of state, Tristan Garel-Jones;
on the left, Tim Hitchens, Garel-Jones's private secretary; on the right,
Alison Pringle, his assistant private secretary.

absolute antidote' to the Foreign Office and 'great fun to work with'. Their personalities were dissimilar: Garel-Jones was 'all mercurial energy and I'm far more logical, straight up and down, not taking too many risks and I think that is a fantastic combination.' Garel-Jones led Hitchens 'to do things I'd never dare to do' and Hitchens occasionally brought him down to earth. '"Thank God it's only a game",' Garel-Jones would say at moments of crisis – a sentiment no diplomat could admit to openly.

The foreign secretary is the overlord. It is he who has to persuade the prime minister and the Cabinet to back his foreign policy, and it is he, too, who is responsible for defending his department against parliamentary assassins and Treasury pirates. He sets the tone of the department, for he determines how much freedom of action is allowed to junior ministers and he has, also, a considerable say in senior diplomatic appointments. Outsiders, assuming the Foreign Office to be inhabited by the privileged and arrogant, would assume that they would be happiest with an Old Etonian aristocrat, and indeed, they get on well with the best of that breed.

Sir Alec Douglas-Home fitted that stereotype and was the second most popular post-war foreign secretary (1970–4). If a little slow, he was highly competent and on top of his job, and he treated everyone, from cleaners to senior officials, with easy courtesy. George Brown fitted another stereotype – the suspicious anti-Establishment politician with a chip on his shoulder – and caused mayhem. The foreign secretary whom the service loved unconditionally was Ernest Bevin, the illegitimate child of a Somerset midwife and domestic servant whose formal education had ceased when he was eleven years old.

The story of Brown and the Foreign Office is the story of what can go wrong; the sadness is that, had he viewed the Foreign Office as a friend rather than as an enemy – and had he drunk less – he might, like Bevin, have been a great foreign secretary. His officials admired his intelligence, his patriotism and his political skills. He had, remarked one, 'a feeling for British national interests, and saw them as important in a way that other foreign secretaries sometimes do not.' And however badly he behaved, he frequently showed flashes of greatness. The *New York Times* reported a meeting of the European Free Trade Association (EFTA) where Brown annoyed everyone by blustering and making 'idiotic' passes at women, 'but then, at the final banquet, he stood up and made a speech about European unity that moved all the delegates . . . to a vision. He suddenly gave sense and purpose to the whole dreary business of toiling over tariffs on cod fillets.'

Unfortunately, from the beginning, Brown's sensitivity about class made him convinced that he was being patronised. When his permanent under secretary, the Old Etonian and well-connected Sir Paul Gore-Booth, said 'With respect, secretary of state', Brown thought he was being ironic. 'The reality', observed an onlooker, 'is that George was bemused by the agonising politeness of the FO, which he took as insincerity. He had the suspicion, deep down, that all these highly-educated public-school types were laughing

RIGHT Tristan Garel-Jones and his private secretary Tim Hitchens discuss a tricky point during the Maastricht Bill committee stage.

at him, or sneering, but, in fact, most of us admired him. It was the English upper-class thing, of everything being understated and cool, that drove him mad.'

Brown's habit of bawling out his officials in public was bad enough. What in the end they found unforgivable was that in his memoirs he disparaged them individually and as an institution, alleging that they were 'striped pants faceless diplomats' (a phrase of Colonel Nasser's) and 'bowler-hatted chaps' who left at six o'clock for home or club.

Unprecedentedly, they struck back. In a letter to *The Times*, Sir Evelyn Shuckburgh, who had been ambassador to Rome in Brown's day, explained why he was breaking with tradition. Although it had suffered grievously from Brown, the Foreign Office 'grinned and bore its tribulations partly because it recognised his remarkable political qualities and force of character and desired to support his policies to the best of its ability.' It was now time, however, that 'something was said by a former member of this Service which he persistently denigrates and ridicules'. Although no doubt Brown had learned much while foreign secretary,

he did not learn the secret of mutual support and loyalty between a minister and his advisers, and between a Foreign Secretary and HM Representatives abroad. . . . When the Foreign Secretary descends from an aeroplane and proceeds to castigate the Ambassador (or members of the Embassy staff) in the presence of local personalities . . . this must affect the Embassy's influence thereafter. Ministers usually understand this.

That was the lowest point in ministerial-official relations, though at times David Owen ran Brown close; he made his mistrust of, and irritation with, his officials clear and criticised them in public. The reign of Ernie Bevin was the highest point. 'David Scott [a deputy under secretary] tells me that the Foreign Office are delighted with Bevin,' recorded Harold Nicolson in his diary in August 1945. 'He reads with amazing rapidity, remembers what he reads, cross-examines the experts, and having once mastered his brief, acts with vigour.'

Bevin was a visionary, a patriot and a pragmatist combined and, even more important, from the beginning, he displayed simultaneously, confidence in himself and confidence in those who worked with him. He trusted, liked and was interested in them. It was he who noticed that the office-keepers on duty at one Foreign Office entrance shivered during the winter from the biting wind and insisted that a glass partition be installed. He was outraged when he found out how little his assistant private secretary, young Nicholas Henderson (public school and Oxford), earned: ' "A good deal less than a tin-plate worker in South Wales," he said indignantly.'

He listened to his officials, he learned from them and he taught them in return. A great negotiator, he rammed home to the young men the importance of avoiding point-scoring. He had acquired his knowledge of the world from what he described 'as the hedgerows of experience' and though he felt his lack of education to be a handicap, it did not make him insecure; 'he was always himself,' observed his daughter. 'I can't help liking Duff,' he remarked of his grand ambassador in Paris. 'He doesn't care a damn what I think of him.' And when bored at a state banquet, he would begin to hum, and when eyebrows were raised around him, ask why they could not all embark on some community singing.

The gratitude of his officials grew to bursting point when Bevin turned on their enemies. When, for instance, the Labour left attacked Foreign Office officials, Bevin told them loudly and publicly 'to try attacking him rather than those who were working loyally for him.' And when the left retaliated by claiming that he had sold out, he was unperturbed.

The Foreign Office referred to him privately as 'Uncle Ernie'. An ex-ambassador, Lord Trevelyan, described him as 'a man loved by all who worked for him, genuine, honest, and full of courage.' And Sir Paul Gore-Booth confirmed his colleague's judgement:

In my diplomatic lifetime, no Foreign Secretary engaged the loyalty and affection of the whole Diplomatic Service as Ernest Bevin did. It is difficult to explain this affection in cold print. Contrary to much invention, the Diplomatic Service could not care less about the social antecedents of its political master. What the Service does understand is reciprocal loyalty. It accepts that you serve the Secretary of State and not the temporary incumbent of the post. But if that incumbent, in addition to his political ability and standing, openly stands up for those who serve him, there can be a coordination of heart and head which is both rare and invaluable. And if, in addition to being powerful and likeable personally . . . the Secretary of State comes to power at a moment which enables him both to demonstrate power and vision and to stand up for his team in public, the Service will do anything for him.

A month before Bevin died and just as – because of ill-health – he gave way as foreign secretary to Herbert Morrison, the Foreign Office held a seventieth birthday-party in his honour. It was financed by a collection of sixpences from everyone in the whole organisation, in London and around the world, from the permanent under secretary and the ambassadors down to the cleaners and the office-keepers. 'They had dancing,' wrote Geoffrey Moorhouse, 'with that great dying bulk of a man beaming at them all from his chair. They had a bit of community singing. They had a cake with candles on top. And when it was all over, Bevin said it had been a marvellous time.'

Flanking the bottom of the Grand Staircase in the Foreign Office which links the permanent under secretary's offices with the secretary of state's are two large marble statues of two great aristocratic foreign secretaries – the Lords Clarendon and Salisbury. In a niche one flight up, facing them and all the grand visitors who climb those stairs, is a small black bust of Bevin, presented in 1991 by one of his private secretaries and unveiled by Douglas Hurd.

Bevin was a wonderful man, and it would be unfair to compare other secretaries of state to him. Yet one cannot but mourn the absence among recent foreign secretaries of warmheartedness and vision. Douglas Hurd, for instance, is exceptionally able, industrious and well-informed. His officials have tremendous respect for him partly because he is clear about what he wants and rejects any submissions he finds wanting. Diplomats speak approvingly of him as 'a master wordsmith' and 'a safe pair of hands'. 'Anybody who has sat in an aeroplane with Douglas Hurd for a couple of hours and had various ideas thrown

ABOVE Foreign secretary Douglas Hurd consults with
senior officials at a meeting in his office.
LEFT Douglas Hurd gives an impromptu press and
tv conference in Luxembourg in which he expresses
support for Boris Yeltsin during the Russian
Parliamentary crisis of October 1993.
OVERLEAF Douglas Hurd flies in an RAF jet to an EC
meeting in Luxembourg.

A Week in the Life of the Foreign Secretary
6–12 September 1993

MONDAY

0845	Inoculations
0900	Australian High Commissioner
0930	Sri Lankan High Commissioner
1000	Call on King Hussein
1100	Office Meeting: Latin America
1130	Nigerian Foreign Minister Mbu
1245	Lunch with Michael Sissons
1430	Talks with Chief Minister of Gibraltar
1600	Mr Battiscombe, Head of Mission Algiers
1615	Japanese Ambassador
1645	Chief Buthelezi
2115	ETD Heathrow for Abu Dhabi

TUESDAY

0800	Arrive Bateen Airport, Abu Dhabi
0830	Arrive Residence
0930	Meeting with British Businessmen at Embassy
1100	Call on UAE Foreign Minister, Rashid Abdullah
1230	Call on Sheikh Zayed, President of UAE
1330	Lunch hosted by Foreign Minister
1530	Call on Sheikh Mohammed bin Zayed, Chief of Staff of UAE Armed Forces
1630	Press Conference
1800	ETD Abu Dhabi
1930	ETA Jedda – Met by Prince Saud
2030	Dinner hosted by Prince Saud

WEDNESDAY

0900	Depart Hotel
0930	Visit Saudi/UK offset project at Savola
1015	Depart Savola
1100	Talks with Prince Saud
1300	Lunch and talks with British Business Group
1415	Return to Hotel
1445	Depart Hotel
1500	Call on King Fahd
1815	Depart for airport
1900	ETD Jedda
2200	ETA Heathrow

THURSDAY

0800	Breakfast with the Prime Minister
0930	Cabinet
1030	Political Cabinet
1130	Permanent Under Secretary
1200	Bilateral talks followed by
1300	Lunch for Argentine Economy Minister
1500	Office Meeting
1530	Mr Tim Lankester, Permanent Under Secretary, Overseas Development Administration
1600	Mr Patrick Wogan, Head of Mission des Doha
1615	German Journalists Interviews
1700	Interview pre-Australia tour
1730	Cypriot Foreign Minister Michaelides
1930	Address Travellers Club

FRIDAY

0900	Call by Lord Owen
0945	Office Meeting
1040	Depart Foreign Office for Northolt
1155	ETD Northolt
1415	ETA Cologne/Bonn Airport
1445	Round Table discussion Bonn
1730	Reception
1915	Dinner
2100	Depart for Cologne/Bonn Airport
2125	ETD Cologne/Bonn Airport
2145	ETA Heathrow

SATURDAY

	EC Foreign Ministers Informal weekend Belgium
0830	ETD Heathrow
1045	ETA Brustem Military Airport
1100	Foreign Ministers Meeting
1330	Lunch at Alden Biesen
1430	Foreign Ministers Meeting
2000	Dinner and Concert

SUNDAY

	EC Foreign Ministers Informal weekend Belgium
0915	Depart for Alden Biesen
1000	Informal talks
1220	Depart Alden Biesen
1300	(Buffet lunch)
1305	ETD Brustem Military Airport
1315	ETA Heathrow
1400	Depart for Sydney

Outside those hours and on aeroplanes he deals with his red boxes, his constituency correspondence, and any urgent communications.

various ideas thrown back as being ill-thought-out, stupid, ill-considered, is not going to conclude that the Foreign Office determines what ministers think,' said Michael Jay, assistant under secretary for the European Community. Yet that could be an account of an aeroplane journey with Sir David Hannay, the British permanent representative at the United Nations. Because in fact Hurd is too like the senior inhabitants of the Foreign Office, unsurprisingly, since he served as a diplomat from 1956–66. A smooth, first-class professional machine should not be led by a mirror image of itself: it needs some fire in its belly. Had the cards fallen differently and had she not been as socially insecure as George Brown, it is possible to imagine Margaret Thatcher as a great foreign secretary. On the rare occasions when she worked in harmony with individual officials – as she did often over the Rhodesian negotiations – there could be magical results.

Though he had tremendous admiration for Hurd's capabilities and considered himself probably not good enough for the job of foreign secretary, Tristan Garel-Jones, who

ABOVE AND OVERLEAF Tristan Garel-Jones in his office.

resigned as minister of state in 1993, had, in many respects, the right temperament to complement the Foreign Office machine, 'I am vehement, like all Celts,' he explained. 'I try to be vehemently moderate and vehemently calm, if that isn't a contradiction,' and that, along with his lightheartedness and his humanity, made him a particular pleasure to his officials. And he liked them.

The chaps are very clever, they're very funny. The nice thing about the Foreign Office is that the task of a minister is to arrive, if you like, laden with prejudices, the prejudices that I pick up in my constituency and with my friends and elsewhere. So one becomes a sort of saloon-bar bore in the Foreign Office, saying, 'Well, I think we should do this, that and the other.' And the officials are very good because they don't actually mind what you say. You can come up with any ideas, crazy as you like, provided you are prepared to discuss them with them and to be argued out of your idea or not as the case may be.

Garel-Jones reckoned his hit-rate at about fifty-fifty.

The most crucial relationships in the Foreign Office are between ministers and private secretaries, whose doyen, Sir Nicholas Henderson, described them as 'the impresarios of Whitehall; and in their private offices the drama and friction between politics and the machine are theatrically audible'. It was a French diplomat at the United Nations who once laughed to the British ambassador, Geoffrey Jackson, 'as one tall and slender young high-flyer after another loped past, each with his master's briefcase – "I think all your British private secretaries are brothers. You must breed them!"'

The relationship is one requiring great delicacy, for unlike most other countries, where a private secretary would be simply his minister's man, the Whitehall private secretary is simultaneously loyal to the minister and the Department. Only the highest of high fliers are chosen, for in addition to intelligence, sensitivity and stamina, they need the courage to be honest with both their minister and their colleagues.

The rewards for both minister and civil servant are enormous. For the private secretary, it is at one bound a leap into a new world. As Tim Hitchens described it:

Until you move into a Minister's office you will have had either responsibility for relations with Malawi or the way the Common Agricultural Policy works and you haven't really had an opportunity to broaden your perspective and to see how a minister views foreign policy. Suddenly you are thrown into a Private Office and you have a minister who has to decide the nuclear policy of this country, who has to decide reforms of the Common Agricultural Policy, who has to think about the position of the Falkland Islands, and you realise the limitations on what he can physically take in, in terms of detail, but also you realise how you actually make policy – how you set priorities.

He found equally fascinating:

the link between the political world of Westminster and the bureaucratic world of the Foreign Office. You are a linchpin in there, because the instincts of politicians are not the instincts of civil servants and diplomats . . . your job is at the centre, explaining to the politician what the bureaucrats are thinking and what is possible and explaining to the bureaucrats what the politicians are thinking; the whole point of government is the way those two interact.

If a minister is strong enough to indicate clearly what he wants, his private secretary will make it possible for him to operate to his highest potential and will harness the Foreign Office to do his bidding. Indeed some of them overdo it, and impose unreasonable burdens on officials down the line.

Michael Jay is one of the management-minded senior people trying to encourage the Foreign Office culture to move towards more oral and less written briefing, but he points out the limitations on radical change. Foreign policy issues are so widespread, varied, detailed and moveable that unless a meeting is about one area in which a minister is an expert, he can be badly caught out. If everything is not covered, there will come a moment when a minister meeting, for instance, a group of MPs, is asked an unexpected question which he cannot answer. A note then goes round the system from his private secretary saying that the minister would wish to draw attention to the fact that when this question was asked there was no briefing available, and that makes the whole organisation feel as if it has failed.

Successful ministers stress the helpfulness of the Whitehall machine. Sir Humphreys flourish only where the minister is weak and there is a power vacuum, or where the minister is poor at playing the system. The way to get round the system is to send a ferret down the rabbit hole; a private secretary who is respected, liked and trusted gets the best out of the machine for his political master. Tim Hitchens summed it up simply: 'My main role will be to make sure that my minister is well briefed, is in the right place at the right time, has his head pointed in the right direction and has full leisure to take the important decisions *and* that I have packets of cigarettes ready for him whenever he wants them.'

LEFT Tim Hitchens grabs lunch at his desk.
OVERLEAF Stephen Smith, assistant private secretary to Douglas Hurd;
behind the desk hang portraits of previous foreign secretaries.

What makes the minister/private secretary relationship so strange to outsiders is the combination of intimacy and detachment. There are of course exceptions; in Whitehall generally there have been close friendships, affairs and even marriages between the two, for not all private secretaries are male. But the Foreign Office people, being more discreet and more proper than those in sister departments, are very good at staying behind invisible barriers. For two or three years a private secretary may live and breathe the same air as his minister up to eighteen hours a day, he may travel half the world with him, he may know his foibles, his defects, hangups, his family problems, his political stresses, yet he is supposed never to forget that ministers are transient and that tomorrow his charge may be replaced by someone else, with a different personality and possibly even from a different political party.

Richard Crossman observed that 'the only operation to which I can compare the Whitehall drill for a change in Government, is the hospital drill for removing a corpse from the ward and replacing it with a new patient.' It is particularly stark for a foreign secretary, who moves from the world stage to the parish hall at dizzying speed. From the moment when his successor telephones the Private Office and is told when it would be convenient for him to arrive, there is just time to say his goodbyes, arrange for the disposal of his personal effects, sign photographs for his erstwhile staff and make his departure with dignity. All the time, if he has any imagination, he will know that his Private Office staff – including his trusted private secretary – are now distracted by hunting for information about the likely needs and habits of the new incumbent.

New ministers may request a change of Private Office staff, but rarely do. (When there is occasion to choose a replacement, a choice of three is offered. Garel-Jones chose Tim Hitchens because he had EC experience, was strong on economics – on which Garel-Jones was weak – the personal chemistry was good and he liked chocolate – an important element in attracting a man like Garel-Jones, who throughout the making of the BBC television series appeared to be permanently half-mad with hunger.)

Ministers come and ministers go – on promotion, demotion, death (political or physical), or very rarely, like Tristan Garel-Jones, elect to retire. Few politicians voluntarily give up the hard, but cushioned and heady ministerial life, which makes them feel every day like a person of consequence.

Their private secretaries mostly stay on in the Foreign Office for the rest of their career. Since they are almost invariably considerably younger than their ministers, they pass them going up the ladder of power – albeit a more discreet form of power – as the ministers tumble down theirs into oblivion. There may occasionally be Old Boys' reunions. They may run across each other socially or meet sometimes overseas, where the ex-private secretary has gone on promotion, and his old boss may be passing through representing Her Majesty's Government in some new role or perhaps doing business on behalf of a company of which he is now a director.

If the law of averages is operating, the ex-private secretary will be running his own Embassy when his old boss dies. If it was an affectionate relationship, the ambassador will be disturbed and moved at the news, and will make strenuous efforts to get back for the memorial service. Even if he hated or despised his old boss, he will write a skilful letter of condolence. Later, if he has become very exalted, is of a literary bent and lives for an appreciable time after his own retirement at sixty, he may in due course write his memoirs. There, at best, he will give posterity a view of an individual politician which is imbued with the understanding that comes from the closest professional relationship either of them ever had. At worst, he will write of his old boss in a way that combines habitual discretion with the occasional feline, slightly ambiguous thrust. In the case of the ferociously competent and private Douglas Hurd – said by officials to warm up slightly, but only temporarily, when travelling in their company – there will be little to say that is not public knowledge.

Sir Nicholas Henderson, assistant private secretary or private secretary to Anthony Eden, Ernest Bevin, R. A. Butler, Patrick Gordon Walker and Michael Stewart, put the relationship in context in a rather chilly way. It brings home that to the civil servants, at the core of their fascination with their job is their closeness to power, embodied physically by the secretary of state's office suite.

It is not . . . the recollection of political motivation, the silhouette of any one personality, or the drama of any particular event that impresses itself most on the retina of my memory as the Private Office flickers in the mind's eye, but the features of that vast room and the awesomeness, however unacknowledged by us Private Secretaries at the time, of our no less vast responsibilities: the high ceilinged expanse of the Private Office, encumbered by the paraphernalia of the past and by the immediate flow of boxes and telegrams and by a procession of visitors, many of them clamouring to impart 'just one word into the Secretary of State's ear'; and the presence hard by, through the heavy swing door, of the Secretary of State himself, the embodiment in retrospect more of abstract political power than of any individual personality, seated in the middle of an even larger room, its windows giving on to the Horse Guards and St James's Park, a view lit in the distance by the lights of Carlton House Terrace twinkling through the willow trees, and highlighted in the foreground by the pelicans, flapping and opening their enormous beaks, as if conducting the orchestra of lesser birds on the lake; and, suffusing the whole place, that sense of self-importance without obtrusiveness, of clandestinity, and, dare I say, of service, that inspires the go-between in all of us (except in those, and few they are, who lack both vanity and the desire to please), a quality that is as vital as is oxygen to the survival of life in the rarefied atmosphere of the Private Office.

OVERLEAF Looking out on to Horse Guards Parade
from the Foreign Office.

· 3 ·

RUNNING IT

In, To and From the Centre

For much of its existence, like many other government departments, the Foreign Office has lived in cramped, often squalid headquarters. In 1782 the Foreign Office inhabited two private houses and by the early nineteenth century it had expanded into a group of houses in and around Downing Street. By the time Lord Palmerston launched a competition for the design of a new, purpose-built Foreign Office, the old one was falling apart: the foundations were giving way and the houses at either end had collapsed.

George Gilbert Scott produced a classical design, and the construction of an Italian Palazzo to house the Foreign Office, the India Office, the Colonial Office and the Home Office began in 1861. Together, the buildings formed a great rectangle to which another storey was added in 1925. Scott saw the Foreign Office as 'a kind of national palace, or drawing room for the nation' and he designed the great three-roomed Locarno Suite for diplomatic dinners, receptions and conferences.

Scott's building deteriorated and by the end of the Second World War there were few Foreign Office people left with any recollection of the grandeur that lay behind the many gimcrack additions. The staff lived in an inconvenient, squalid, rodent-ridden slum – the kind of offices that only an East End sweatshop owner, or a government, would expect its employees to work in without complaining.

In 1963 Sir Leslie Martin devised a master plan for the rebuilding of Whitehall. His ideas were ugly and modernity was his maxim (he designed the hideous Department of the Environment building in Marsham Street which is about to be demolished). Parliament was told that Scott's Foreign Office building was to be knocked down and replaced with modern offices, but the Victorian Society succeeded in whipping up a sufficient outcry and the decision was reversed: the classification of Scott's building as a Grade One listed building left ministers unsure what to do next.

LEFT The recently-restored Durbar Court in the Foreign Office.

TOILETS

ABOVE Catering staff taking a breather in a corridor just off the Durbar Court.
RIGHT A back staircase in the Foreign Office.
PREVIOUS PAGES Murals of Britannia, painted by Sigismund Goetze during the
First World War, which decorate the Grand Staircase in the Foreign Office.

The Colonial Office died, the Foreign and Commonwealth Offices merged and the Home Office moved, so the pressure on space was reduced and in the end the Government bit the bullet. Scott's building was restored to its former glory at much less cost than would have been incurred by building something new somewhere else.

Somehow the Foreign Office system threw up a diplomat who proved to be the perfect man to oversee the job. David Brown, a diplomat from a family of architects, has a passion for European classical architecture. His commitment, enthusiasm and understanding of the subtleties of restoration have ensured that the great rooms and staircases are a triumph. And as an experienced survivor of the appalling working conditions of the Office, he has gradually provided, side-by-side with the grand restorations, revamped offices that are comfortable, efficiently lit, decently decorated, and free of vermin. The reprographic section in the basement could be a modern purpose-built office anywhere. The only inappropriate note is struck by the bomb-proof curtains that hide the magnificent windows, but the Foreign Office has to take account of current realities.

Every phase of the rejuvenation has uncovered forgotten and breathtaking treasures of carving, painting and mosaic. There are marvels of over-the-topness like the politically deeply-incorrect murals, painted throughout the First World War at his own expense by Sigismund Goetze, which depict 'the origin, education, development, expansion and trials of the British Empire, leading up to the Covenant of the League of Nations', in a series of vast portraits of Britannia in her various roles of warrior, daughter, mother and so on. Overhead is a great dome painted with comely maidens representing the countries which had diplomatic relations with Britain in the 1860s. And the restorers have paid tribute to Palmerston and Scott, who are featured in the hall of the main entrance.

Foreign visitors love the building and only the most humourless native can fail to enjoy the spectacle. For the Foreign Office – bludgeoned on all sides for failing to recognise that the UK is all washed up – it is the cause of many an ironic grin.

If the occasional Roundhead working there sighs for a more workmanlike building, the Cavaliers – and they are in the majority – exult in this unapologetic environment. Admittedly it is not convenient. The corridors are so long that scooters should be provided, and there is still not enough room to bring in badly-housed staff from nearby offices. But these are minor matters. The Foreign Office headquarters has a soul.

Running the Foreign Office

Only two people who work in Scott's Foreign Office headquarters are expected to know something about everything: the foreign secretary and the permanent under secretary. The permanent under secretary is the head of the Diplomatic Service and the manager of all the Foreign Office's resources both human and capital. He must also keep in touch with all areas of foreign policy.

The current incumbent, Sir David Gillmore, became permanent under secretary in 1991. He joined the Foreign Office in 1970 at Grade 5 through a special recruitment scheme

Sir David Gillmore, permanent under secretary of state
and head of the Diplomatic Service since 1991.

for mature entrants. He served in London, Moscow and Vienna, and as high commissioner in Malaysia, before becoming deputy under secretary for the Americas and Asia.

The permanent under secretary's role has changed substantially during the past decade. The demands of the job have grown and it has become impossible for one person to fulfil the policy direction and coordination, management and representational functions, as well as being the foreign secretary's closest advisor. Now there is a political director who supports the permanent under secretary. He (now she) is a free-wheeling thinker, whose job includes looking after the policy planning staff, who ponder likely global developments, contemplate various scenarios and suggest contingency plans.

The permanent under secretary requires an immense capacity for absorbing detail while maintaining a balanced overview, but an outstanding political intelligence is no longer the only important prerequisite for the job. Sir David Gillmore, like his predecessor, Sir Patrick Wright, was given the job above all for his managerial and human qualities. During the past decade the Foreign Office has become uncomfortably aware that the low morale of its staff is a product not only of cut-backs and low pay, but also of a culture in which being a rotten man-manager was no bar to promotion. Gillmore's priorities include making sure he sees every British head of mission privately to talk over what they are doing and to listen to any personal problems.

At a time of financial stringency, managerial experimentation and global political upheaval, being head of the Foreign Office requires huge stamina. In 1966 the then incumbent, Sir Paul Gore-Booth, was handed a questionnaire on an aircraft which enquired:

'How many hours do you work a week?' Counting the business meals, formal and informal, the red boxes taken home and the solid backlog of papers done during the week-end, I conscientiously wrote 'eighty hours'. The sharp end of this calculation was that five nights a week there was an hour and a half's work to be done between 11.30 pm and 8.00 am. I started by doing it at night; my physique took charge at half time and indicated a strong preference for 6.30 am to 8.00 am.

Sir David Gillmore, asked a similar question recently, discovered that the length of his average working day was eighteen hours, making ninety hours for five weekdays. And on three out of four weekends he is away on business, and paper follows him everywhere.

Morning Prayers

Every morning at 10.30 am the permanent under secretary plays host to his senior colleagues. There is no confusion about the *placement*: the deputy under secretaries of state and the head of news department sit with him at the table and around them, against two walls, sit the assistant under secretaries. One of the Foreign Office men on secondment to the Cabinet Office sits on the window seat and the permanent under secretary's private secretary sits a discreet distance away listening hard. Sitting alongside the deputy under secretaries, often at the centre of attention, is the comparatively youthful private secretary to the foreign secretary. And should the permanent under secretary be away, the most senior (in terms of date of appointment) deputy under secretary will take the chair.

With remarkable economy of language (the discipline of communicating by telegram has its effect on oral communication as well) and crisp though courteous chairmanship, in exactly thirty minutes the gathering identifies the priorities for the Office in terms of briefing, instructing, reporting and so on. All deputy under secretaries of state say something each day, but usually only a few of the assistant under secretaries intervene.

It is an intensely well-mannered occasion: the atmosphere is not conducive to a 'bloody-hell-I-never-heard-such-a-load-of-nonsense-in-my-life' approach. Nor is it the forum for profoundly questioning basic assumptions: twenty people cannot sort out the new world order in half an hour, but they cover the key developments in the world and determine today's tactics.

What most strikes the outsider is the incredible range of issues the permanent under secretary has to keep up with. He will have read the large batch of telegrams his private

Morning prayers: the PUS (second from the left) at his daily meeting with
senior officials. Deputy under secretaries and the head of news department
sit around the table, in the outer circle are the assistant under secretaries.
On the PUS's right is John Sawers, Douglas Hurd's private secretary.

secretary has selected for him and will be up-to-date on all significant global events. As
much as the permanent representative at the United Nations, the permanent under
secretary has to keep a detailed grasp on fast-changing, complex events and apply to them
his understanding of the interlocking nature of international relations. And on top of that,
he has to keep an eye on all the non-political work of the Office and manage and motivate
his staff.

Similar meetings occur at around the same time in missions around the world – the
frequency depends upon staff members. To a novice, Sir David Hannay's meeting at the
UK Mission to the UN is an impenetrable avalanche of acronyms and foreign place-names.
Less frenetic, but still perplexing, a conclave in most European capitals will discuss how

complex lobbying instructions from London on matters concerning the European Community – from competition to social policy – are being implemented, and whether the key person to bring round to the British way of seeing things is – depending where you are – Herr Doktor Ranke, Madame Balzac or the new chap on smoke emission, Signor Bellini. By contrast, a meeting in a medium-sized Middle or Far-Eastern post is a gentle, intelligible affair taking place often only once a week and with time for the odd joke or anecdote. Unless, of course, the populace are on the rampage.

Telegrams

Telegrams whizz around the Foreign Office and its outposts keeping too many people too up-to-date with too much information. At the height of the Falklands crisis, there were 2000 daily; in the case of the Gulf, 12000. In the year to July 1992, Tokyo sent 4054 and received 13141; Rome sent 2477 and received 27950. The disparity has to do with multilateral as opposed to bilateral diplomacy. Rome needs to know what is going on all round the European Community.

One of the major management problems facing the Foreign Office in this era of instantaneous communications is how to confine political reporting to the essential, how to avoid duplication of press agency information and how to ensure that information is copied to those who need it, but not to those who do not.

The volume of telegrams from a post depends to a considerable extent on the inclinations of the individual head of mission. Some are slow to adapt to the realities and cut down on unnecessary political reporting. There are frustrated people in chanceries around the globe who are desk-bound and duplicating the work of Reuters. They are well aware that they are simply not getting around the country enough, making the right government contacts, getting close to opposition parties and, where possible, cultivating politicians of all parties.

The purpose of political reporting is to put a British spin on the news. There is no point in telegraphing London to say that the finance minister has just resigned: Reuters can do that. The embassy's job is to send a telegram at top speed saying that the finance minister has resigned and what the consequences are for the forthcoming European Community meeting; or to explain the reasons for the resignation and then say what that means for British interests. That is the value of these instant reaction telegrams.

Later the embassy's job will be – in the case of something like a major political crisis – to give a complete picture. Journalists will not necessarily be objective: Foreign Office staff are required to be. In Tienanmen Square the journalists were running the tragedy and the human interest material. The embassy's job was to talk about the implications in terms of the political stability of China in the short and long term.

What the foreign secretary needs, when there is a major crisis on which he is going to be quizzed as soon as he puts his nose out of his office, is guidance on how things are likely to go. It is the job of the ambassador to call on his contacts to give him information not available to the press.

In the case of the constitutional crisis faced by Yeltsin in Moscow in October 1993, if the international community was to have any effect on the progress of events, it had, said Simon McDonald, Sir David Gillmore's private secretary:

to get its act together quickly . . . be singing the same tune, and to give clear signals. I think they did play a part and it was valuable to Yeltsin that he had Western, strong Western support with certain conditions very early on; the telegrams provided the means for John Major in Kuala Lumpur, Douglas Hurd in London and Bill Clinton in Washington to get their act together. The prime minister was in Malaysia when the news came through, but because of the telegraphic system his line was very clear and completely cogent very early on. Because he was in touch with people, he was able to give a properly thought-out reaction.

ABOVE The telegram distribution room in the Foreign Office; the distribution
list includes a box of telegrams for the Queen, the prime minister,
the foreign secretary and all senior officials.
OVERLEAF The post room at the Foreign Office.

The telegram is the crucial medium for confidential communications (a restricted telegram is encoded at the sending station and decoded at the receiving station) and the information on how the cards are going to fall can be in the hands of 200 people very quickly. Then there are numerous international meetings where the press will be interested in a couple of items on the agenda but the Foreign Office is interested in all the events that are not newsworthy but are important. Simon McDonald again:

the best journalists know much more than they print, but their editors don't want that amount of detail, and frankly some of the most important pieces of paper are secret. The sources are secret and so there's a role for the telegram there. Reuters cannot compete.

There are also countries of potential strategic significance which journalists rarely cover where straightforward political reporting is necessary.

Confidentiality, inside information, analysis, the British angle and speed are the elements that drive the drafting of a telegram. The instruction that used to be given in the days when cyphering and decyphering was a major undertaking was that 'Telegrams should be written as from a miser to a fool.' Understanding the art-form is vital.

Below is a telegram from Sir Brian Fall in Moscow on 6 October, at the beginning of the 1992 Russian constitutional crisis. He sent the telegram at 14.40. The prime minister was likely to telephone Yeltsin at 15.30 primed with what Yeltsin would be saying at 16.00.

```
FCO PLEASE PASS TO PS/NO 10

RUSSIAN CONSTITUTIONAL CRISIS; YELTSIN TV ADDRESS
SUMMARY
1. YELTSIN INVITES ALL SOVIET POWER BODIES TO DISSOLVE THEMSELVES AND SAYS THAT
THEY WILL IN ANY CASE FACE REELECTION AT THE SAME TIME AS THE DUMA ELECTION ON 12
DECEMBER
```

and some of the detail:

```
2. I UNDERSTAND THAT THE PRIME MINISTER MAY BE TELEPHONING YELTSIN AT 1530Z.
IT MIGHT BE USEFUL TO PASS ON WHAT WE UNDERSTAND WILL BE THE MAIN POINTS OF
YELTSIN'S TV ADDRESS DUE TO BE BROADCAST AT 1600Z.
- PARTICIPANTS IN THE ARMED REBELLION TO BE BROUGHT TO JUSTICE:

THERE CAN BE NO MORE TOLERATION IN RUSSIA OF COMMUNIST-FASCIST INCITEMENT TO
VIOLENCE AND BLOODY DICTATORSHIP:

- HEAVY RESPONSIBILITY OF THE CONSTITUTIONAL COURT (NOTE: THE COURT'S CHAIRMAN,
ZORKIN, FINALLY ANNOUNCED HIS RESIGNATION TODAY):

- DIRECT RESPONSIBILITY OF THE MAJORITY OF SOVIET POWER STRUCTURES FOR MAKING
POSSIBLE THE TRAGEDY IN MOSCOW: SOVIETS INVITED TO TAKE THE DECENT AND COURAGEOUS
DECISION TO DISSOLVE THEMSELVES:

- FREE AND FAIR PARTICIPATION IN THE ELECTIONS GUARANTEED FOR ALL PERSONS AND
PARTIES NOT STAINED WITH DIRECT PARTICIPATION IN SUNDAY'S ATTEMPTED PUTSCH.

FALL
```

Diplomatic Bags

Despite all attempts to remind staff of the rules, there were the usual crop of oddities. Two whole fresh salmon, a large pungent cheese, whisky, wine and a packet of frozen cranberries, whose thawing juice left a gory trail across the bag room floor, were among the items left unsent! In return, we received a Christmas cake, two porcelain horses and three parcels of dates.

So wrote the chief clerk in January 1988 in his newsletter to all posts.

Until the 1963 Vienna Convention on Consular Relations, customs officials in the receiving state had the right to challenge a bag which seemed suspect; since then the diplomatic bag has been inviolate. Bags are supposed to contain documents or items for diplomatic use only. In practice, they also include such comforting features as private mail and presents from home or valued commodities (like bacon in Islamic countries) which exiles can no longer bear to be without.

Vital though they are to the people at post, bags are extremely unglamorous to look at. They are prison-made, rough, grubby, off-white canvas bags with OHMS stamped on them. They are also extremely difficult to open and normally only those diplomats who have started at the bottom in a Registry or one-man head of mission ever have to do so. John Everard was recorded wrestling with his first bag.

Bags are curious animals. They're tied with, for obvious reasons, tough string, and you need a particular kind of clipper to open them. . . . Whoever tied this bag did so with a great deal of loving care. I shall make a point of counting how many fingers I've got left after this operation.

The bags come in several sizes, though a pantechnicon can be classified as a bag for customs purposes. They also come in two categories, classified and unclassified; in 1992 480 000 kilograms of unclassified bags were sent overseas from the Foreign Office, transported by a private company. The classified bags, which are supposed to contain only confidential material, are handled by a combination of Queen's messengers and casual couriers.

Conditioned always to play by the rules, Foreign Office staff use the diplomatic bags less creatively than do their opposite numbers in less conscientious foreign services. Interesting cargo found in other service's bags include drugs and guns, and on some occasions, people. In 1964 the customs authorities in Rome violated the immunity of an Egyptian bag because of the moans emanating from it; a drugged and kidnapped Israeli was found inside.

Diplomatic life is full of the unexpected.

OVERLEAF Diplomatic bags awaiting collection in the reception area
of the British Embassy in Moscow.

The Technological Revolution

Fifty years ago, it would have taken ten hours to encode a 1000-word telegram, five hours to transmit it by morse and another ten hours to decipher it. Twenty years ago, the Diplomatic Wireless Service connected half the missions to London and an electronic device called Piccolo cut down the whole process to around forty-five minutes. Nowadays, a 'flash' telegram from abroad takes seconds.

The Foreign Office had some bad experiences with technology in the 1980s. The complexity of their requirements in terms of security and geographical spread caused headaches and, as the Stock Exchange was to do later – and even more expensively – the Foreign Office made the error of trying to be in that dangerous spot – the forefront of technology.

Recently however, Jeffrey Ling, a physicist and a diplomat with a particular gift for management, has revolutionised information technology throughout the Foreign Office. Radio communication, which requires an expensive aerial infrastructure, has been phased out and substantial manpower savings have followed. The new telephone-satellite-based system has achieved a 20 per cent increase in the speed of communications and fax is proving a boon for non-confidential traffic.

Crisis management has also become sophisticated. The old crisis room in the Foreign Office was an attic a long way away from the centre of power, with a few telephones, teleprinters and a television set. Nowadays in a crisis the Emergency Unit have direct lines to all the relevant posts abroad and to key departments in Whitehall, and closed-circuit television links appropriate officials around Whitehall.

Then there is the Flying Foreign Office, an RAF VC10 converted from a troop-carrier in 1974 on the instructions of Jim Callaghan. With today's technology on board, the unfortunate foreign secretary can be sure he will never be left in peace. The equipment makes it possible to communicate with the Foreign Office in London and with Embassies in the capital cities he is passing – and vice-versa.

The Foreign Office's efficiency in communicating information has always been the envy of other diplomatic services; the drawback is that it encourages centralisation. Scope for individual initiative and improvisation is much reduced when approval or advice can be sought from, and provided by, the centre within seconds. Some ambassadors are very grateful for a time-lag that leaves them master of their own decision-making for just a few hours a day while their masters in London are, reluctantly, asleep.

· 4 ·

OF DIPLOMATS

Immunity, Precedence, Protocol, Language, *Esprit de Corps* and Other Timeless Matters

S ir Harold Nicolson suggested that the father of the diplomatic profession was an anthropoid ape who lived in a cave and was covered in hair. There having been a particularly unpleasant run-in with the tribe next door over hunting-grounds, he drew the short straw when the chief decided to send him as an envoy to negotiate a truce. By coming back alive he proved he was a diplomat: by not slaying him, the neighbours proved they saw the need for diplomatic immunity. (One suspects that when he arrived home he was told he had compromised too much, accepted too much hospitality and developed some funny foreign ways and was stoned to death.) Nicolson's was intelligent conjecture: more recently a Finnish anthropologist and diplomat backed up this theory with evidence. Dr Numelin has concluded that even very primitive societies work out procedures for making war and peace and negotiating trade deals, and that as part of this process they allow envoys personal immunity and freedom of movement.

In essence, a diplomat is one who practises diplomacy, the definitions of which are legion. Sir Ernest Satow, a great diplomat who became famous for his *Guide to Diplomatic Practice* (published in 1917 and periodically revised by a Foreign Office luminary) summarised it stolidly as

the application of intelligence and tact to the conduct of official relations between the governments of independent states, extending sometimes also to their relations with vassal states; or, more briefly still, the conduct of business between states by peaceful means.

The word diplomat comes from diploma (the Greek word for doubling, thence a document 'twice folded': a document by which a privilege is confirmed: a state paper, an official document, a charter). It was a term known to the *cognoscenti*, but did not come into popular use until the nineteenth century.

Modern diplomats have a wide range of activities. Sir David Hannay, our man at the UN, who appears on our television screens self-confident and unruffled in every new crisis, is a diplomat; so too is the most junior clerk filing papers in his overburdened Registry.

Sir Robin Renwick, British ambassador to Washington, in his office.

Sir Brian Fall, whizzing around the former Soviet Union from impoverished new capital to impoverished new capital, is a diplomat, as is Stephanie Bee, who sits in cramped and tatty offices in the grounds of his embassy, revelling in her work as an assistant accountant. Jean Sharpe, consul in Bangkok, visiting British prisoners in Thai jails is a diplomat quite as much as the new ambassador to Riyadh, David Gore-Booth, answering a summons to visit a senior prince of the Saudi royal family. Glynne Evans, trying to organise humanitarian relief on the ground in Bosnia, David Hawkes, advising businessmen on how to sell successfully in the Thai market and Kit Burdess, recommending manpower cuts in the Washington Embassy, are diplomats too. All of them – from Grade 10 up to Grade 1 (for in the civil service you go up the ranks in descending numerical order) – belong to the Diplomatic Service and for all of them international mobility is a requirement of their contract of employment. It makes no difference whether you are a secretary, an ambassador, a registry clerk or a security man: for the purposes of the United Kingdom, all are members of the Diplomatic Service.

What do diplomats do?

The work that diplomats used to do is vaguely comprehensible to outsiders, who can see why it might have been necessary – in the days of primitive transport and poor communications – to send representatives abroad to fly the flag, to smooth the path of trade and become involved in occasional negotiations to try to prevent an outbreak of war.

Life for the diplomat abroad in days gone by was both easier and harder. It was easier, because he was not expected to know much beyond what was going on in his own patch and harder because he was more isolated and frequently lacking in the necessary guidance for taking important decisions. Yet there was in this world a certain exhilaration, and for the adventurous it was rather more exciting than the more cocooned living of today.

One paradox of the diplomatic life is that as communications have been transformed, as countries have come closer together and as politicians have begun to jet around the world conducting negotiations, the diplomat's workload has increased beyond measure. Another is that as the better-informed press and public call ever more shrilly for success in negotiating peace deals, trade deals and so on, they make negotiation more difficult by demanding to be informed at every stage, while simultaneously rubbishing the negotiators who represent their interests.

As early as the 1930s, a famous French diplomat, Jules Cambon, wrote gloomily about how much more difficult and complicated diplomacy was becoming.

The activities of the press, the parliamentary lobbies and the business world, and the ignorance and impatience of the public which insists on being told everything, though very often none the wiser therefor, do not help to create an atmosphere favourable to the prosecution of far-reaching political designs.

He defended diplomats against the critics who thought that the League of Nations could, and should, replace them: good international relations depended on permanent representation in all the capitals of Europe.

Some people nowadays . . . never seem to be able to visualise public affairs save in connection with the noise and turmoil of a popular chamber; they are unable to grasp the fact that the bargaining which affects the result of so many important divisions in every parliament of the world does not take place in the chamber but in the lobbies.

One of the most fascinating aspects of diplomatic history is its timelessness. Not only is what Cambon wrote in 1931 relevant to the United Nations, but in his explanation of the importance of permanent diplomatic activity, he was echoing Louis XIII's great minister, Cardinal Richelieu, three centuries earlier, when he wrote

that it is absolutely necessary to the well-being of the state to negotiate ceaselessly, either openly or secretly, and in all places, even in those from which no present fruits are reaped and still more in those for which no future prospects as yet seem likely.

So modern critics, who think that modern conditions no longer require diplomats, are merely making a very old case.

'Why not replace Her Majesty's Foreign and Commonwealth Office with a fax machine?' asked Andrew Roberts in the *Daily Mail* in March 1993.

The function of the personal representative abroad is virtually obsolete in today's world; faxes, telexes and now face to face conference telephone facilities could easily be installed in place of our smug, expensive diplomats.

Similarly, with foreign Ministers constantly jetting around and summits taking place almost monthly, the day of the grand embassy is over. The 18th century concept of a large legation in every foreign capital has been made progressively redundant by technological advance; and if prestigious ambassadorial jobs were not expected and demanded by diplomats as the climaxes of their careers, half of the legations could be closed down tomorrow.

An ex-ambassodor, Sir Geoffrey Jackson, twelve years previously, explained why diplomats and their embassies are necessary.

Diplomacy has over the millenia evolved into a marriage institution of sorts. As in matrimony, the high points, the humdrum, the ecstasies and parturitions are all part of an enduring and uninterrupted relationship, and have their rules, written and unspoken, for quarrel and for reconciliation too. With nothing but a summit diplomacy the nations risk exchanging marriage for a mere mating, an intermittent rut in which a frenzied collision of the parties briefly and single-mindedly interrupts long intervals of mutual aversion.

Yet if you look closely at who wants the diplomat abolished, you will observe that it is not the summiteers, for they know, more than most, that almost everything they achieve is a result of steady, humdrum work in the diplomatic backrooms.

Or as Douglas Hurd put it when discussing the huge amount of work that went into handling the Edinburgh European Council Summit in 1992: 'Multi-dimensional diplomacy like that needs clarity in understanding what our partners and we want, and can live with, ingenuity in constructing a package, and vigour and integrity in selling it.' A clear understanding of what is required, and the ingenious construction of the subsequent package, can only be achieved by constant communication between the permanent diplomatic representatives on the ground in the different countries. The better each knows how the other thinks, and what each wants, and could live with, the more likely it is that summits – which are the end, not the beginning, of negotiations – will be successful.

In bilateral diplomacy, ie, two-nation diplomacy, the diplomat's main job is to try to

LEFT Part of the 'Ambassadors' Board' at the Foreign Office which hangs in the Head of Mission section. The section provides assistance to ambassadors while on visits back to the UK.
OVERLEAF Tim Barrow (left), second secretary in the British Embassy in Moscow, in discussion with the Armenian ambassador to Moscow.

promote his country's interests peacefully. The bulk of his most successful work is invisible at home, for, as Douglas Hurd put it, a crucial element in playing 'a pivotal role in both European and global diplomacy . . . is having diplomats on the ground with access and influence'. So it is foreigners who know if he does his job well and with them his influence must be used sparingly and discreetly.

Diplomatic failures get a great deal of publicity. As Douglas Hurd lamented:

we are to some extent fair game. If a British subject ends up in a foreign jail, if a British firm is in danger of losing a contract, if abuse of human rights is not checked, if a cruel war rages and is carried on our television screens, then the Foreign Service is expected to act. If the mischief is not then remedied the Foreign Service is easy to blame. The messenger gets a beating if the message is unwelcome. The Foreign Service carries upon its back the sins of that quite significant part of the world inhabited by foreigners.

Successes, by contrast, awaken little interest. There are occasions when, after hours and days – even weeks and years – of tedious negotiation, decisions are arrived at, flash points are circumvented, crises defused and wars prevented. But effective diplomacy is rarely dramatic and almost never visual: it holds little attraction for the media.

Martin Wight, an international theorist, recently divided diplomacy into three types: Grotian[1], Machiavellian[2] and Kantian[3]. The classical diplomacy in which British diplomats are brought up is Grotian, that of the old Soviet Union was pure Machiavellian and the Kantian, being Utopian, is practised by no serious diplomats but is much recommended by idealistic socialists everywhere.

GROTIAN DIPLOMACY springs from moderation, courtesy and sympathy for others, defined by Harold Nicolson as in its essence 'common sense and charity applied to international relations'. Wight summed it up as 'a reconciliation of interests, a composing of differences, even, perhaps, creating a common interest'.

MACHIAVELLIAN DIPLOMACY springs from a position of strength and uses 'coercion and bribery', 'stick and carrot' and is the opposite of the Grotian's attempt to understand the other side's position. 'It assumes a hostility and irreconcilability of views, discounting the other side's views in advance.'

KANTIAN DIPLOMACY springs from an assumption that mankind is fundamentally benevolent and will respond to open diplomacy and to unilateralist gestures of goodwill. A recent dramatic manifestation was among the feminist, would-be unilateralist nuclear disarmers of Greenham Common.

---

[1] After the Dutch theologian, diplomat and lawyer, Hugo Grotius, whose masterpiece was *De Jura Belli et Pacis* (About the Law of War and Peace), published in 1625.

[2] Machiavelli has been much misrepresented. A pragmatist who believed that strong government was essential to keep Italy free of the French, his *The Prince* (1532) was intended to be a handbook on how to maintain authority: he considered that all necessary means were legitimate, but did not advocate unpleasant behaviour for its own sake.

[3] Immanuel Kant, the eighteenth-century philosopher, whose essay on *Perpetual Peace* (1795) argued in effect that the facts of the human condition 'are so horrible that one must make a leap of faith and believe that progress is going to transform them.'

So the British Foreign Office is Grotian as usually are British foreign secretaries; prime ministers vary. Grotians can easily be dismissed as temporisers and compromisers by contrast with Machiavellians, who appear decisive because they beat their chests and rarely alter their views. It is no wonder that Mrs Thatcher, one of the great Machiavellian practitioners, could not stand the Foreign Office. Yet Grotians are trusted and Machiavellians are not. Machiavellians can win great victories but can also crash to great defeats: Grotians have staying power and take many of the less public tricks. For a relatively weak country like the UK, the ideal combination is Grotian diplomacy with an occasional timely infusion of dynamic Machiavellianism.

ABOVE Tristan Garel-Jones meeting a Polish Government delegation
at the Foreign Office.
PREVIOUS PAGES Morning meeting of the UK delegation to the United Nations
chaired by Sir David Hannay, the British permanent representative.

Alastair Goodlad, a junior Foreign Office minister, remarked in a speech in 1993 *apropos* the *Daily Mail*'s complaints about the 'sheer chickenheartedness' of British diplomats, that Oliver Cromwell had made the same point less subtly 300 years previously when he said 'A man-of-war is the best ambassador.' Yet,

We have no choice but to be in the business of persuasion. If we want the Netherlands to support us in some European Community business we cannot place Cromwell's man-of-war outside Rotterdam. We have to identify common interests, consider deals, compromises. If our objective is crucial, we may press extremely hard – the Falklands is the obvious example – but in pressing that hard for support we may have to accept that our objectives on other subjects will fall by the wayside. There will always be costs. That may appear to be sheer chickenheartedness to some. But it is the only way to do business in the international world today.

Who does it best?

In 1973 in *Corps Diplomatique*, Eric Clark wrote,

British diplomacy has a reputation developed during the country's days as a great power. It is still highly regarded; its own diplomats, certainly, almost universally regard it as the best. British diplomats impress as being unbeatable in crisis situations. They rarely take pains to impress; boasting or displaying abilities are, somehow, not good form.

The French rival the British for the position of the best diplomatic service in the world. The French are easily the most disliked and also the most admired. 'It's a diplomat's diplomacy,' said one ambassador. This is partly because the French believe they own diplomacy, having dominated international diplomacy throughout the seventeenth and eighteenth centuries. French took over from Latin as the language of diplomacy and still dominates diplomatic jargon: in the eighteenth and nineteenth centuries it was the language used in most correspondence between all ministries for foreign affairs and their own ambassadors. To the chagrin of the French, after the First World War, English began its steady progress towards becoming the lingua franca.

'French diplomats', said Clark,

are a mixture of great charm and yet self-superiority. They are conscious of their 'eliteness', are very formal, professional and cynical, believers in the right of their own country, in the supremacy of their own culture, and quick to take slight at any imagined offence. . . . It is striking that though most non-French diplomats dislike these characteristics, they also admire them.

The temperamental differences are graphically illustrated in attitudes to showing off. British heads of mission living abroad in magnificent residences play them down, and explain how they have been acquired by historical accident and are very draughty anyway. The very existence of these buildings is permanently under attack from the Treasury, the media and a host of other critics. 'I do not believe in moving out of our handsome embassy buildings abroad into suburban villas,' said Douglas Hurd in 1993. But then he had to

The main hall of the ambassador's residence in Washington, which was designed by Sir Edwin Lutyens in 1926–9.

justify such a bold utterance. 'I do believe in using those buildings to good effect. In 1814 the Duke of Wellington bought our embassy in Paris from Napoleon's sister. In 1993 Rover launched its latest model in the forecourt. The Duke would have approved.'

The Duke would have been far more likely to curse the critics and make no apologies. The great embassy in Paris is a museum of French architecture, decoration and furniture and as such is hugely appreciated; a suburban villa would make the British an object of ridicule. Indeed the French are notorious among diplomats for never stinting on anything to do with the ambassador's representational function. As in every aspect of their lives, they understand the importance of appearance. 'They are not,' observed one British diplomat in the Far East, 'so good when it comes to office facilities or communications systems or indeed the conditions of the ordinary staff, but anything which is to do with the image that France presents to the world is made available almost unquestioningly.' It is for that reason that the Queen's visits to France make such an impact.

The British and the French are temperamentally an unlikely pair to be widely recognised as operating the best diplomatic machines in the world. The French diplomatic culture is Machiavellian; the British, Grotian, but no one questions their superiority. They have always been diplomatic pacesetters, whose chief distinguishing characteristics became apparent early on. France was the trail-blazer in developing the philosophy; Britain was the pioneer in turning diplomatic theory into law.

In the European Community and on the United Nations Security Council, the British and the French operate at a level of professionalism that often leaves everyone else standing. The French score on two fronts. First, their foreign policy is far more consistent and more visionary than the British. As one reflective, retired British diplomat, Sir James Cable, put it: 'Ever since the inauguration of the fifth Republic . . . French foreign policy had been characterised by "premeditated and predetermined intention".' It has been, within the limits of the possible, positive, independent, assertive and even flamboyant. By contrast, in the words of one critic, 'the regular pattern of British foreign policy is one of reaction to international developments'. Second, the French are utterly ruthless in pursuit of self-interest. 'Le fair play' is not to them a sensible concept, whereas resolute British fair-mindedness does afflict British officials. 'My impression', said Tim Hitchens, 'is that the British Foreign Office in Spanish or Italian eyes is ludicrously fair-minded and open.'

(It is alleged that after a very long period of wrangling about whether the aeroplane should be called 'Concord' or 'Concorde', the chief French negotiator suddenly burst into tears and his English opposite number said in deep embarrassment, 'Oh, my dear chap. Let it be Concorde.')

Fair play does however confer some advantages, and, in any case, if British diplomats ceased to operate *'le fair play'*, they would cease to represent the essential character of the country they represent. People who know about diplomacy trust the word of the British and are resigned to dirty tricks from the French.

The French also score intellectually. For connoisseurs, at their best they are stunning. Sir James Cable, discussing international meetings of foreign policy planners, said 'most of our foreign colleagues were highly intelligent, but a French intellectual, on a good day, can give discussion a sharp glitter unobtainable by the best minds of more stolid nations.' Other British diplomats, however, would suggest that the reason is that the French diplomats are better-educated. As they are. Except where hard languages are concerned, the British approach is still that of 'Sitting Beside Nellie' and having the occasional few weeks training on specific subjects. The French recruits are graduates who have gone through the intensely high-powered École Nationale d'Administration. But then in France, unlike in Britain, elitism is not a dirty word.

Where the British score is on teamwork. As Sir David Gillmore, addressing the Foreign Office Carol Service at Christmas 1992, said, 'We have to work together and live together and rely on each other', and that, compared to their rivals, is what they do superbly. The French and the British may level-peg on hard work and skill in negotiation, but the British culture shares information while the French tend to hug it to themselves. Back-biting and back-stabbing is notorious in the Quai d'Orsay; compared to most institutions there is very little of that in the Foreign Office.

The devotion to communicating information is awe-inspiring. Everybody takes notes about everything and promptly relays it to everybody who might conceivably have an interest in it. If the secretary of state has a conversation on the telephone at 3.00 pm with his American opposite number, either his or his private secretary's notes of the conversation will be on the desk of the British ambassador in Washington within a couple of hours, and if necessary, within a few minutes. A British diplomat in the Middle East coming across a Japanese with something interesting to say about the General Agreement on Trade and Tariffs (GATT) negotiations will instantly commit his information to the system. The drawback is that the Foreign Office risks being drowned in paper and many individuals are overwhelmed by it. But in the world of multilateral negotiations, this information system confers an advantage which frequently puts the Foreign Office ahead by a nose. And in the European Community it needs to be, for there, the UK is almost always outnumbered by opponents and usually under-resourced.

Why do diplomats have immunity?

While special envoys can be traced from ancient times, resident ambassadors were a mid-fifteenth century Italian innovation which rapidly became a feature of European life, producing ceaseless arguments about the limits of immunity.

Most mature societies subscribe to the essential principle of diplomatic immunity, summed up by Charles Thayer, an entertaining retired American diplomat: 'You may not kill, jail, or even poke the nose of a diplomat no matter how much he may seem to deserve it.' Britain seems to have been the first nation to make this customary immunity law. In 1708, the Russian ambassador in London was pulled out of his coach and arrested by bailiffs acting for his creditors. Despite an apology from the secretary of state and a promise to try his attackers, he rushed home to complain. Peter the Great demanded of the British ambassador in St Petersburg that the attackers be summarily executed and to mollify him, not only did Queen Anne apologise publicly through her ambassador, but a law was enacted giving immunity from arrest to ambassadors or their servants.

Diplomatic immunity is often resented by the general public, who are aware of its abuse but not of its justification. The Nigerians struck a major blow against diplomatic integrity in 1984 when they used the diplomatic bag in a kidnap attempt, but it was the shooting in the same year of the young British policewoman, Yvonne Fletcher, from the window of the Libyan People's Bureau (as they called their embassy) in London which created the greatest public anger. Britain broke off diplomatic relations with Libya and sent the Libyans home: but immunity law prevented the British from charging the Libyans.

This gross abuse of diplomatic immunity prompted Yvonne Fletcher's mother to organise an international petition calling on 'civilised' governments to stop the abuse of diplomatic immunity. Her petition was backed by the British media but was a non-starter. Without all-encompassing diplomatic immunity, unscrupulous states could frame foreign diplomats with impunity, so the existing system cannot be radically reformed, only tinkered with. As the 1961 Vienna Convention on Diplomatic Relations, accepted by almost all the international community, explained: 'the purpose of such privileges and immunities is not to benefit individuals but to ensure the efficient performance of the functions of diplomatic missions as representing States.'

When it comes to freedom of movement, the Vienna Convention was able to achieve little, for there East and West have always seen matters differently. The Western practice is to offer the legal protection necessary to allow an ambassador and his entourage the greatest possible freedom: the Eastern tradition has always been to curtail an ambassador's movements as much as possible. For many centuries, pointed out Thayer,

diplomats in Eastern countries have been frustrated and thwarted, sometimes with Oriental tact and courtesy, sometimes with brute force. . . . The Western code of immunities has been built up during those centuries in the belief that diplomacy is useful in preserving peace. In the East diplomacy is, to paraphrase Clausewitz [the military strategist], an extension of war by other means.

The constraints upon foreign diplomats in the old Soviet Union dramatically reflected this tradition.

Precedence and Protocol

Diplomatic protocol has always seemed absurd to outsiders, but it has been devised painfully over a long period in order to stop quarrels and bloodshed over the unimportant. In these quarrels, the French displayed that grandeur that characterises their ruthless pursuit of self-interest.

One colourful example occurred in 1633 during discussions about the forthcoming wedding of the Crown Prince of Denmark. The ever-reasonable Danes were trying to solve the problem of precedence between the French and the Spanish and offered the French ambassador a number of solutions, including a choice of sitting next to the King or to the Imperial Ambassador. His response was: 'I will give the Spanish ambassador the choice of the place which he regards as the most honourable, and when he shall have taken it, I will turn him out and take it myself.' Recognising when he was beaten, the Spanish ambassador discovered urgent business elsewhere.

Nowadays there is no formal precedence recognised among nations. The relative seniority of ambassadors in the country to which they are appointed is determined by the date on which they presented their credentials. This makes them one straightforward element in the international protocol game, which continues to be of the most amazing complexity. The only guiding principle is that the local chiefs of protocol have the last word. It is they who decide such matters as that at Elizabeth II's coronation her great-uncle and great-aunt took precedence over 'representatives of monarchical States not being themselves Royal personages' and that the representative of the German Federal Republic followed hot on the heels of 'cousins of Her Majesty not being Royal Highnesses'. It is easier than the Vatican, where decisions involve the relative importance of the Quartermaster Major of the Sacred Apostolic Palaces, a Supernumerary Privy Chamberlain of Sword and Cape and the junior Monsignor Participating Privy Chamberlain.

Critics of foreign ministries everywhere think that their country's own diplomats are stuffy and formal to an unnecessary degree, but this is an inevitable part of their job. The only way of avoiding the possibility of involuntarily insulting representatives of another country is to stick rigidly to diplomatic etiquette. Being able to keep your face straight on ceremonial occasions, whatever the provocation, is as much a prerequisite of the job as being able to look interested while being bored to the depths of your being.

Usually, on the appointed day, an ambassador is taken to the head of state by a court or state official, with one or more cars for himself and his suite: local custom determines the degree of formality. In Britain for instance, the marshal of the Diplomatic Corps calls at the Embassy in a state carriage to take the ambassador to Buckingham Palace. Similar carriages follow with senior members of his staff. Carriage attendants are in royal scarlet and two footmen stand on the footboard at the back of each carriage. Dress is uniform, national dress or European full evening dress and decorations. The ceremony that follows is relatively simple and the official dramatis personae are restricted to the Queen, a lady-in-waiting, the vice-marshal of the Diplomatic Corps, the permanent under secretary of the Foreign Office and the comptroller of the Lord Chamberlain's Office.

Sir Marcus Cheke, vice-marshal of the Diplomatic Corps, in his instructions to tyro diplomats on how to behave, considered in 1949 the reaction to diplomatic protocol of the young Englishman who says:

'Good heavens! is all this sort of thing really necessary *in these democratic days*?' To such an exclamation it can only be replied that political changes, however vast, produce, in fact, little or no change in human nature or in the national temperament of peoples, so that not only is ceremony likely to continue to be dear to foreigners, but a comprehension of its forms will continue to be the most useful lubricant to negotiations to them.

Talleyrand said '*seuls les sots se moquent de l'etiquette; il simplifie la vie . . .*'. ('only fools mock etiquette; it simplifies life'.)

Reception of Vo Van Kiet, the prime minister of the Socialist Republic of Vietnam, visiting the Foreign Office in July 1993.

Diplomatic language

Protocol extends to language. As parliamentary language was developed to compel adversaries to observe the decencies of debate, so a diplomatic idiom was devised to convey messages in terms which will not needlessly antagonise. 'In matters of language', explained a recent edition of Satow,

the art of the diplomatist, as observed by André Maurois, 'is that of expressing hostility with courtesy, indifference with interest, and friendship with prudence'.

When an ambassador, speaking on behalf of his government, says that they 'cannot remain indifferent' to a particular situation or course of action, he is understood to mean that, should that situation arise, they will intervene. If they are said to 'view with concern', or 'with grave concern', a matter under discussion, this means they are proposing to take a strong line about it. 'My Government will reconsider its position', is a warning that a present state of friendliness may not continue. 'Is obliged to tender grave reservations', means in effect 'will not allow', while 'will be obliged to consider its own interests', indicates that, however its obligations have hitherto been interpreted, it will claim a free hand, which could result in a severance of relations. 'My Government will regard this as an unfriendly act', means 'will regard this as a threat of war'. He may add 'and will decline to be responsible for the consequences', with the corresponding intention.

Politicians and diplomats engaged in public diplomacy have developed a means of conveying disagreement in similarly understated terms. 'While I have deep respect for the distinguished delegate' means, 'I disagree with the delegate'; 'We have reached substantial agreement' means they disagree on at least one major issue; and, of course, as all followers of politics now know, if participants in a meeting have shared 'a full exchange of views', they disagreed about almost everything; if they had 'a full and frank exchange of views', the meeting was acrimonious.

Esprit de Corps

Diplomats are a breed apart because they have to be and like all breeds apart, they understand each other better than outsiders can. As a body, they are more correct, more courteous, more cautious and more impersonal than are ordinary people. And among their fellows in 'the corps diplomatique', as it has been known since the eighteenth century, they feel at home and, within limits, that they can trust each other. François de Calliers said in 1716:

Since the whole diplomatic body labours to the same end, namely to discover what is happening, there arises a certain freemasonry of diplomacy, by which one colleague informs another of coming events which a lucky chance has enabled him to discern.

And diplomats need to like each other, for they will keep crossing each other's paths throughout their careers. They refer to each other as 'colleagues' and wherever they meet up they will be experiencing similar problems with local customs and conditions. They will also have, unless they are very junior, many acquaintances and some friends in common. So when one speaks of *esprit de corps* in relation to diplomats, one is referring to the whole diplomatic community in the same capital as well as to a particular foreign service.

In 1967, a retired ambassador, Sir Douglas Busk, defined diplomacy as both an art and a craft. As an art it was 'conducting relations with foreign powers on the basis of a policy decided at high level in the home country; keeping your headquarters properly informed of events and negotiating in accordance with instructions received from them'. This required the diplomat to put himself 'up against people often of different culture in a strange environment and trying by entirely peaceful means to influence their thinking, to live in comity with them and to reach agreement in matters often highly abstruse and fraught with prejudice or preconception'. The 'craft of diplomacy', about which Busk wrote an amusing book, is the creation of the right instrument for the conduct of that art.

Some diplomats may be artists; some may be craftsmen. David Gore-Booth thinks in artistic terms, reflecting on how much of a contribution can be made by 'the application of personality to problems'. Glynne Evans, head of the UN Department in London, while struggling to bring some effective humanitarian aid to Bosnia, thought 'in terms of cogs, small cogs; and you're putting one cog with another cog and trying to make them mesh together so that a machine is set in motion . . . the cogs try and sort things out and make the well-oiled wheels turn', while the politicians think about the concepts. Tristan Garel-Jones, after an exhilarating period as minister of state, talked about the conduct of foreign affairs also in craft terms, as being 'like most other aspects of life: it's doing the little things competently and carefully all the time that build up to success.'

The public does not see consular officials, entry clearance officers and administrators as diplomats. To them the term is restricted to those dealing in political work in embassy chanceries, in foreign ministries or in delegations to international bodies – what might be described as the paper pushers and the negotiators. As Jules Cambon put it more than sixty years ago:

the public in general look upon diplomacy as mere intrigue, and fancy that, apart from the time when he is thus engaged, an ambassador is a mere idler whose life is one long round of junketings and feastings. There is indeed another class of people who refuses to subscribe to so hasty a verdict and who tries to get down to realities: they look upon the world as a theatre, and are given to talking about what is going on behind the political scenes. In fact they look upon it as a stage where everything is artificial and mechanical and arranged for a scenic effect. As they are firmly convinced that everything that happens has been prepared and thought out beforehand, they credit diplomatists with the qualities of Machiavelli and hold them responsible for whatever disasters occur. You cannot persuade these folks that these things happen much more straightforwardly in real life . . . political skill does not consist so much in creating opportunities as in turning them to advantage.

Of all the allegations made about them over the centuries, the view that they are nothing but intriguers wounds good diplomats even more than the notion that they are wastrels, for most of them would put integrity highest of all on their list: it has been drummed into them since time immemorial that their profession is based on trust. Sir Henry Wotton, who did such damage to the profession in the early seventeenth century by his jest about ambassadors being sent 'to lie abroad' said late in his career that 'an ambassador, to be serviceable to his country, should always speak the truth'. Jules Cambon said that a diplomat must be 'a man of the strictest honour'. Harold Nicolson defined the main quality as 'reliability', and analysed its five components as 'truthfulness, precision, loyalty, modesty and a sense of proportion'.

Office Skills and Practices in the FCO, a booklet which is given to new entrants to political work, points out that the 'value of intellectual honesty in a diplomat is obvious. Without it, there can be no mutual trust; and the whole basis on which the Office works crumbles away.' That does not, of course, preclude – in the phrase of Edmund Burke that Sir Robert Armstrong made famous – 'being economical with the truth'. Honesty does not require a diplomat to volunteer information that damages his country's case. Nor, like any businessman, will a diplomat engaged in sensitive negotiations be forthcoming about what he is up to: he may, on occasion, feel it right to lie. Foreign Office involvement in certain aspects of the Middle East peace process is, for example, most effectively conducted in secret.

The tabloid press see the time-honoured British system of giving MPs only the information they have asked for as duplicity, but that is an issue to address to politicians. As journalists protect their sources, civil servants protect their ministers. In 1993, in his evidence to the Scott Inquiry on the sale of arms to Iraq prior to the invasion of Kuwait, David Gore-Booth defended the practice of providing a partial answer to a Parliamentary Question. He is not a man for weasel words, and his open refusal to answer certain of the chairman's questions fully, attracted criticism in the press. 'He may have been to Eton and Oxford,' said the *Sun*, 'but we'd find it easier to take the word of Arthur Daley.'

The Diplomatic Platypus

I had a duck-billed platypus when I was up at Trinity,
With whom I soon discovered a remarkable affinity.
He used to live in lodgings with myself and Arthur Purvis,
And we all went up together for the Diplomatic Service.
I had a certain confidence, I own, in his ability,
He mastered all the subjects with remarkable facility;
And Purvis, though more dubious, agreed that he was clever,
But no one else imagined he had any chance whatever.
I failed to pass the interview, the Board with wry grimaces
Took exception to my boots and then objected to my braces,
And Purvis too was failed by an intolerant examiner
Who said he had his doubts as to his sock-suspenders' stamina.

The bitterness of failure was considerably mollified,
However, by the ease with which our platypus qualified.
The wisdom of the choice, it soon appeared, was undeniable;
There never was a diplomat more thoroughly reliable.
He never made rash statements his enemies might hold him to,
He never stated anything, for no one ever told him to,
And soon he was appointed, so correct was his behaviour,
Our minister (without portfolio) to Trans-Moravia.
My friend was loved and honoured from the Andes to Estonia,
He soon achieved a pact between Peru and Patagonia,
He never vexed the Russians nor offended the Rumanians,
He pacified the Letts and yet appeased the Lithuanians,
Won approval from his masters down in Downing Street so wholly, O,
He was soon to be rewarded with the grant of a portfolio.

When, on the anniversary of Greek emancipation,
Alas! He laid an egg in the Bulgarian Legation.
This untoward occurrence caused unheard-of repercussions,
Giving rise to epidemics of sword-clanking in the Prussians.
The Poles began to threaten, and the Finns began to flap at him,
Directing all the blame for this unfortunate mishap at him;
While the Swedes withdrew entirely from the Anglo-Saxon dailies
The right of photographing the Aurora Borealis,
And, all efforts at rapprochement in the meantime proving barren,
The Japanese in self-defence annexed the Isle of Arran.
My platypus, once thought to be more cautious and more tentative
Than any other living diplomatic representative,
Was now a sort of warning to all diplomatic students
Of the risks attached to negligence, the perils of imprudence,
And, branded in the Honours List as 'Platypus, Dame Vera',
Retired, a lonely figure, to lay eggs at Bordighera.

Patrick Barrington, 1908

· 5 ·

STAFFING IT

Streaming

The Foreign Office takes on recruits in two categories: fast stream and main stream. About 2000 hopefuls apply annually to join the fast stream (previously called the administrative, or 'A' stream); approximately twenty succeed. And over the last few years there have been anything from 1000 to 3000 applications to join the main stream (previously called the executive, or 'E', stream); between nine and thirty-five were taken on.

The qualifications required for the fast stream are a second class honours degree in any subject, with an aptitude for languages being an asset, but not a prerequisite. Some applicants who fail at fast-stream level subsequently apply to join at main-stream level, along with other graduates who have applied directly for the main stream because they lacked either the minimum fast-stream qualifications, or the confidence to apply directly for the fast stream.

Foreign Office jobs fall into ten grades (see table on page 88). Fast streamers skip the first two grades and join directly at Grade 8. Main streamers join either at Grade 9 or, if they fail at that level, they opt to be considered for Grade 10 along with those who have specifically applied for Grade 10 positions. Fast streamers and main streamers have separate grades at Grade 7 and fast streamers skip Grade 6 altogether.

In the last recruitment for Grade 10, fifty-five out of 1000 applicants were taken on. No one has been recruited to Grade 10 since the spring of 1992.

'There are enormous intellects in the Office that deal with questions that I wouldn't know how to cope with', declared Jean Sharpe, the consul in Bangkok, 'so I think we've each got our place. But I do think that a greater knowledge of what we do in the functional jobs would improve morale no end amongst those of us who are doing it – who feel that there is a lack of understanding of what we do because no one in the senior grades in the Office has ever done it. We're unlike any organisation anywhere, in that the people that run the organisation come from only one part of it.'

Jean Sharpe reflects the feeling among many of the main streamers. Almost all those in the senior grades are fast streamers.

In the days when Grade 9s were mainly school-leavers and the Grade 10s had few educational qualifications, the different career paths of those who entered at Grade 8 (with a degree), and those who entered at Grades 9 to 10 caused much less resentment than nowadays, when Grade 9 in practice has become all-graduate entry and most Grade 10s have good 'A' levels; some even have degrees. Yet the quality of the work given to main streamers has not changed significantly and the staff structure is so top-heavy that people at the bottom of the tree have far too little responsibility.

Caught in work that is usually beneath them intellectually, the Grades 9 and 10 complain. And as they realise they are on a career path that will always be undervalued and where promotion comes slowly, they look at the small number of their contemporaries disappearing past them on a fast track and they become resentful. And the Foreign Office deserves much of the blame.

In 1862, Walter Bagehot, while praising the introduction of qualifying tests for the civil service, gave a warning about the perils of making them competitive. Reformers had

adopted the idea that the state wanted, in its junior and inferior civil servants, not only competent men but superior men; that, as carrying on the highest and most important work of the country, it was entitled to claim the chief talent of the country; that, in a word, it must have not only good men, but the best men. . . . [It was] simply wasteful and cruel to turn a young man of cultivated and aroused intellect into an ordinary . . . clerk.

He worried additionally that competitive examinations favoured the merely clever over those more valuable candidates who – though slower – had judgement and sense. These days more sophisticated examining techniques ensure that more qualities than cleverness are taken into account, but the system has remained greedy. It still takes in the very best available applicants, regardless of the kind of work they will be given. As more people stay on at school or go into higher education, applicants have become progressively over-qualified, a trend exacerbated by the recession that began in the late 1980s. All too many people in the last few years have joined one grade down from where they had hoped to be or might have been a generation ago, and promotion prospects have become correspondingly worse. At the bottom of the heap, almost everyone is doing a job one or two grades beneath their capabilities.

The Grade 10 registry clerks, for instance, most of whom enter the Foreign Office with 'A' levels – some even have degrees – have to keep detailed records of all Foreign Office communications. They must copy, sort and file material and make sure that each piece of information is delivered to its correct destination under the correct classification, in the correctly coloured box. This work, self-evidently, does not require 'A' levels.

I met one Grade 10 who had functioned just about adequately in his sequence of mindless, boring jobs. Fate suddenly caused him to have to take over for some months from someone three grades his senior. His superiors were delighted with his performance, and for the first time in eight years he was enjoying his work. Later, inevitably, he had to return to his old job, for which he is seriously over-qualified.

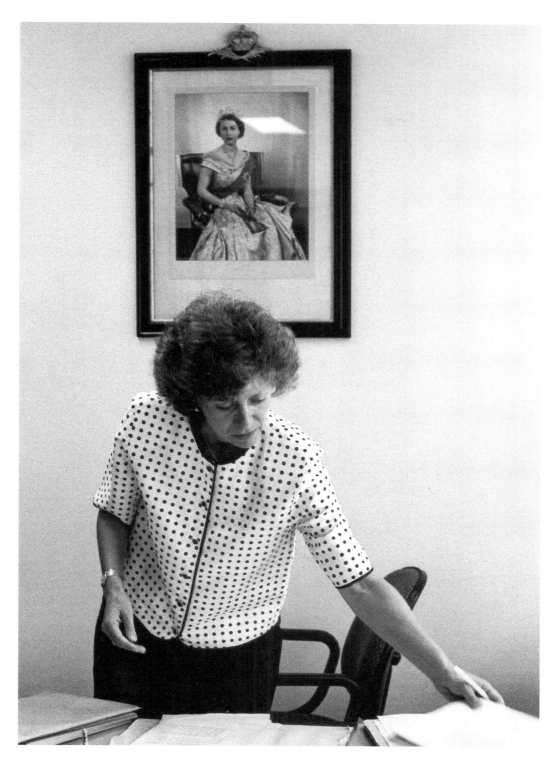

Main streamer Jean Sharpe, consul in Bangkok.

Grades, Job Titles and Salaries

Grade	Title	Salary (at 1 April 1993)
1	Permanent under secretary Senior ambassador	£104,860 £90,148
2	Deputy under secretary Ambassador High commissioner	£75,328–£64,307
3	Assistant under secretary Ambassador High commissioner Minister Senior consul general	£62,990–£54,751
4	Head of department Counsellor Ambassador High commissioner Consul general	£51,540–£39,339
5S*	First secretary (London only)	£40,977–£34,735
5	First secretary Consul	£37,769–£27,080
6	First secretary Consul	£27,586–£20,039
7D**	Second secretary	£25,039–£17,645
7E†	Second secretary Vice consul	£21,994–£17,776
8	Third secretary	£16,477–£14,416
9	Third secretary Vice consul Attaché Executive officer	£17,940–£10,378
10	Clerical officer Registry clerk	£13,812–£7,289

SECRETARIAL

Grade	Title	Salary
S1	Personal assistant	£17,553–£14,948
S2	Secretary	£14,226–£11,602
S3	Secretary	£11,940–£9,357

*S = Special: denoting heavy responsibilities
**D = Development: those selected for fast stream career development
†E = Executive: or main stream

Ambassadors and **high commissioners** are usually graded according to the importance of their post. **Private secretaries** range between Grades 4–7, depending upon the seniority of the minister they serve.

Fast streamers start at Grade 8. **Main streamers** start at Grades 9 or 10. Fast streamers and main streamers have separate grades at Grade 7 and fast streamers skip Grade 6 altogether.

When living abroad, diplomats are given various **allowances** which always include free accommodation and utilities.

While the Foreign Office undoubtedly needs a substantial number of brilliant people of the calibre of the Hannays and the Kerrs (Sir David Hannay is the UK permanent representative to the UN, and Sir John Kerr performs the same function within the European Community), it seems to overvalue the abstract, and undervalue the practical, intelligence. One of the quickest and most intelligent diplomats I met on my travels had come up the hard way, and was obviously being promoted at a ludicrously slow rate considering his ability and experience. I asked why. Had he failed in political work, perhaps? Could he not draft well? No, he said. But one day his personnel manager had told him that his was essentially a practical intelligence, and he felt the glass ceiling come down on his career. Like Jean Sharpe, who knows that her slow start means she will never be an ambassador, he has only a slim chance of ending his career at Grade 4, still one below what he deserved.

The Foreign Office places a relentless emphasis on the importance of being 'policy-capable', yet there are many areas of policy – particularly the management of the Service – where movers and shakers and competent people of sheer common sense might make better decisions. In the early 1980s one of the few voices raised in Personnel against the policy of always recruiting the best was that of a Grade 7 main streamer, but her policy-capable superiors thought her misguided.

Here is a parable about James and Robert, two fictional characters devised to incorporate the experience of many Foreign Office recruits. They are graduates with similar social and educational backgrounds who, being adventurous and anxious to travel, simultaneously apply to the Foreign Office. They read about the two streams.

The red brochure, for the fast stream, called 'Making the Difference', says: 'Expert all-rounders, all-round experts: the successful diplomat must combine interpersonal and analytical skills, management know-how with political acumen.' The blue brochure says: 'Developing Main Stream skills: variety is the key to main stream career development in the Diplomatic Service. Our aim is to see you develop into a diplomat with a battery of readily adaptable, high level skills to carry you through your career.'

For a twenty-one year old, the distinction is somewhat blurred. The last page of each brochure tries to make things clear:

FAST STREAM
The people we want to bring into the Fast Stream must demonstrate a mix of quick, confident analytical thinking, interpersonal skills and an interest in international affairs.

MAIN STREAM
The people we want to bring into the Main Stream must demonstrate a combination of analytical thinking and an interest in international affairs with good practical and interpersonal skills.

Essentially, they mean that the fast-stream people have to be brighter than the main stream – according to traditional Foreign Office criteria.

If James and Robert are very alert, they will note two significant differences between the two brochures. The first is that those in the fast stream are likely to spend half their working life abroad, while those in the main stream will spend two-thirds. (This is because London is the hub of policy-making.) The second is that everyone featured in the fast-stream brochure thinks they are doing something very important, but one of the main streamers quoted remarks that the downside of her work is that 'I could handle more responsibility. I enjoy going to meetings on my own, but I generally only get to do that when my bosses are busy themselves.'

Her complaint is echoed in the equivalent Grade 10 recruitment brochure. One of the endearing characteristics of the Foreign Office is that they are so anxious to be honest that they permit their own staff to criticise them in their recruitment videos and literature as well as in the BBC television series.

Most of the intake comes straight from university, though the literature encourages recruits between the ages of twenty-one and fifty-two. From time to time in the past, having found it needed an injection of talent half-way up the tree, the Foreign Office held a competition for mature people to come in directly to Grade 5. By that means it netted the present permanent under secretary, Sir David Gillmore, who joined at the age of thirty-five. These days, unfortunately, since the present structure is groaning with Grade 5 talent wailing about the promotion blockage, no such recruitment is taking place. There are therefore too many bright young people who have gone straight from one institution into another, for few older bright people want to come in at the bottom of the heap.

(The rigidities of the Foreign Office promotion system are primarily the fault of trade unions who have blocked fast promotion for main streamers between Grades 10 and 6. It is no longer possible, as it used to be, for someone who joined at Grade 10 to rise up the main stream and become a senior ambassador: with a system of Buggin's turn holding them back for the first thirty years of their career, there simply is not time.)

James and Robert both apply for the fast stream. They have been warned that because of the number of applicants (as well as the need for medical tests, positive vetting and so on), the whole process could take a year between application and appointment. They take temporary jobs and set off simultaneously on the Foreign Office quest, which is organised by the Civil Service Selection Board (CSSB – pronounced Sizzbee). They both pass the qualifying test in 'verbal usage and general reasoning', and some months later go through stage two, which consists of a two-day selection board in London. There they take further tests and are asked 'to analyse a fictional but typical problem of the sort you might encounter as a civil servant and recommend a course of action. There are, in addition, group exercises to determine your interpersonal, leadership and negotiating skills'; and a series of interviews with, among others, a psychologist and an ex-ambassador, 'to explore your background, intellect and motivation.'

The results come out and to their excitement, they are both asked to go forward to the six-man final Selection Board. James sails through his thirty-five minute interview; Robert, who has a nasty cold, feels afterwards that his fuzzy head made him a little leaden by his normal standards. He is right. James comes twenty-first of the twenty-one who succeed; Robert comes twenty-second.

After he has assuaged his grief, Robert decides to accept the offer of a main-stream job. But he feels very fed up. He hopes, however, that in due course he will be able to get across into the fast stream. The Foreign Office is pretty fed up too, for, despite all its efforts to attract applications from science graduates, women, ethnic minorities and the products of state schools and provincial universities, they have a result very like last year. For the early 1990s the figures look like this:

	1990		1991		1992		1993	
	FAST STREAM	MAIN STREAM	FAST STREAM	MAIN STREAM	FAST STREAM	MAIN STREAM	FAST STREAM	MAIN STREAM
Total	**27**	**55**	**19**	**39**	**14**	**9**	**21**	**16**
Per cent								
Oxbridge	67	12	78	8	64	0	66	6
Independent schools	56	27	78	42	64	67	66	37
Science graduates	0	13	0	7	7	11	5	13
Graduates	100	96	100	97	100	87	100	100
Women	26	70	36	77	21	56	19	75

Personnel groan at the thought of the inevitable Parliamentary Question that will elicit this information and the usual accusations that will follow. Ironically, since grammar schools were abolished, the proportion of entrants from independent schools has gone up.

James and Robert join on the same day, and are together on the three-week induction course, for in the interests of efficiency and economy, training for the two streams was merged some time ago. 'It was', observed a fast streamer, 'an interesting example of the Office introducing what seemed like a sensible reform, which then wreaked more damage than the old system of divided courses.'

These young people come on the induction course treating each other as equals. Then they are separated for one unforgettable session with Personnel. The fast stream are told that their minimum expectation should be Grade 4 – junior ambassador – by the age of fifty, and the main streamers are told that they will be doing well if they ever reach that grade at all.

James and Robert learn many practical things on the induction course and spend a whole five days on drafting, after which they both take up their first jobs. They are given identical jobs as assistant desk officers in geographical departments in London.

They occasionally meet. Robert is continuing to make the best of it, but he is resentful because his job is, if anything, more demanding than James's, and yet he is paid less and he now realises that he will almost certainly be lagging almost fifteen years behind James in the promotion stakes.

At the end of his first year Robert gets a good report and his superiors urge him to apply again for the fast stream; this is the only route across the grading structure. This year they are taking only fourteen: Robert comes fifteenth.

After eighteen months they are both sent off for hard-language training and then posted. They exchange Christmas cards, but do not meet again until six years after they joined. James has been using his fluent Arabic in Saudi Arabia, where he hopes some day to be ambassador. Having gone there as third secretary, he was then promoted to second secretary (Grade 7D). He is expecting his promotion direct to Grade 5 (first secretary) within two years.

Robert has been using his excellent Japanese in Tokyo, on the commercial side. The job is extremely taxing, and he has done well, but he knows he will be lucky to be promoted to Grade 7E (second secretary, main stream, less well-paid) in three years. With luck he will progress to Grade 6 in his late thirties and Grade 5 in his late forties. He could opt to take the fast-stream exams once more, but he has lost heart and can no longer face trying again. As one fast streamer explained to me:

When they join the Office, you can't tell fast streamers and main streamers apart. Within a few years you can always tell which is which, because there is a slightly defeated look about the main streamers, whereas all the fast streamers know they are on their way. They get metaphorically patted on the head by ambassadors.

Life will not be all promotions even for James, who will probably spend almost a decade at Grade 5, mostly working in London and working harder and longer and earning much less than many of his university contemporaries. But he loves being with bright people and enjoys the buzz of being close to power – especially if he becomes a private secretary. And in due course the rewards will be his.

Traditionally, most main-stream jobs have largely been in the less fashionable areas of Foreign Office work, particularly consular, visa and administration, but fast streamers, whose work is almost exclusively political and economic (with occasional forays into the commercial side) are destined to become the main streamers' bosses. The main streamers are, in increasing numbers, protesting that like policemen doing time on the beat, fast streamers should know what it is like at the bottom, where as well as finding out about the work for which they will some day have to take responsibility, they might acquire the common sense which their main stream colleagues feel many of them lack.

Many young fast streamers agree; some of them even think they might enjoy the beat. Not every bright youngster necessarily thinks it more exciting to sit at a desk in London when he could be discovering what it is like to deal with visa applications in Bangladesh or distressed British drug-traffickers in Bangkok. Most of the working lives of those who end up flying high, will, of course, be spent on the political side, but more and more, there is a feeling that the ambassadors of the future should know what goes on throughout their whole embassy and should have had experience of all the work; they might even do a short time in a registry, so that they understand the boredom and complexity of the jobs there.

And some of them may discover a talent for other aspects of Foreign Office work, and by opting for it from time to time, raise its status.

Increasingly the Foreign Office stresses the importance of management skills, but, in the end, it takes an exceptional person to come in half-way up a structure and have any grasp of what life is like at the bottom. The contrast with the Army is striking. The military attachés whom I met almost all condemned Foreign Office man-management. One summed up its greatest deficiency. In the Foreign Office, he said, people look up; in the military they look down: in the Foreign Office, you are judged by how you perform according to your personal objectives; in the military you are judged on how you get the best out of your men.

These days main streamers and most young fast streamers believe that streaming on entry is unjustified. 'I feel permanently guilty,' said a young Grade 5, 'that my colleague next door, who does a job as taxing as mine and as well as I do mine, is worked harder and is four grades down from me. It is totally unfair.' There is a general feeling among many of the young that all graduates should enter together and be promoted on performance, with perhaps, a fast stream then emerging.

The conservatives are terrified that the most intellectually able will refuse to join if there is no fast stream and if they are required to deal with prisoners and disappointed visa-applicants. Others are more confident. 'If there were no fast stream,' said one fast streamer, 'I fear I am arrogant enough to think that I would still make my mark.' 'I hear on the grapevine,' observed another very bright youth to me, 'that you think we should all be sent out to work at the coal-face. And quite right too.'

In the Foreign Office, the fast streamers have traditionally made management and personnel policy as well as every other kind of policy. Because the policy-makers had no experience of most of the work of the Office and underestimated its subtleties, they failed to grasp that each kind of work required different talents. 'My bosses have never done consular work, have never done visa work, have never done management work, have never done commercial work,' said Jean Sharpe. Therefore they vaguely assumed that these were all straightforward jobs which any competent person could do and should do, for the buzz-phrase was the need among the main stream for 'the fully-rounded officer'. A main streamer might successively do consular, visa, administrative and commercial work. He might even do a spell in political or information work. The occasional exceptional person could do all these jobs well; most discovered that their talents lay in two or three of those areas and they had to be forced back into the others resignedly, or kicking and screaming, depending on temperament. So people who loved consular work would be sent off to be administrators while those with a natural talent for management were dispatched to look after the distressed British nationals at consulates abroad.

'I want to stay in commercial work,' said a main streamer who had slipped through the net and had four commercial posts in a row. 'No, no', he was told. 'You are mono-skilled. You must take a job in administration.' He forbore to mention that by that criterion every ambassador he had ever worked for was mono-skilled.

Fast streamer
John Sawers, private
secretary to the
foreign secretary
Douglas Hurd.

The difficulties caused by the Foreign Office's opposition to any main-stream specialisation has been compounded by the inevitable inflexibility of a bureaucratic promotion system. A main streamer who is brilliant in one line of work will be sent off, after his three or four years are up, into another that bores him rather than be given a promotion before his turn comes up.

The simmering discontent among the main streamers which led to a personnel upheaval at the end of the 1980s is gradually altering the climate. The Foreign Office has responded positively to advice from consultants to enable people to specialise more. It will take a long time to effect the culture change necessary for many of those at the top to recognise that there are gifts as unusual and valuable to the Service as being 'policy-capable', but at least there has been movement in response to harsh criticism towards trying to help all staff to develop a career that suits their talents.

The Foreign Office is also trying to deal with over-qualified Grade 10s. A long debate goes on about the advisability of abolishing the grade in favour of an executive support group on short-term contract to do secretarial-cum-registry work. Like all the Foreign Office's personnel problems, every solution – whether devised by consultants or by the policy-capable – throws up a raft of new problems. In this case the problems include the possibility of losing the valuable intake of career-minded school-leavers which has traditionally leavened the graduate recruits.

The success of the Foreign Office in recruiting high flyers and inspiring dedication amongst them is remarkable, but the present streaming system is divisive and unfair. The Foreign Office seems to be moving inexorably towards an integrated graduate entry: the key issue is whether in practice the Oxbridge firsts will do time in non-political work.

An outsider, Kevin Fuller, a Home Office secondee running the visa side of Jean Sharpe's office in Bangkok, talked about his bafflement at the streaming system. 'I think it's the most obvious cause for morale problems within an embassy . . . the people in the "E" stream who've worked their way up are quite often subordinate to people with minimal experience and expertise.' Since it was 'harder to work abroad than it is at home' and the personal pressures were greater, it was, he felt, particularly important to address the low morale evident among main streamers.

I think, you know, the obvious answer would be for everyone who works in the Foreign Office, absolutely everyone, however they enter the Foreign Office and whatever their career plan may be, to experience all the jobs that the . . . diplomatic service has to offer. It [would] give them the broadest base of knowledge and experience.

What was more, he believed, they would discover that what he called 'the service end' of the Foreign Office 'can provide some of the most interesting moments of anyone's career and without doubt some of the most demanding jobs that anyone's going to do.' Jean Sharpe's was a job which 'would stretch anyone in any part of the diplomatic service regardless of what they aimed to do in the future.'

Getting such a strange notion through to the policy-capable may take a little time.

· 6 ·

WOMEN

The Long March

The marriage bar was not formally abolished in the Foreign Office until 1972. Equal pay was granted in principle in January 1955, and fully implemented by 1961. Yet despite the slowness of the change in the rules, women who joined the Foreign Office in the 1960s have few complaints about discrimination at work. Like the Civil Service as a whole, the ethos of fairness has meant that women were always treated far better than in private industry.

Although her career was interrupted temporarily until the lifting of the marriage ban, Marian Binnington, born in 1940, whom the BBC filmed while inspecting posts in the United States, is one of those who look back on her career with delight and would do it all again. From a working-class background, she had relatives who had served abroad in the armed forces and the Colonial Office, and who gave her a taste for travel. At eighteen she joined the Commonwealth Office and was sent overseas after two years. She was first appointed to Colombo, but rejected by the high commissioner, who decided that as it was a one-person registry, 'the bag work would be too tough for a girl.' Then came Karachi. 'It was a dream come true, that's all. I went at a time when the age of majority was twenty-one . . . my parents had to sign over guardianship to the high commissioner in Pakistan to allow me to go at the age of twenty.' It took three weeks to get there by liner, and she loved it.

In the sixties you didn't leave home unless you got married or your job made you leave home so . . . this was the first time I'd had my own place. It was lovely and hot – also very smelly, but I got used to the smell and I loved the heat. I had a servant, for heaven's sakes, and I had a fabulous time in Karachi, loved it, every minute, a social life that would never have come my way if I'd stayed in the East End of London or if I'd stayed anywhere in the UK . . . it was the sort of social life that the Sloanes have in London nowadays.

She went up the Khyber Pass, was posted to Delhi and then visited Afghanistan. Diplomatic bags notwithstanding, she did not find the service discriminatory. It gave unimaginable freedom to women of her generation, not just to travel, but to spread their wings in career terms and achieve the kind of professional success that they would never have dreamed of as young women.

The major battles of principle are long over, but there are still very few women in the senior ranks of the Foreign Office. The statistics are all too predictable. Out of 580 secretaries all but two are female, as are all the nurses. Women make a reasonably good showing in the legal and research cadres, with 31 per cent and 34 per cent respectively. This was the situation in April 1993:

Number of women in the Diplomatic Wing of the Foreign Office

Grade	Total men and women		Number of women in grade		Women as per cent of total
	1993	[1992]	**1993**	[1992]	**1993**
1-3	147	[146]	5	[5]	3.4%
4	278	[281]	10	[10]	3.5%
5	453	[450]	54	[49]	11.92%
6	265	[274]	29	[30]	10.94%
7M	444	[424]	92	[81]	20.72%
7D-8	157	[160]	49	[51]	31.21%
9	783	[806]	385	[388]	49.16%
10	541	[581]	222	[237]	41.03%
Total:	**3068**	[3122]	**846**	[851]	**27.25%**

M = main stream
D = development, direct entrant fast stream

In other words, in 1993 women made up 27.25 per cent of the Diplomatic Service proper, with 72 per cent of them clustered in the bottom two ranks. Of the five women at senior grade in October 1993, Maeve Fort was ambassador to the Lebanon, Maureen MacGlashan was on loan to the Civil Service Selection Board, Pauline Neville-Jones was on secondment to the Cabinet Office as chairman of the Joint Intelligence Committee, Rosemary Spencer was minister in Berlin and Veronica Sutherland was deputy chief clerk and responsible for the personnel departments. Only Veronica Sutherland is married.

The reasons for the shortage of women at the top are the old familiar ones about differing priorities that explain the lack of substantial numbers of women in top jobs anywhere, but there are, of course, in the Foreign Office, additional factors that exacerbate

RIGHT Jean Sharpe playing tennis in the Bangkok compound.

the problem. If there are increasingly few well-qualified women prepared to tag around the world after their husbands, there are even fewer well-qualified men who are prepared to follow their wives. So a woman joining the Foreign Office has to face some stark choices.

In the secretarial grade the position is relatively straightforward. Young women join to see the world, or some of it; for the sake of travel and adventure they accept a very low salary in London, and in most instances a longish and extremely boring period working in a typing pool regardless of their previous experience. From the typing pool they go forth into the world, and for those that strike lucky it is a terrific experience.

A secretary with professional ambition may sit tests and interviews to break into the main stream at Grade 9 or 10; she would be unlikely to hang around for several years waiting for an ill-paid vacancy at the top of the secretarial tree, and there are fewer posts at that level abroad. Only those biding time until their next posting overseas, or people who are institutionalised, want to stay in London on Foreign Office rates of pay. The secretarial turnover is high, for most settle with someone and only a few partners or husbands are venturesome enough to go abroad as accompanying spouses.

Women make up just over 40 per cent of those at Grade 10. Like the secretaries, they join for the adventure and because in some cases joining enables them to escape from small-town or provincial life. They can afford to move to London because of accommodation at Foreign Office hostels, where they live while waiting to be posted abroad or to find some like-minded friends to share a flat with. The hostels are pretty basic and some find them grim, but they do at least offer companionship.

A constant complaint from the Grade 10s is that nobody at the recruitment stage ever told them how tedious the work would be; they sit glumly in the registries in London and abroad, filing telegrams and reports and briefing papers and longing to be allowed to use their minds. 'Monkeys could do it,' said one disconsolate Grade 10 in Washington. Some of them are trained in communications – transmitting and receiving telegrams, and distributing them to the right people. This forms the bulk of work at that grade, and for all the brave statements in the recruitment brochures about the importance of knowing that you're at the centre, the hub, the axis of the office or the embassy, it is mind-numbingly boring work for most of these bright girls and boys. They long for a posting which yields something a little more interesting, on the administrative side, for instance. But unless they are exceptionally lucky, they will have about eight years of untaxing labour before they get a chance of promotion to Grade 9.

The women are less inclined to stay than the men, but at that level there is quite a lot of intermarriage. For the lowest grade, marrying a colleague poses fewer problems than further up the tree, because there are many more posts abroad and so joint postings are feasible. Yet if they are roughly the same age and experience there will often come a moment when someone's career has to take a back seat.

One grade up, at Grade 9, where the gender balance is fifty-fifty, the system bears down particularly hard. Recruits are required to have two 'A' levels; almost all of them now have degrees. Many of them failed the examination for the fast stream and feel like

11+ rejects and there is little likelihood of transferring into a higher grade: promotion is likely to take seven, eight, or nine years.

Main-stream people spend a higher percentage of their time abroad than do those in the fast stream, so for women this grade brings particularly difficult choices. They go abroad to do entry clearance work, consular work, administration and so on. They have transient relationships, and – unlike the men – rarely marry foreign spouses. A Grade 9 observed that she had had two Japanese boyfriends. Had she met either in London she might have been tempted to marry, but having served in Japan she knew she did not want to be a Japanese wife. So in terms of looking for marriage partners, women tend to be restricted to people they are involved with at home, or colleagues or expatriates.

Like the fast-stream women, many of the main-stream women who stay and go up the tree (and turnover is high) stay single. Boyfriends at home get fed up, relationships founder and they settle for occasional affairs or opt perforce for celibacy. 'The pool from which you might draw a prospective spouse is always narrow if you're constantly living a nomadic life . . .' said Marie-Louise Childs, a Grade 9 entry clearance officer in Bangkok.

That's the price you pay for joining the Office. I had an elderly school teacher who . . . said 'Well, you know, if you join the Foreign Office you'll have to be prepared to be a spinster for the rest of your life.' That's not entirely true. I've got lots of colleagues who are married, but it's a possibility because of the way the job takes you from pillar to post.

Over the past few decades, with its customary virtues of decency and integrity and its customary vices of lack of imagination and inadequate consultation, the Foreign Office has struggled to forget its old assumptions and adapt to the needs of its women. But as with most institutions, line managers tend to be much more cautious than the recruiters, trainers and personnel departments. Ambassadors, who used to have the right to reject staff offered by London (nowadays they are able to turn down only their deputy or their personal assistant), could often be extremely rigid about where they thought it appropriate to place women.

The British fear of embarrassment has made the Foreign Office slow to send contentious individuals to particular posts. They advanced very slowly and cautiously in sending women of middle or senior grade to Arab countries. The Americans were more afraid of law-suits at home, citing discrimination, than of upsetting the susceptibilities of foreigners, so they sent women to the most unlikely places. Arab governments rapidly adjusted and chose to accept the female diplomat as an honorary man, so young British female Arabists are now becoming numerous in most Arab countries. The three junior posts in the five-man consulate in Jerusalem which deals with the Palestinians were, in mid-1993, occupied by women. However where the religious police rule, women diplomats cannot function properly; it will be some time before our man in Saudi Arabia is a woman.

In 1986 the chief clerk, Mark Russell, reported in his newsletter on the case taken by

Mrs Sue Rogerson, who alleged discrimination because her posting to Lusaka as deputy high commissioner had been cancelled.

The decision not to go ahead with the posting was taken on the basis of the judgement that an all-female Political Section in the Lusaka Chancery would not, in the local conditions, have been as effective as an all-male, or a mixed one. There was never any suggestion that women *per se* could not undertake political work, (or any other work) effectively in Zambia. The essential point in the Board's final decision was the question of balance and a judgement on the effectiveness of the post.

A settlement was reached without the case going to an Industrial Tribunal and the Foreign Office formally acknowledged 'that while acting in good faith the decision to abandon Sue Rogerson's posting was mistaken and could not be reconciled with Section 7 of the Equal Opportunities Act', which stated that for a women to be excluded from a job, it must be shown that that job can *only* be done by a man. Mrs Rogerson had accepted that the Foreign Office's

stated policy as an equal opportunities employer was to develop the careers of each member of the service on the basis of individual merit irrespective of sex. She also accepted that we recognised our obligation that her career should not suffer as a result of the cancellation of the Lusaka posting.

Sue Rogerson would be 'pursuing her career without any detriment to her promotion or future prospects. . . . We for our part learned some valuable lessons and are looking carefully at all our procedures in the light of this case. We are determined that every officer in the Service should as far as possible receive equal treatment.'

Sue Rogerson was promoted and posted as consul general to Perth, Western Australia, where she stayed a relatively short time; she was offered a better job outside the Service and parted from it amicably.

In a valedictory lecture in 1989 the same chief clerk spoke about the continuing efforts being made to give equal treatment to women. Measures taken included joint postings of married couples, flexible and part-time working, and leaning on heads of missions to help find jobs for spouses. 'But', he concluded, 'at the end of the day I do not think that twin careers can be managed in the Diplomatic Service without, at some stage, periods of separation, or the subordination of one career to another. That, it seems to me, is a reality. But within that reality we shall do all we can to help spouses who want to work.'

Unfortunately, yet again, a solution generated a new problem. Management were downcast when the realisation broke through that while a joint posting is welcome to the couple involved, it is usually deeply resented by single people or those married outside the Service, for by their nature, especially for the higher ranks, joint postings are available only in the most sought-after jobs in the big embassies. Most people are keen to go to Brussels and New York, Washington and Paris. So now, in the new selection procedure, which is cumbersomely geared to fairness, joint postings occur only if each party is the best applicant for the job.

The higher up the tree you go, the more difficult become issues like flexi-time and part-time working, while long hours for both partners put a great strain on their marriage and cause tremendous difficulties with child care. So the much-valued female half of a married couple of first secretaries in Moscow concludes that she wishes to see her baby during the week as well as at weekends, and the ambassador is faced with allowing her to work half-time (without anyone to take over the other half) or losing her completely.

Vivien Life and Tim Dowse, a married couple who are both first secretaries in Washington, have managed to work full-time so far, despite having a young baby, but they will have severe difficulties when they return to London, where 'the interesting jobs are the ones where you end up working ten or twelve hours a day . . . which is not easy with a small child.' When Tim met Vivien he was in the Foreign Office and she was in the Treasury. They approached the Foreign Office, told them their situation and the Foreign Office took Vivien on. They said they would like to go to the United States and the Foreign Office gave them a joint posting.

Job-sharing may be the answer for them when they return to London, but though the Foreign Office has been exceptionally helpful about unpaid leave, like most employers, it has proceeded at a snail's pace on job-sharing except at the most junior levels.

There are other problems that come with the very traditional male culture. The Foreign Office rather resembles an all-male boarding school which has taken in a handful of girls in the sixth form, a larger number in the first form, but has only a couple of token women as teachers. It takes a very confident woman to resist the unconscious pressure to be an honorary chap with all the virtues of the chaps – loyalty to the school, respect for its traditions, deference to the head, and a dedication to *mens sana in corpore sano* – as well as their vices – reverence for a hierarchy, unquestioning obedience and a desire to keep the new bugs in their place and see that they go through what you went through. 'The only good and responsible officer is the one who works long hours!' wrote one disaffected officer and mother in 1992, briefing a management review team investigating long hours and working practices.

And as the officer rises so do the number of hours expected. This is the expected culture in the FCO. The pressures placed on middle:senior women officers trying to combine work with family (or just a non FCO husband) are as a result greatly increased. Unless she relegates family to second place she is faced with either accepting a less demanding post with more reasonable hours but consequential lower promotion prospects or, in a higher profile job, risking claims of inability to cope, especially if a job suffers regular overload, no matter the quality and quantity of her daily output, because she is limited to some form of conditioned hours (ie childcare cut-off).

There are difficulties from the outset. To be recruited into the fast stream, women have to be extraordinarily tough. Not because they face discrimination in the normal sense of the term, but because the recruiters – like recruiters everywhere – look for people in their own image, and they look for the time-honoured male diplomatic qualities. There are still men around the institution who think that warmth and intuition, and an interest in people,

are more useful in a sewing circle than in a chancery. Foreign Office women may let their hair down in private but most of them take care to avoid doing anything to attract such dangerous adjectives as 'emotional', 'mercurial' or 'lacking in detachment'. Some of them go down the Mrs Thatcher route. Indeed one of the fascinating aspects of observing large numbers of the young fliers today is that there are several rather gentle, concerned, new-mannish chaps working with deceptively fierce women, who dare not let their façade crumble.

Yet the climate is improving. The majority of women feel little deliberate discrimination. In 1993, Glynne Evans, one of two female heads of department, had three women as heads of section and considered that

it is a great mistake to be self-conscious about being a woman in a world that is largely dominated by men, and I never have been. As it happens I have a large number of extremely able women in my department. One doesn't see them as men or women, one sees them as officers and I think that's the way one should always see oneself.

And there are many rising stars, like Frances Guy, until recently Iraq desk officer in London, and Glynne Evans who are unafraid to talk passionately about their idealism and their humanitarian concerns, and who take being a female career diplomat and, in Frances's case, bringing up a young family at the same time, in their stride. But it isn't easy. The Foreign Office faces problems keeping high-flying women. According to a report prepared by the Office's trade union in November 1992, the percentage of women graduates coming into the higher grades is rising, but many more women apply for the main stream than the fast stream, and the percentage of women resigning from the higher grades is also climbing. If these women continue to leave at their current rate (of the six women in the 1983 Grade 7D and Grade 8 entry, all but one have resigned), the trade union says that the Foreign Office may ultimately face structural personnel problems. The report also states that the Office's 'current working practices demand from women an unacceptable number of sacrifices. Women are not fake men. They face social and other pressures as a result of child bearing which need to be accommodated . . .'

Overseas posts can be less demanding in terms of the numbers of hours worked, provide better facilities for looking after young children, and the allowances augment low salaries, but they can also be much more demanding in terms of stress and, often, personal safety. It is still possible to find a diplomat near retirement wringing his hands at the dangers that may be facing young women on his staff, but the women themselves show no such worry. Glynne Evans spends many days wearing a bulletproof vest, travelling in and out of Sarajevo and other parts of war-torn Bosnia, while Frances Guy went across the Turkish border into northern Iraq to visit the Kurdish-controlled-areas. As officers (and, indeed, as spouses) they have always tended towards the intrepid. A story from Peking

LEFT Vivien Life and her husband Tim Dowse, both first secretaries at the British Embassy in Washington.

Frances Guy, then Iraq desk officer in London, on a trip to the Kurdish controlled areas of Northern Iraq, taking a rest with her *peshmerga* escort.

Glynne Evans, head of the UN department, clad in a
flak jacket, visits Sarajevo.

during the cultural revolution is a classic. During one attack on the embassy, which involved physical assaults on many of the women, one young girl was hit on the forehead by a flagstaff. Typically, one of her male colleagues urged her not to cry. 'Cry in front of these bastards?' she said. 'Not likely.'

Maeve Fort – attractive, humorous, intelligent yet practical and in every respect her own woman – lately ambassador to the Peoples' Republic of Mozambique during a civil war, and now sailing calmly around the Lebanon in her armoured ambassadorial jeep, is as good a role model as any young female diplomat could want. As long, that is, as she is prepared to sacrifice family life.

· 7 ·

LANGUAGE

Going Native

In order to be eligible to apply for a job with the Foreign Office you must be a British citizen, and at least one parent must have been a citizen of a Commonwealth country or of the Irish Republic for the previous thirty years. It is the job of the Security Service, including the Foreign Office's own 'field investigating officers', to decide whether you possess the requisite qualifications and characteristics.

Positive security vetting can cause long delays between being offered a job and taking it up. Negative vetting is necessary for non-secret work: in other words you are acceptable if the Security Services have nothing on you and no reason to suppose that you present a risk. But if, like most diplomats, you will inevitably be seeing secret documents, you have to be positively declared safe after an arcane, elaborate and lengthy procedure.

For a twenty-two-year-old straight out of university the procedure can be reasonably swift. For a fifty-year-old secretary who has moved around and lived a little, it will take longer, especially if her origins are more exotic than the Security Service is normally used to. The positive vetting of one woman of Hong Kong origin whose birth had not been documented took eighteen months.

The initial vetting involves a thorough scrutiny of the background, the friends and the travels of the would-be entrant. Membership of Communist or Fascist parties is a disqualifier. Visits to Communist countries, or over-indulgence in drink, sex, or anything else perceived as a vice is deeply suspect. Anything which involves breaking the law, like taking drugs, automatically rules out the candidate and indeed is a sacking offence.

Members of the Diplomatic Service have to adhere to a strict code of conduct, laid out thus in the regulations:

The following general principles govern your conduct as a member of the Diplomatic Service:

(a) you must give your undivided allegiance to the State on all occasions when the State has a claim on your services;

(b) you must not subordinate your duty to your private interests, nor put yourself in a position where your duty and your private interests conflict;

(c)   you must not use your official position to further your private interests, nor act so as to create a reasonable suspicion that you have done so;

(d)   you must not engage in heavy gambling or speculation;

(e)   you must not engage in private financial transactions in connection with any matter on which members of the Diplomatic Service might be suspected of having access to information which could be turned to private gain;

(f)   you must not engage in any occupation or undertaking which might conflict with the interests of the Diplomatic Service or be inconsistent with your position as a member of that Service;

(g)   you must not fall short of the professional standard expected of members of the Diplomatic Service or act in a way which might bring discredit upon the Service.

This is quite a tall order and the security procedures for ensuring an officer lives up to these principles can seem harsh and insultingly intrusive. On the five-year check up, the security vetters are entitled to talk to two of the officer's friends, who are asked questions about the subject's sex life, the state of his marriage, if they have ever seen the individual drunk, gambling and so on.

On the plus side is the sheer efficiency of the system. Whether because of its effective security precautions, its recruitment methods or its ethos, the Foreign Office has rarely been betrayed by its own people. The spies Philby, Burgess and Maclean were all the more infamous because of their rarity. In the last decade, say Personnel, only five officers were sacked, 'three for financial misdemeanours, one for gross misconduct and one for a serious abuse of position. The three financial cases were all the subject of court proceedings prior to disciplinary proceedings.' On average, there are twenty minor disciplinary cases in any one year which result in the relevant officer receiving a written warning as to future conduct. This usually works, though occasionally someone is fined, downgraded or has his promotion delayed.

Security of information

Keeping information secure can also be a cumbersome business. Cautious people tend to over-classify everything, and ensuring that Foreign Office information does not fall into the hands of foreign spies puts an enormous burden on the communication system: cypher clerks work round the clock.

In 1993 there were four classifications for official documents, defined as follows:

RESTRICTED Information and material the unauthorised disclosure of which would be **undesirable** in the interests of the nation.

CONFIDENTIAL Information and material the unauthorised disclosure of which would be **damaging** to the interests of the nation.

LEFT Gurkha soldier guarding the British Embassy in Bangkok.

Despite the end of the Cold War, the morning meeting at the Moscow Embassy is still held in the 'safe' room which is specially designed to prevent eavesdropping.

SECRET Information and material the unauthorised disclosure of which would cause **serious injury** to the interests of the nation.

TOP SECRET Information and material the unauthorised disclosure of which would cause **exceptionally grave damage** to the nation.

To over-grade material say the instructions (which are themselves restricted), is damaging, though under-grading means 'that the material will be at risk through the absence of appropriate security measures'. And security breaches of any kind are serious offences. Communications technology has added to the irritating aspects of security. There are places in embassies where a lap-top computer may not be taken lest it interfere with the system; tape recorders pose a threat in other rooms. Only the positively vetted are allowed unaccompanied on certain floors.

There is much criticism within the Foreign Office these days that paper is still guarded as if the evil empire were alive and well. Security standards are maintained, yet – as with so many aspects of Foreign Office activities – financial constraints have led to the function being maintained by exploitation of the staff. As security guards are made redundant, already over-worked main streamers are required to become security duty officers every fourth week or so.

In Moscow, confidential meetings have, for many years, been held in a large safe which contains a table around which a dozen or so people can sit, with just enough room for another layer to sit close behind them. When the ambassador enters he closes the door of the safe and conversation becomes KGB-proof: even with the collapse of Communism, there is a perception that some of the old guard may still be plying their trade in the old way. There is a similar perception that some of them are doing likewise in MI6 and that valued resources which could be put into greater diplomatic effort are, as one diplomat in Moscow bitterly observed, 'probably being spent on the same clutch of die-hards sitting in a basement reading three-week-old Russian newspapers'.

Protection of personnel

In these violent times, however, the major Foreign Office security headache is the protection of its people. On the ground floor of the headquarters building in London is a plaque which reads:

In memory of members of HM Diplomatic Service, victims of terrorism while serving their country

Christopher Ewart-Biggs, CMG OBE Dublin 1976

Sir Richard Sykes KCMG MC The Hague 1979

Percy Norris OBE Bombay 1984

Today, because of terrorism and an increase in aggressive behaviour, most embassies are no longer user-friendly. Guards quiz you at entrance gates; receptionists, consular officials and visa clerks sit behind reinforced glass; passes are worn by everyone and at

IN MEMORY OF
MEMBERS OF H.M.
DIPLOMATIC SERVICE
VICTIMS OF TERRORISM
WHILE SERVING
THEIR COUNTRY

CHRISTOPHER EWART-BIGGS
CMG. OBE.   DUBLIN 1976
SIR RICHARD SYKES
KCMG. MC.   THE HAGUE 1979
PERCY NORRIS
OBE.   BOMBAY 1984

Memorial in the Foreign Office.

all times; impregnable doors inside cannot be opened unless you have coded cards or know the combination for the buttons; ambassadors travel in armour-plated cars.

In terms of personal protection, United Kingdom security people are effective but unobtrusive, unlike their American equivalents, who are a standing joke internationally because of the fortresses they build and the manner in which they maintain them. In Beirut, when the American ambassador drives out, he is in a convoy of six armoured vehicles, one with two mounted machine guns and several of them crammed with armed guards. The klaxon sounds from the moment they leave the embassy and locals' cars are forced to the side of the road as the Americans race through, disrupting the traffic and focusing the attention of all Beirut on the ambassadorial trail.

The British of course are different. 'We like to keep it nice and low-key,' observed a member of Maeve Fort's Close Protection Team. No sirens are sounded unless there is a very good reason and the British ambassador can pass through Beirut without attention being drawn to her.

'Security threat to Maeve?' observed an ambassador in another Arab country. 'Why she must be the safest diplomat in the Foreign Office.' At peaceful times in Beirut this may be true, but in today's world there is no possibility of an ambassador simply eschewing such protection. Every European Community ambassador in Beirut has similar protection, and for one to lower his guard means becoming a soft target. So when Maeve Fort takes her dog for a walk, six men go too, and in her house there can be little privacy, in her garden none.

Many ambassadors have adapted to a regime in which they are always shadowed by silent, watchful men and they leave for their offices at irregular times and by irregular routes. The German police escort for the British ambassador in Bonn is highly visible: whenever he stops to get out, plain-clothes police men and women brandish machine guns.

Rather like British commuters who would prefer the police to be less inclined to respond to suspicious packages on the trains, many diplomats would prefer to be freed from what they see as security excesses and instead take their chances. 'I don't want all this,' observed one senior ambassador, 'but my wife insists.' So of course does the Foreign Office, which suffers great corporate grief and guilt when it loses one of its number to a terrorist attack.

In October 1993 there were Close Protection Teams from Britain (military police and SAS) in operation in Colombia, Cyprus, the Lebanon, the Sudan, Uganda and Zaire. There are twenty posts where there are local close protection arrangements with police, security authorities or private organisations and ninety bullet-proof vehicles at various posts around the world.

First Day

Once you have been positively vetted, you can start work.

The day-to-day political work of the Foreign Office is notoriously difficult to explain, but their document *Office Skills and Practices in the FCO*, makes a brave shot at spelling out the basics. One section describes, at enormous length, a novice's first day in a political job, sitting in what is known in the Foreign Office as the Third Room – so-called because the head and assistant head of department each has a room of his own nearby. The on-the-job training is essentially the responsibility of the assistant – an experienced Grade 5, who has had two overseas postings as a first secretary.

RIGHT Security desk at one of the entrances to the Foreign Office.

The Third Room contains two or three people and is responsible for a subject of its own – perhaps one or two countries. The novice has to get to know his designated country as quickly as possible. He is advised to put the best available map of Lilliput (the imaginary example used in the guide) on the wall, steep himself in its history and culture, get to know the members of its embassy and learn from them about who and what counts in Lilliput. He should learn how the registry system works and how to extract material from it.

Detailed instructions are given about initialling telegrams, passing them on – what to read and what not to read. Everything about Lilliput should be read, but the novice should also keep abreast of major areas of diplomatic activity worldwide, such as a UN peace initiative in the Middle East or a negotiation between the European Community and developing countries. He can learn general principles from circulated speeches by the secretary of state and drafting skills from telegrams and ambassadorial despatches.

There is a system for dealing with each piece of paper in the in-tray: letters must be registered and copied to all appropriate people and replies drafted and cleared with all concerned. The work encountered ranges from organising a sight-seeing tour for a visiting basketball team to drafting a reply to a Parliamentary Question. Most important is to learn to organise work in order of priority and get everything done on time.

Security reminder in the lavatory of the Bangkok Embassy.

There is a discipline about working in the Office which is very real despite the informality in which it is clothed. If your Head of Department 'wonders if you would try to produce a draft reply to a Parliamentary Question by 3 o'clock,' what he or she really means is that you must ensure that your draft is written by then, cleared with everybody else who ought to see the draft reply and if you have to miss your lunch, that's too bad. Only a bad Third Room puts up beautifully written drafts half an hour after the deadline.

By now the novice should have grasped that most Foreign Office business cannot be dealt with by any one department: the views of others, inside the Foreign Office and around Whitehall, must be sought and differences 'reconciled or overruled; and the draft – a piece of paper not yet in final form – is the vehicle for establishing a consensus. The same process of consultation goes on internationally.' His other discovery is that work flows upwards, giving him 'a considerable power of initiative', for he decides what should be submitted to his superiors: 'When to submit is one of the most difficult tricks of the trade you have to learn.' The guide gives an example:

You turn again to your in-tray and pick up a minute on blue paper signed by your Head of Department a week ago and addressed, in the top left-hand corner, to your Superintending Assistant Under-Secretary. It is a submission recommending that the Lilliputian Foreign Minister be invited to visit London. The AUS, over the page, has written a short minute agreeing with the Department's recommendation: since it would be useful to have the Foreign Minister's views on a number of subjects. The AUS had submitted the minute to the Permanent Under-Secretary who had written on it 'I hope you will agree that the Secretary of State should find the time for this. The Foreign Minister is worth talking to and will anyway be coming back through London after the General Assembly.' The PUS had marked the minute to the Minister of State's office, who had written 'I agree' on it. The submission had then gone to the Secretary of State's office (known as the Private Office) where the Private Secretary had put it into the Secretary of State's overnight box, with a little ephemeral slip saying 'Secretary of State: if you want to, you could fit him in on pm 15 October'. The Secretary of State, in his red pen, wrote across the bottom on the page 'All right. Try for 15 October'. And the submission the next day went back down the line so that the Minister of State, PUS, AUS and Head of Department all saw the Secretary of State's decision. Attached to the submission the Assistant had written an ephemeral note saying 'Mr/Ms X. Pl spk'. The Assistant will want to discuss with you the mechanics of translating the Secretary of State's wishes into action. So you start thinking ahead: the Lilliputian minister is in New York now, so we shall probably need to send a telegram to our Mission there so they can catch the Minister before he leaves; better repeat the telegram to our Ambassador in Lilliput to keep him informed; perhaps the Lilliputian Ambassador should be asked to call at the office so that he could be told why the Secretary of State attaches importance to the visit.

No day is 'typical' in the FCO, and every Department is different. But this glimpse of the kind of situations that occur may give you an idea of what goes on in the Third Room.

It sounds tedious and much of it is, but although the booklet goes no further, one can predict how the novice will become enthralled when, for instance, Lilliput's tribal tensions threaten to destabilise the region with serious implications for UN peace-keeping forces in next-door Brobdingnag. The Department of Trade is pressing for a licence to be granted for the export of equipment which the new King claims is to make machine tools, but MI6 think may be used to attack Brobdingnag to distract attention from domestic troubles; this would be very damaging to the substantial British investments there. After a couple of bloody border-incursions by Lilliput, Brobdingnag starts a huge row in the United Nations and the United States tries to push a UN Resolution through the Security Council threatening sanctions against Lilliput, which for at least two weeks becomes a place everyone can find on the map. Every day the novice is in at dawn to read the telegrams from Lilliput and Brobdingnag and his analyses wing their way up to the secretary of state. In one day he has to draft a House of Commons statement and a speech.

Prince Bernhart von Bülow, a pre-First World War German Chancellor, said that 'diplomacy is a "first class stall seat at the theatre of life"'. It is that closeness to big events that hooks these bright young people and keeps them poorly-paid but uncomplaining at their desks for sixty and seventy hours a week. 'Do you enjoy it?' people ask. 'Oh, yes', they reply. 'It's tremendous fun.'

LEARNING THE LANGUAGE

There are several languages to be mastered if you want to make yourself understood inside the Foreign Office. Here are some examples.

Arabic and the Arabists

'For all their pin-striped suits and old school ties, Foreign Office top men would feel happier dressed up like the Sheik of Araby,' explained the *Daily Mirror* in May 1991. It is a popular view of British diplomats. On a notice-board in the office of a Jewish third secretary in Tel Aviv there is a Jak cartoon from the time of the 1973 war between Egypt and Israel which features Sir Alec Douglas-Home and a collection of officials – all dressed in Arab robes – pausing on their way into the Foreign Office to gaze at a small perplexed colleague in suit and bowler hat. 'Oh, come on, Cohen,' one of them is calling to him. 'Everyone at the Foreign Office dresses like this these days.'

A Foreign Office Arabist is a person who has learned Arabic and who has a job which David Gore-Booth, the British ambassador in Riyadh, has defined as that of trying 'to put himself into the mindset of the Arabs and not to become an Arab or behave like one but to be able to predict or judge how Arabs would react in certain circumstances.' Of course Arabists have to be watched to make sure they do not go native. 'X has had one Arab posting too many,' one senior diplomat said to me. 'How does it show?' I asked. 'Circular thinking.'

It has always seemed faintly sinister to the outside world that the Foreign Office contains so many Arabists. Part of this is bound up with popular culture, festooned as it is with images of sexually-ambiguous Englishmen careering around the desert with burning-eyed Bedouin. The reality is usually more prosaic. Most Arabist diplomats did not start out as inveterate romantics in love with the desert: such people, like Wilfred Thesiger, become explorers. While a few people arrived in the Foreign Office with Arabic degrees, most of them were pushed towards learning the language because they were excellent linguists or else they opted for Arabic because it was beneficial in career terms: there are many posts where a knowledge of Arabic is necessary whereas Hebrew, for example, is required in only a couple. And there are even more pragmatic reasons. David Gore-Booth, whom the *Daily Mirror* suggested in 1991 would feel more at home in 'an oasis in the middle of the Arabian desert', expected when he joined the Office in 1964 to be asked to build on his Russian 'O' level. When he was told instead to learn Arabic, he agreed happily when he discovered that he would be sent immediately to study in the Lebanon, thus qualifying for enough allowances to save him and his new bride from a penurious start to their marriage.

Yet there is a solid basis to the longstanding perception of Arabist cliquishness. Very young people spent usually about sixteen months together at the Middle East Centre for Arab Studies (MECAS) in Shemlan, a village near Beirut. It was hardly surprising that they developed the mentality of a cadre – with its inevitable sense of superiority – along with such British distinguishing marks as a MECAS tie and nicknames. (A young first secretary told me of his delight at hearing a middle-aged colleague in London speak of the need to send a telegram to 'Baggers' – i.e. Baghdad.) Their colleagues habitually referred to them as the Camel Corps or the camels. Even now, many years after the Lebanese civil war closed MECAS, its graduates still have a certain bond, for over the years they have served together in many locations or been in constant communication as they ploughed their particular Arab furrow in the Middle Eastern Department or in an embassy abroad.

For younger Arabists, trained now in London and Cairo, there is no longer much more of a bond than is likely to be found these days among the large numbers of youngsters being trained in Russian or Chinese. And the sense of being a crack corps has considerably diminished. These days being an Arabist is less important than spending time at one of the centres of multilateral negotiations. An Arabist of the old school might have spent almost all his service abroad in Arab countries. Sir Donald Maitland, for instance, whose jobs at home included being principal private secretary to the secretary of state, joined the Foreign Office in 1947, served abroad in Iraq, Lebanon (as director of MECAS), Egypt and Libya and did not leave that particular track until at the age of fifty-one he was appointed UK permanent representative to the United Nations. David Gore-Booth, by contrast, served in Iraq, Zambia, Libya, at the office of the permanent representative (UKREP) in Brussels, Saudi Arabia and at the UK mission to the UN (UKMIS) New York, before becoming an ambassador.

Yet, because of the high emotions aroused by Middle Eastern politics, the Arabist legacy is still seen to dominate the Foreign Office. There is a common media perception that to be an Arabist is to be pro-Arab and hence anti-Israel. In this caricature, says

Gore-Booth, the Foreign Office Arabists are 'conducting Middle East policy entirely to satisfy the Arabs and to jeopardise the interests of Israel.' His statement at an off-the-record meeting that there were grave breaches of human rights in the Israeli-occupied territories led to a demand by the *Mail on Sunday* for his resignation. Yet whatever Zionists may fear, much of the effort of the Foreign Office Arabists is spent on trying to help along a peace process that will not only respect the Palestinian desire for self-determination, but maintain the security of Israel.

Whatever leavening may be provided by other postings, most Arabists have a life-long fascination with their specialism. Arabism offers something for everyone. The scholarly can immerse themselves in an astonishing ancient culture and history and the highly political have the most volatile part of the world to deal with. When he was assistant under secretary in charge of the Middle East, Gore-Booth once explained, in a speech to British businessmen, the five main reasons why the British were so strongly involved there. First, they had a tradition of expertise in the region, which was greatly envied by other foreign services. Second, the Middle East was the scene of two of the major unresolved disputes of our time – Arab/Israel and Iran/Iraq – 'both of which threaten international peace and security and both of which are connected.' Third was trade – 'and no harm in that for a nation of shopkeepers': apart from sub-Saharan Africa and the Commonwealth overall, the Middle East was the only region in the world where the United Kingdom had a substantial surplus on visible trade – £3.2 billion in 1992. Fourth was Europe – 'which is the Middle East's backyard, or vice versa.' And the fifth was – 'and I do not deny it, fascination. As Sir Anthony Nutting once said: "It is almost impossible to forecast their [the Arabs] future. Some change or upheaval always occurs which contradicts what has gone before and similarly proves false the wisest of prophecies as to what may follow."'

In a profession where the greatest rewards come from the sheer interest of the job, it is no wonder that the under secretaryship in charge of the Middle East is greatly coveted. 'I've got the most interesting job that an Arabist can ever have,' said David Gore-Booth during his last few months in London, 'because I'm having to deal with and be knowledgeable about twenty-one countries or whatever it is and the disputes that affect the region – of which there are many, alas. And being closer to ministers gives one a greater degree of influence than ambassadors tend to have these days. Yes, it's a pulsating job and it's been absolutely fascinating.' He also admitted it had been exhausting, hardly surprisingly, after a period that included issues like the Rushdie *fatwa*, British hostages in the Lebanon, the Gulf war, the Kurdish safe havens, the civil war in the Sudan, the reopening of the British Embassy in Syria, the deployment of British troops under a United Nations mandate in the Western Sahara and, of course, continuing efforts (both in London and by British ambassadors throughout the Middle East) to help move matters along in the Arab–Israeli peace negotiations.

And for the diplomats posted abroad, there is a continuing joy in the sheer variety. Saudi Arabia is nothing like Syria, and Tunisia might be in a different world. Similarly, the issues vary hugely. An Arabist could be trying to alleviate the massive humanitarian problems of the Kurds or the Palestinian refugees, or tracking the implications of the clash in Egypt between religious fundamentalism and secular politics, or he could be dealing with the situation thrown up in the Gulf states where a sudden accession of easy money has caused a loss of soul which is creating a backlash against the corruption of Western materialism.

And then there is the poetry of the desert. Just because most Foreign Office Arabists started out as conscripts, they are not immune to romance. My most stunning sensual experience in a trip around many countries occurred in the Occupied Territories. I stood with a companion at the top of a mountain looking across the desert towards the Dead Sea and Jordan. The heat was dry, the air was still, the landscape consisted of uncluttered shapes and the silence was absolute. Just below were the caves used by anchorites over the millenia and a few hundred yards behind was a small Bedouin encampment. I stood mesmerised for a long time and then uttered some inarticulate sound to the British diplomat beside me. 'Now you know why people become Arabists,' he said. 'It's about this. It's not about the politics.'

Jargon

Press metaphors are military: diplomatic language is mainly related to sport – particularly team sports. Boxing metaphors are as violent as it gets. There is extraordinarily little vulgarity, swearing or blaspheming.

Here is a small selection of terms I heard or read during my time observing the Foreign Office. It is hard to avoid the inference that the culture tends towards the male.

Sport

GENERAL
Level playing field
Certain matters play badly back home
Blow the whistle

CRICKET

Bowling a fast one	Batting first	Putting a spin on it
Bowling a googly	Opening bat	A sticky wicket
Fielding a question	Hitting for six	Caught out
Acting as long-stop		

Bat in as you see fit when you know what line we're taking.
It's the man at the crease who counts, no matter how many wiseacres there are in the pavilion [re the secretary of state in Cabinet]
Officials alone knew precisely how the pitch was playing that day and whether or not the ball was beginning to swing through the air.
The progress of an EC negotiation is quite as intricate and subtle as a game of cricket.

BOXING
Punching above our weight
I've got to come in with all fists flying

RUGBY
The Cabinet Office full-back caught the ball
Clear that change right round Whitehall then table and run with it

BASEBALL
I'll have to play some pretty hard ball
Touch base

ROWING
Rowing back

SNOOKER
It's outside the frame

SAILING
The British Presidency is trying to steer a pretty battered ship back into a safe port. . . .
At Birmingham they're just looking for a puff in the sails. . . . You can feel the secretary of state's hand on the tiller

CARDS — MAINLY BRIDGE
Playing the right card
A diplomatic mission is rather like a card player: it has to play the card it has been dealt, but skilful play can squeeze more out of any particular hand
Finessing
Trumping
Taking a trick

ATHLETICS
Going through hurdles

Business-speak

Getting into bed with (as in 'getting into bed with the Iraqis')

Run it past him
Up to speed
Knock-on effect
Blank cheque

Losing momentum
Hanging on the edge
Chicken-and-egg situation

Civil Service

Taking a line
Giving a firm steer
Ministers must decide
A water-tight piece of paper
Give a lead

Safe pair of hands
Bringing out the salient points
Would you like a piece of paper on this?
We're just having a wash-up meeting
    [post-mortem]

Mainly Foreign Office

That young man is policy-capable

The dog that didn't bark

Seen from here

Helpful

Unhelpful

Inappropriate

Widgets [everyone engaged on the commercial side talks of selling widgets]

A little bit of quiet advice

You might perhaps hint

You might perhaps stress

The Queen is minded to offer you a CBE

It was nip-and-tuck right to the very end of the conference [the only female imagery – though from the permanent under secretary]

We are custodians of the holy places as far as the conference is concerned

A little massaging might be in order

On his way to Australia he decided to cycle through Iraq, which seems to me to be one of the less sensible things he might have done

A song we've been singing for the last six months

It sends out the wrong signals

We'll need a pre-cooked statement

That's a bogus point

Will someone alert the PM?

Working with the grain of public opinion

I can foresee considerable difficulties

Tirets [pronounced: Teeray. Hyphens in the margin indicating separate points]

That was a useful exegesis on the Oslo text

One is seeking the pressure points in Government

Clutch card (ie what the foreign secretary takes with him into meetings)

The speech has some munchy bits

Their relationship is a fragile one

QBP – Queen's Birthday Parties

Brits

Trying to get the gate open

Let him know on a background basis

We don't think we're ready to draw a line

Rules of engagement

Outside its mandate

We'll hope to push them as far as we possibly can on the steps that they
can take and visibly implement

Maximising the pressure on the parties to improve what happens on the ground

Concessions

Preconditions

Wholly unrealistic proposals

Transparent
Colleagues [diplomats in other services as well as Foreign Office people]
Analogues [people of equivalent rank at home and abroad]
Partners [European Community member states]
Boil down the action so its very sort of punchy *Express* and *Mail*
The clock has started ticking

Alan Judd, a pseudonymous Foreign Office novelist, produced the following exchange between a head of chancery and a young novice:

'I hope you've taken all that on board. You're going to have your hands full trying to keep all these transport balls in the air. As for your own posture during the visit, I think a low profile would be about right. Hull down but antennae up in case the Lower Africans try to bowl any fast ones, logistically speaking. Also, make sure London don't slip anything through the net on the run-in. 'Course, Miss Teale thinks all this ought to be in her parish, really, and so it should in a sense but horses for courses. I mean, she's mad so you'll just have to have a light touch on the tiller where she's concerned. Keep her briefed by all means but don't let her run with the ball. I'll be long-stop in case there's real trouble, but I don't want to have to take flak unless I have to. I shouldn't say this but I must be about due for an award – you know, something in the honours list – and so I don't want the minister walking into any trip-wires and us all ending up with egg on our faces.'

'Roger,' said Patrick.

Hard-Language Training

Part-time courses in what are considered easy languages – French, German and Spanish – are available in London. There is a general assumption that anyone with any language ability should either know such languages already or be able to pick them up very quickly in their spare time. The big training effort goes into teaching what are called 'hard' languages to those with linguistic aptitude – particularly the fast stream.

One odd feature is that the young are given little guidance on what to choose, being merely told which languages are required at present by the administration and asked to pick which they would like. Considering that the choice largely determines where an officer will spend a major part of his career, this is a rather bizarre form of neglect. They are told nothing about, for instance, the culture of the place in which they might afterwards be spending much of their life. One young man chose Japanese purely because he had an image of cherry blossom. As it happened, he has been very happy there and has a Japanese wife, yet it is all too easy to think of someone spending two years learning Japanese only to find that they were temperamentally better suited to consort with Russians.

There is also the career angle. Unless their parents are in the trade, these young people have very little idea about how their career is likely to develop. A smart youngster takes Arabic, for there are around twenty ambassadorships where Arabic would be a considerable asset. Whereas if you take, for instance, Indonesian, Japanese or Thai, the value of your asset is more limited.

Standards are very high and the British Foreign Office is superior to all other services in its linguistic depth and professionalism, even for instance ahead of the big-spending Americans in providing the Russian-speaking ambassador to Azerbaijan with a crash course in Azeri.

Tim Hitchens summed up the difference that mastery of a language can make in dealing with foreigners.

My character changed when I spoke Japanese. I became far more polite than I am; I became far more demure. I became far more persistent in some ways and in all those ways I entered the Japanese world through the Japanese language . . . I know people who spoke English, American, whatever, found enormous problems with the Japanese because they found them obtuse or they found that they said one thing, meant another. But a lot of those are the problems of translation.

Including salaries, it can cost up to £60000 to train a young diplomat in a hard language, but no one within the Office questions the value of this investment. The regret is rather that because of the eternal squeeze on financial and manpower resources, the Office can be slow to react to new market demands. It was only recently that the teaching of Chinese (Mandarin) expanded, which is why there is an unfortunate preponderance of young people in the Peking Embassy. And why, asked one of these young people, have they not yet got going on teaching Cantonese, which will be a vitally important language in Hong Kong after 1997?

The Foreign Office assess competence in a language at four levels: Survival, Functional, Operational or Extensive. Taking the Riyadh Embassy as an example of the spread of competence, in July 1993 they could muster two whose overall standard was Extensive, four Operational, three Functional and four Survival: not a bad total for a country where many senior Saudis and most businessmen speak English.

In the last five years, the following numbers of diplomats have been trained to Operational standard in the following languages:

Arabic	35	Greek	11	Korean	3	Serbo-Croat	10
Bulgarian	14	Hebrew	2	Malay	5	Swahili	6
Burmese	2	Hindi	2	Persian	6	Thai	5
Chinese		Hungarian	11	Polish	13	Turkish	7
(Mandarin)	16	Indonesian	8	Romanian	7	Urdu	2
Czech	11	Japanese	14	Russian	19	Vietnamese	1
Finnish	5						

Humour

And finally, to the language of Foreign Office humour. The first recorded joke by a British diplomat misfired. In 1612, Sir Henry Wotton, an envoy of King James 1, wrote what he described as a 'merry definition': 'An ambassador is an honest man sent to lie abroad for the Commonwealth.' Kings are rarely partial to jokes if they appear to reflect on them, so Wotton was dismissed.

For 350 years people have been using this phrase against diplomats and for 350 years diplomats have been explaining vainly that a joke is a joke and that in fact Sir Henry in his serious moments stressed the importance of telling the truth at all times.

So the Foreign Office uses humour carefully. It is no hotbed of custard-pie throwers or blue comedians and there is no effing and blinding. Although it is awash with Celts, it is the understated 'English' sense of humour that prevails; the culture is impregnated with low-key ironic, self-deprecating wit. However the products of different parts of the British Isles delight in gently mocking each other.

In India, the high commissioner has a framed tea-towel on his wall that he brought with him from his last posting in Ireland. Irish and Indians enjoy it; it would be unlikely to go down well in Germany or North America:

As Others See Us

There were the Scots
Who kept the Sabbath
And everything else
They could lay their hands on

Then there were the Welsh
Who prayed on their knees
And their neighbours

Thirdly there were the Irish
Who never knew what they wanted
But were willing to fight for it anyway

Lastly there were the English
Who considered themselves a self-made nation
Thus relieving the Almighty
Of a dreadful responsibility

Such humour is all part of the Foreign Office ethos, which is to maintain perspective and never lose sight of the joke. How many organisations – in a booklet instructing newcomers on how to conduct themselves – would include the instruction, 'maintain a sense of the ridiculous'. For contrary to public perception, pomposity or self-importance are not viewed in the Foreign Office as attributes, but as cause for derision.

Sir Marcus Cheke, advising on how to deal with foreigners, tried to explain:

The late Prince Arthur of Connaught rightly instanced the following lines as an example of humour that every Englishman delights in, which is unintelligible abroad:

I was playing golf
The day the Germans landed,
All our troops had run away,
All our ships were stranded,
And the thought of England's shame
Nearly put me off my game

The humour of these lines depends on the fact that England's ships are *not* all stranded. England has not been invaded for a thousand years, and 'he jokes at scars who never felt a wound.' But there are many foreign countries which know only too well what defeat and invasion are, and for them it is not a subject for joking at all. In the same way the Englishman can joke about politics, for England has not suffered the horrors of violent political convulsion since the 17th century . . . politics are a no more suitable subject for humour in these foreign countries than invasion is, and Mr Bull must not expect to amuse a Spaniard with a joke about communism.

Tristan Garel-Jones tells a story of a difference of opinion between officials about having an open session at the Edinburgh European Community summit, which produced a typical ironic one-liner. '[Michael] Jay has this romantic attachment to openness which is incomprehensible to the rest of his colleagues. A guy from the Treasury leant over to him and said, "It's all very well for you to say that as a human being, but *I* regard myself as a representative of her Majesty's Government."'

Irony is a closed book to many cultures, whose diplomats are resigned to not knowing when an Englishman is making a joke. Referring to foreign ambassadors' surprise at 'the extraordinary licence allowed to the pigeons around the Foreign Office, whose portals they render so perilous,' Sir Nicholas Henderson remarked that 'they come to accept this in time, perhaps, as a reflection of the English attitude to animals – and foreigners – or at any rate as a manifestation of the well-known British sense of humour, the scourge of the Diplomatic Corps.'

A good example of how the British use humour as a diplomatic tool concerns one of the Foreign Office's legendary figures, Sir Donald Maitland. As permanent representative at the UN in the 1970s during the UK–Icelandic Cod War, he was commanded by London to make urgent representations to his Icelandic opposite number, but was anxious to make the gesture as unaggressive as possible.

Maitland was just over five feet four inches: the Icelander was about a foot taller. Maitland allegedly arrived in the other's office bearing the telegram with his instructions: 'I have been told', he announced, 'to make representations at the very highest level', and climbed onto the ambassador's desk.

Gentle humour creeps into the Foreign Office training literature. For instance, warning against the mixing of styles, a drafting guide called in aid the anonymous author of an epitaph on Queen Victoria:

> *Dust to dust, and ashes to ashes:*
> *Into the tomb the Great Queen dashes.*

Funny despatches get buried in archives and a nomadic life encourages people to jettison their favourite absurdities, but they lurk here and there. David Gore-Booth was the provider of the minutes of the magnificent 1937 drafting session (see page 167). The following letter from the British ambassador to the Soviet Union during the Second World War was discovered by an academic researcher.

Sir Nicholas Henderson, who knew Sir Archibald Clark Kerr, described him during his subsequent period in Washington: 'In a long career abroad he had become so bored with small talk and polite responses that he longed only for the unusual and unexpected. He would say things in order to shock and so to produce some non-automatic reaction, a temptation he found irresistible in Washington's Victorian society.'

The letter was written from Moscow.

Lord Pembroke
The Foreign Office
London
6th April 1943
My Dear Reggie,

In these dark days man tends to look for little shafts of light that spill from Heaven. My days are probably darker than yours, and I need, my God I do, all the light I can get. But I am a decent fellow, and I do not want to be mean and selfish about what little brightness is shed upon me from time to time. So I propose to share with you a tiny flash that has illuminated my sombre life and tell you that God has given me a new Turkish colleague whose card tells me that he is called Mustapha Kunt.

We all feel like that, Reggie, now and then, especially when Spring is upon us, but few of us would care to put it on our cards. It takes a Turk to do that.

Archie

Their sense of humour can be wintry, even arid – too rarefied and too cultivated for the outside world. There is an arrogance in enjoying humour so arcane that most outsiders do not realise it is there. Many of them, because of their intensely proper behaviour, appear staid and dull. And though, of course, some of them are, I have been frequently frustrated to hear a friend or acquaintance describe as humourless diplomats people I know privately to be wickedly funny at the expense of themselves, their calling and the people with whom they deal professionally.

But they have to be discreet. It would do little for international harmony to have it known, for instance, that one ambassador described the country in which he was serving as 'a low-lying, fertile country, full of low, lying, fertile people.'

· 8 ·

CONFORMING

Behaving Yourself

Like all large organisations, the Foreign Office has its own culture, habits, expectations and quirky ways. Here are a few of them.

Demeanour

'I'd like to make the whole darned Foreign Office tight', announced Ernest Bevin once in gales of laughter to Nicholas Henderson. It is an ambition I, and no doubt many others, also share, but we know it is doomed. The combination of Britishness and the caution of the disciplined diplomat makes for a rather bland and homogenous exterior. The Office comes across as British without the wilder Celtic shores. There are Irish and Welsh in the Foreign Office but the veneer is English with a strong Scottish input. Indeed Scots are said to represent about 40 per cent of the Service.

It is an efficient combination – a veneer of diffidence, of reserve, of fastidiousness and irony on a base of tough-minded, hard-working prudence. But English manners predominate. While there are, of course, exceptions, in general Foreign Office people are polite; they say 'Please' and 'Thank you'; they know whom to shake hands with and whom to kiss; they usher their guests ahead of them; they never jostle; they speak unassumingly about themselves; they listen rather than talk; they write thank-you letters; they come at the time appointed and they leave at the time their hostess would wish – not earlier and not later. They do not drink to excess; they do not gorge themselves; they are never rude to waiters; they eschew profanities or obscenities or anything that might cause unnecessary offence. They do not ogle those to whom they are sexually attracted or nudge people in the ribs. In their studied formality and exceptional courtesy they can make one feel at times uncouth, although they are straining every sinew to put one at one's ease.

There is a terrible necessity to appear respectable which rubs off on those in close proximity: the BBC cameraman and sound recordist both wore suits for the nine-month filming period, a rare sight when they are filming anywhere else.

131

One diplomat talked about how unnerving it was that husbands and wives are so excessively polite to each other; 'Would you awfully mind getting me a drink as well, dear?' 'Oh, thank you *so* much.' You don't hear couples indulging in affectionate abuse or having arguments lest somebody gets the idea that they have marital problems. 'There is,' he said, 'a tremendous amount of pretence even with the closest of colleagues.' Get drunk in the wrong company and you are in trouble. One diplomat who had a few too many at a dinner party and called his ambassador a shit was sent home on the next plane. The training also encourages the containment of emotion. 'Stay calm', is the advice.

Much of the work of the Office stems from things going wrong abroad: crisis with deadlines; rows. These are our bread and butter. To get het-up is a poor way to transact business. Business, either oral or written, can be done more efficiently and agreeably when it is done politely. And the more hectic life becomes, the calmer one should try to be.

The Private Office, where the ministers' private secretaries work, is the extreme example of this. When the pound was forced out of the Exchange Rate Mechanism (ERM) and the future of the Maastricht Treaty seemed bleak, the Private Office still had the quiet, calm demeanour of the Reading Room in the British Library.

It is a certain boredom with the emotional repression and sheer order at home that has the English falling in love with the deserts of Arabia, with the Russian steppes, with the craziness and colour of India, with the paradoxes of Ireland and with the inscrutability of the Orientals, for the English are among the most romantic of peoples and their travellers and diplomats are the most romantic of all. They respond to the easy warmth of less-disciplined peoples. You never hear of British diplomats being seduced by Germany or Scandinavia. They may see northerners as allies or potential allies in the European Community against the profligate southerners, but they do not give them their hearts.

Many diplomats – particularly the middle-aged and older – speak with passion about their country, their vision, their disappointments or their wounds. They would like to be more loved than they are, but it is hard to be loved if you project an image of discipline and self-containment: it can be confused with moral superiority. And their patriotism is a quality that is out of touch with the present mood of Britain. It is difficult for people whose job is to talk-up their country to return and find the residents relentlessly talking it down.

'I think you have to be intensely patriotic, which is not the same thing as saying you have to be chauvinistic or to be of the view that Britain is always right and everybody else is always wrong,' said David Gore-Booth. 'Despite imperfections I continue to believe that this country is run as well as, if not better, than any country in the world.' That statement would arouse incredulous laughter in Hampstead.

There are of course exceptions to all this: Sir David Hannay's rather engaging egotism is a case in point. It is always welcome to find a few obvious vices to leaven the perfection of behaviour. No amount of discipline and no pressure from the politically correct has so far stopped Sir David Gillmore or Sir John Kerr from being heavy smokers. Indeed Gillmore braved American disapproval while on a sabbatical at Harvard in 1990. Finding himself literally out in the cold with other lepers smoking behind the bike sheds, he considered the situation, pronounced it ludicrous that he was back where he had acquired the habit forty years earlier and insisted on being permitted to smoke in his own room; this then became a focal point for the similarly afflicted.

Haughtiness used to be added to the characteristics of some ambassadors and their wives. 'Are all ambassadors megalomaniacs?' I asked one deputy head of mission. 'Most', he said. 'If you have a tendency that way, it is hard not to let being God go to your head.' It is a heady experience to have some of the brightest minds of several generations leaping to obey your every whim; to have a shimmering manservant treating you with exaggerated respect and to be the Queen's representative. But megalomania does not go unnoticed in the Foreign Office and its manifestations are noted, relayed to colleagues and give rise to gentle chuckles around the Office.

David Gore-Booth again:

I like to think I'm not a pompous person but . . . the buttresses are in place to push an ambassador upwards . . . after all that is actually part of the function . . . he is supposed to be somebody to whom both the nationals of the country concerned, and his own nationals in the country concerned, look up to, so it's a very interesting balance that has to be drawn between being too pompous and being too informal. Very difficult.

Nowadays, though, megalomania has more checks on it. Speedy communications and constant travel mean that ambassadors no longer have the freedom of action that they used to. They get ticked off for being poor managers and their wives are more critical. 'Devotion and disrespect' is what Mary Gore-Booth says she offers her husband. She shared his excitement when they arrived in Riyadh and David took up his ambassadorship in Saudi Arabia, but

as long as he doesn't have an attack of ambassadoritis . . . and [take himself] more seriously than [his] job . . . [we'll be all right]. It's the job that's important [not the person]. There are people who are inclined to get very pompous because the trappings are there, you know, a lot of things enable you to be pompous. [But] I have no reason to believe that he will, and if he tries he'll have to deal with me.

Entertaining and Being Entertained

One of the worst aspects of a diplomat's job in many parts of the world is the social burden, yet it is a vital part of what he is paid to do. The Foreign Office's modern guidelines on entertainment describe it as 'one of the tools of our trade' which 'often marks the starting-point in making official contacts which can last throughout our careers: we should be as scrupulous in this as we are in the performance of our other professional duties.' The booklet is commonsensical and it certainly puts paid to any naive notions that diplomats and their wives spend their lives with their heads greedily in a trough of caviar and cocktails.

CONFORMING

The three main purposes to diplomatic entertainment are, explains the guide: 'to build and maintain a wide range of friends and contacts among officials, "opinion-formers" and private citizens of your host country; to introduce British visitors to an appropriate selection of the above; and to maintain contact with diplomatic colleagues, both British and foreign.'

There are also occasions, such as National Days, 'when you must simply attend in order to be seen there, signifying the Queen's or the Government's approval by your representational presence.' In London, there are 139 National Days. Most celebrate monarchs' birthdays, or are simply called 'National Day', or 'Independence Day'; among the small number of others, Cuba celebrates 'Day of Liberation'; Ireland 'St Patrick's Day'; Mongolia 'Anniversary of Mongolian People's Revolution' and Norway 'Constitution Day'. 'I had to go to two last night', groaned one ambassador. 'The Malaysian one was dry and cavernous and the French one was wet and absolutely crammed; they're just two different kinds of torture.'

While everybody dreads National Days, it is the hosts that dread them most. The British National Day occurs at a suitable date close to the Queen's birthday on June 14. The first strain is that a vast number of people are insulted not to have been invited. At one time it was the custom that the National Day catered more for local expatriates than anyone else, but for countries with vast expatriate communities around the world this has become impossible.

It is up to the ambassador to decide what mix of influential locals, diplomats from other embassies and members of the British community is appropriate. The people who have to be invited are of course those who least want to be there, yet they have to be there. The people who least need to be invited are those who are desperate to come, so every QBP – as it is known – causes a lot of sensibilities to smart. In Saudi Arabia for instance, I heard bitter complaints from the local British community about the failure of 'their ambassador' to invite them to what they saw as a party which should specifically be for them. The fact that there are 31 500 British in Saudi Arabia did not change their view that, by excluding them, the embassy was showing that it rated foreigners ahead of its native sons. It is one more reason why British diplomats, already reviled at home, also attract obloquy from their compatriots abroad.

What particularly breaks the hearts of diplomats is the allegation that they enjoy cocktail parties. 'I would do anything, anything,' wailed a young Australian diplomat in Saudi Arabia, 'to get out of going to a cocktail party.' For overworked diplomats the

LEFT Cocktail party in the Foreign Office's Locarno Suite for Marshall scholars from the USA. In the centre is Mark Pellew, head of the North America Department.
OVERLEAF Bob Harris, chargé d'affaires (left) and Tim Barrow, second secretary (right), arranging the placement for a lunch in Almaty in Kazahkstan for Sir Brian Fall, the British ambassador, and various Kazahk dignitaries.

problem is compounded by the fact that the higher up they go in the service the more representational duties fall to them and the more insulted people are if they fail to turn up. So an ambassador who has been up since six, may have to leave the office at 5.50pm to attend two National Days in sequence, then rush back to his office to continue his work before proceeding to a formal dinner, which he cannot leave until the guest of honour leaves, at the end of which he dashes back to deal with urgent messages from London.

All that is bearable. What isn't are the 'Aren't-you-lucky-to-have-such-a-wonderful-social-life' comments from visitors and friends at home, and the tabloid headlines about the diplomatic highlife. 'Ludicrous ordeal at the Château St Anne [the international club],' wrote Christopher Ewart-Biggs, 'where the Chief of Staff of the Belgian Air Force has invited a head-splitting superfluity of people, packed tight. It is not a cocktail party but a demographic experiment. What unspeakable pretention to inflict such a thing on people under the guise of entertaining them. And where is a society that sees its pleasures thus?'

The Office guide to entertaining gives much space to the most hideous of all problems in entertaining on the diplomatic circuit: *placement*. Seating people correctly is necessary to avoid 'uncertainty and confusion' and take into account 'national sensitivity. While there is some truth in the old crack, that someone who matters doesn't care where he sits, and someone who cares doesn't matter, diplomacy requires that you take care to avoid giving offence.' That over, the hard work begins.

Social conversation can be heavy going, especially if there is a language problem. Another difficulty is ladies who are not used to the company of gentlemen outside their immediate families and who find small talk difficult. (Your wife may have the reverse of this problem at the other end of the table, with her male neighbours inclined to talk across her.) All you can both do is to grit your teeth and persevere.

And then there is the sheer nervous strain of getting it wrong, as when a diplomat guest who felt that he had been given insufficient precedence turned his plate over and refused all the dishes he was offered. Or the horror of having a bad memory for names and faces, something not unknown even among successful diplomats.

I watched a senior diplomatic couple performing their duty at a National Day. The place was an anonymous hotel in a Far Eastern capital. The hosts represented an extremely poor country which had just come out from under the Soviet yoke. The understanding in the trade is that as long as you show up and have a drink (usually non-alcoholic: diplomats spend their lives trying to avoid alcohol), pay your respects to the host and hostess, warmly greet and say an appropriate individual word to various ambassadors and do a little business with a couple of people from the local ministry of foreign affairs, you can disappear after fifteen to twenty minutes, with everyone's honour satisfied.

On this occasion the hosts pulled a fast one, trapping the guests with a twenty-minute film extolling the virtues of the republic in question and then requiring them to go into another room where the host – whose Communist training died hard – addressed the gathering in his obscure native tongue for a considerable period, after which an interpreter went through the whole speech again in English. Then and only then could the ritual drink and exchange of pleasantries be conducted. The British diplomat was aghast at this departure from precedent.

Misperceptions dog diplomats on the entertainment circuit. They get duty free but not free liquor, yet visitors happily swig it under the impression that somehow they are entitled to it because they are taxpayers. Nor do they see the petty regulations that force the ambassador's spouse to account for every bottle of wine used in the exercise of representational duties. 'It would be nice,' said one senior wife pensively, 'to be trusted with a budget.' It would, and random auditing could ensure that such a system did not suddenly turn senior staff into monsters of corruption, but bureaucracies are slow to adapt. The Treasury is ever-vigilant lest a cocktail onion go down an inappropriate throat, so in the grand residences of the world, Lady This and Lady That laboriously count up the breakfasts and lunches, dinners and drinks, teas and coffees, consumed in her residence in that financial year, and instructions of a relentlessly nit-picking and cheeseparing variety come from home as the budget is squeezed further.

Servants

'I worry about what will happen to my maid when I leave,' observed one registry clerk in Delhi. 'I'll have to find her a job with someone else.' When a twenty-one-year-old returns home from his first foreign posting, he has formidable enough problems in trying to describe his life abroad to his old school pals; he is unlikely to cement his friendships by discussing his servant problem. Yet domestic servants are a very important part of life abroad.

In countries where servants come cheap, it is virtually impossible not to employ any, unless you are happy to keep the poor poorer. What can an egalitarian, working-class youngster, who has never even seen a servant, do when begged by his predecessor to keep on Amita or Purnima or Lakshmi? She will do his cleaning, his laundry and his shopping for about £3 a week and she relies on that sum to keep her family eating. Embarrassed, initially even a bit ashamed, he takes her on, of course.

Further up the tree, if you are not cut out for it, the problem is nightmarish. A head of mission inherits a large number of dependent people. In some missions – like Delhi – some of them wear uniforms which seem absurdly elaborate to the Western eye, but the wearers are tremendously proud of them. In a country which reveres tradition and has very clear notions of social responsibility, drastically changing the *status quo* would be both brutal and diplomatically disastrous.

So whether she likes it or not, the ambassadress is a memsahib. She is supposed to look after the welfare of the vast extended family of servants who occupy quarters on the compound. She tends sick wives and sick babies, and many of her kind find themselves dipping constantly into their own pockets to pay for the medical needs of wives and children. More difficult, again, are the cases where servants come very cheap, it is customary to have them, many have anyway been inherited from your predecessor, and they're either useless or bloody-minded.

Having servants can mean – as in one Third World post – having to hire someone who is nominally a cook, but is in fact an animal slaughterer, because the only way to get meat is to buy animals in the market, bring them home and kill them on the premises. Since the cook is a man of consequence, it is necessary to have a second servant to be his assistant and do his carrying for him. Ordinary diplomats who endure circumstances like that find it much simpler not to mention servants at all when they go home.

Sex

Until recently, a member of the Foreign Office could not – at least in theory – be a practising homosexual, since the security services feared that homosexuals would be a security risk, liable to be blackmailed by foreign spies. Also, those running the Office worried about the potential for embarrassment in countries where homosexuality was unacceptable. Nothing was said in the rules about lesbianism. Presumably, like Queen Victoria, the Security Service did not believe it existed.

Homosexuals who were determined to be diplomats, therefore, had no option but to lie their way through the positive-vetting procedure and at their five-yearly security interview. Paradoxically, perhaps because of its public-school image, the Foreign Office was often alleged by its domestic enemies to be populated by 'queers', as well as 'pinkos', 'wimps' and 'papists'. On one occasion, when hysteria about homosexual spies was at its height, the head of news was asked, at a press conference, if it was true that the Foreign Office was riddled with homosexuals. 'I've been in the FCO for thirty years,' he said, 'and I've never been riddled.'

In 1991 John Major announced that 'in the light of changing social attitudes towards homosexuality in the UK and abroad, and the correspondingly greater willingness on the part of homosexuals to be open about their sexuality, their life-style and their relationships', homosexuality would no longer automatically be a bar to joining the Diplomatic Service. The word 'automatically' needs further definition. Candidates are not yet queueing up to confess their proclivities. And Foreign Office staff who have been in the closet cannot come out without showing themselves to have been lying to the security people throughout their careers.

The Service is liberal (some of the old school would say permissive) about heterosexual sex. Cohabiting couples are treated as husband and wife when bidding for a joint posting. And illegitimate children are accepted on equal terms. For decades, an officer could have two illegitimate babies without being fired. Nowadays there are no limits whatsoever.

When officers are quizzed about their sex lives by security colleagues, the tacit understanding is that no eyebrows will be raised about sexual relationships with non-suspect single people, though people are reluctant to test how security men feel about serious promiscuity. It is believed they would frown if sexual partners proliferated like confetti.

Mostly, the sexually active or those of slightly unusual tastes offer their investigators a sanitised account. The trick is to give them enough information to reassure them that you are normal and not hiding anything, while concealing that which might make them think you were flighty and potentially a worry. Rules at missions abroad are very strict. A liaison with a married colleague or with a colleague's spouse is absolutely forbidden on penalty of being sent home immediately.

Dodgy foreigners should also be avoided. Anyone having a sexual relationship with a native, in a country where fraternisation is discouraged, would be viewed askance. So quite a lot of people are off-limits for diplomats.

Loneliness often forces people into relationships they would never have contemplated had more choice been available. Male diplomats are sought after in many countries where there is fierce competition among the locals for British husbands, who not only offer access to the Western way of life, but who have a reputation for being far better husbands than most other nationalities: their image is one of reliability, courtesy, and decency. Women diplomats fare less well: they are more likely to be pursued simply for sex than for marriage.

What makes sexual problems additionally difficult for diplomats is the absence of close friends to confide in, and the necessity at all times to appear strong and in control of your life and emotions. One young woman in a Far Eastern embassy found herself pregnant by a local who ditched her immediately on hearing the news. She was new to the embassy and had no friends. On a Friday afternoon she left the office on a pretext, had an abortion, spent the weekend alone and went back to work on Monday morning. No one at the embassy ever knew. Colleagues might well have been kind, but on the other hand someone might have regarded her behaviour as reckless. In any case, in a culture permeated with reserve, talk about matters of such intimacy does not come easily.

There is the occasional scandal. One ambassador had to be recalled from Moscow after being set up with a woman by the KGB, but generally diplomats are more circumspect than most of their contemporaries. Their affairs are less blatant; their divorces are low-key. One hears the odd tale of occasional excess, of South American prostitutes or other manifestations of the low life, but having a vigilant security service on your neck keeps most on the straight and narrow. They are required – but then they have been trained – to be discreet.

Religion

Religion has little place in the Foreign Office, which on the whole emits a vague and low-key Church of England aura. The occasional embassy has a chaplain. And in London, at Christmas, the permanent under secretary leads a carol service in the Durbar Court and reads Betjeman to his troops.

However, diplomats can hold whatever faith they like – or none at all. It is immaterial if they wish to worship in synagogue, mosque, temple, church or chapel, as long as they do so in their own time and do not let their beliefs intrude on the proper conduct of their work. Being a Christian Scientist did not stop Sir Paul Gore-Booth becoming permanent under secretary.

The Foreign Office, of course, is not the kind of institution that attracts fundamentalists. If you are likely to spend a large part of your life dealing with people whose beliefs are frequently exotic, visceral and strongly-held, it would be unhelpful to be, by instinct, a proselytiser. One of the British values the Foreign Office practises and sells abroad is tolerance.

A perfect example of religious and cultural sensitivity occurred recently in Bangkok, where for many years the embassy compound had been protected by a Buddhist guardian housed in a tiny temple inside the gates; but the structure on which it stood was becoming increasingly unsteady. The vigilant management officer realised that the day the structure collapsed and the guardian bit the dust would be the day when many of the locally-engaged staff would probably down pens, typewriters and telephones and retire indefinitely.

In the days before local budgeting provided posts with flexibility there would have been prolonged correspondence with London seeking to justify the erection of a new temple; it might have been authorised six months after disaster had struck. Treasury-inspired regulations have yet to wrestle with the notion of providing, at public expense, appropriate accommodation for gods. On this occasion, the management officer discussed the matter with the locally-engaged staff, who between them took up a collection amounting to about £1500, which he topped up with the necessary amount from his own budget.

The project was more expensive than might have been expected for such a small structure, for the guardian has to be located higher than the nose of the head of the household and the British ambassador to Thailand was six feet four. Built for a long life, the temple was secured on a pillar on a solid, raised plinth. A ceremony was performed by a local Buddhist priest, with all due involvement by the ambassador and staff. There were rumblings from some of the local Christian community about pagan practices, but everyone else was happy.

The religion with which the Foreign Office is periodically accused of being riddled and therefore that attracts most attention, is Roman Catholicism. In the 1930s there were completely baseless allegations of a conspiracy of Catholic appeasers. The Anglo-Irish Agreement started another such round of suspicion, not least – though coincidentally – because two of its prime British architects were Catholic. One Protestant Unionist announced grimly: 'You can hardly hear the clatter of typewriters in the Foreign Office for the rattle of rosary beads.'

In meetings connected with the television series and the book, the only Foreign Office people who talked about their own religion were Catholics – and that happened only a few times. Those in question were devout and were driven in their working lives not only by that commitment to public service, common to many in the Foreign Office, but by an additional spiritual quality – a longing to help bring about a better world. 'The only good Catholic is a saint,' says Glynne Evans, although she does not aspire to be such.

Yet despite the fears of anti-papist conspirators, there is no freemasonry among Foreign Office Catholics. They practise their religion individualistically and openly, and they appear to spend their working lives implementing ministerial policy rather than hanging around the corridors plotting a papal *coup d'etat*.

Friends

'I wouldn't join the Office if I had my time over again,' said one woman, 'because of the way it destroys relationships.' It had wrecked her love-life and badly damaged her friendships. 'You disappear out of people's lives for four years.' The telephone helps a little with the devastating loneliness of some diplomats abroad: some of the young single people in Peking spend hundreds of pounds every month, which they can ill-afford, phoning parents, girl or boyfriends or ordinary friends.

The diplomatic life is inimical to friendship. The typical fast-stream diplomat makes his friendships at university, then disappears at the age of twenty-two into the Foreign Office, where for three years, aping his superiors, he works till seven or eight at night and has little energy for the nurturing of friendships. He makes some friends at the Office and is then posted abroad. If he goes to Paris, friends will visit him; they are less keen on Riyadh or Kampala. An inveterate letter-writer might keep relationships going but that tradition no longer flourishes and a young second secretary, posted far from home, cannot afford the lengthy telephone conversations that keep a long-distance friendship in working order. As one woman put it: 'When my friends realise it is costing me £1 a minute, they think they should talk only about earth-shattering matters. They don't tell me the children have measles.'

It is always a shock when the young come home for the first time and find most people at home are totally uninterested in what they have been doing and where they have been doing it. 'People know nothing about where you've been, can't understand what you do and most of them can't be bothered finding out,' said several of the Grade 10s. A high commissioner laughed when I told him that. 'In my case', he said, 'what happens is that I'm given a lecture about the country I'm working in.'

The diplomats are handicapped too by being rather out of touch with Britain. One woman talked about going home and arriving in on serious discussions about British politics, with teachers and academics complaining about the educational system in enormous detail. She had nothing to contribute on what preoccupied them and no one cared about what was happening where she had been: all she could do was keep quiet.

Lower down the scale the experience is the same. 'What's it like?' an old school-friend asks a registry clerk, who notes the glazed boredom that settles in after a minute-and-a-half trying to describe life in Peking. 'And of course I can't join in on the things that concern them,' remarked another Grade 10. 'After Delhi, how can I get excited about the failings of British Rail? You can buy a ticket quickly, you don't have to bribe anyone to get a seat, the trains are more or less on time, and they're even clean. But try explaining to the folks back home that they're well off! You just keep your mouth shut.' And for those who come back with foreign spouses, picking up where you left off is even more difficult.

There are other barriers. People at home are envious of the perks of the diplomat's life, yet determinedly uninterested in the drawbacks, and are put off by the formality and studied politeness that the diplomats acquire as part of their training, and fearful that they cannot live up to the standards of hospitality of the returned diplomat. They prefer not to invite them to their houses.

Permanent deep friendship then is difficult for most diplomats to acquire. A four – sometimes an eight-year absence – with an occasional visit in the middle, is not conducive to keeping your old university friend, or maintaining an intimacy with your neighbour. You rarely meet the parents of your boarding-school children's friends. Relationships with office colleagues tend to be transient. You might become close to somebody for two years in Belgrade and never again be posted anywhere together. The joy that is evinced by a happy posting coincidence for old friends is a rare experience.

There are acquaintanceships – sometimes friendships – with other members of the Diplomatic Corps, but postings elsewhere disrupt these relationships in exactly the same way. The same is true with the indigenous population, even in those places where it is possible to become friendly with them – and of course until the collapse of Communism there were many posts where such friendships were by definition impossible: anyone who came to your house got into trouble with the secret police. It is overwhelmingly a world in which the intimate friendship can rarely flourish.

· 9 ·

TIDYING-UP THE WORLD

Political Work

Let us pause to consider the English,
Who when they pause to consider themselves get all reticently thrilled and tinglish,
Because every Englishman is convinced of one thing, viz:
That to be an Englishman is to belong to the most exclusive club there is:
A club to which benighted bounders of Frenchmen and Germans and Italians et cetera cannot aspire to belong,
Because they don't even speak English, and the Americans are worst of all because they speak it wrong.
Englishmen are distinguished by their traditions and ceremonials,
And also by their affection for their colonies and their contempt for the colonials.
When foreigners ponder world affairs, why sometimes by doubts they are smitten,
But Englishmen know instinctively that what the world needs most is whatever is best for Britain.

from *England Expects*, by Ogden Nash

One of the Foreign Office's two basic aims is 'to promote and protect British interests overseas'. And for any trading nation, self-interest starts with global stability. Nations bring to international diplomacy what strengths they have: military, political, financial or diplomatic. Until recently, military strength ruled. Now, with the collapse of the Soviet Union, it is a diminishing asset even for the United States, which has a military machine built on the scale of Goliath at a time when what the world needs is a collection of nimble Davids.

Politically, the world is trying to find a new way and the politicians are overworked. There is the same desire for collective security that dominated the 1920s and 1930s, allied to a desperate fear that the United Nations, like its predecessor, the League of Nations, may fail, through a lack of international will, to marshal and employ properly the resources necessary to contain international aggression. As Douglas Hurd said in a speech in 1993, the Secretary General to the UN is in 'the extraordinary position of someone who is being asked to manufacture a vehicle, while he is driving that vehicle on the road.'

OVERLEAF Douglas Hurd at an EC meeting.

145

Politicians are blamed for an absence of leadership, but in the new climate of teamwork, few are in a position to lead. The European Community, the UN Security Council, NATO, the Commonwealth, G7 and all the other groupings are under increasing pressure to speak with one voice, which most of them have not, as yet, found. President Clinton struggles with the role of the Big Kid on the Block, but the Big Kid is less confident than he appears to be. And his attempts to discipline the small kids often have him abused for bullying.

The Japanese throw money (and often highly inappropriate equipment) at the problems in the Third World (where they are now the largest donor) and – to a lesser extent – in the former Soviet Union, but with fundamental political changes going on at home, they are uncertain about what to do with the influence they thus acquire. Like so many others, they want status without responsibility.

As the global ant-heap strives to right itself after its latest huge upheaval, its inhabitants long for tranquillity. As the politicians flail around, the diplomatic ants scurry around behind the scenes doing what they do best – in the words of a retired British diplomat – 'putting small and accurately moulded bricks into buildings for which other men will take the credit.'

The public see every argument, every disappointment, every war, every unsuccessful negotiation as failure. All grand meetings of politicians, bilateral or multilateral, are expected to produce results. Impossible expectations are dashed with the maximum publicity and television shows a small selection every day from the hideous spin-offs of political failure all over the world.

Amid all this confusion, the over-stretched British diplomatic service attempts to bring reason and decency to bear on world affairs, yet because it is often carrying out a foreign policy that annoys more people than it pleases, its effectiveness is greatly limited.

Europe

There is one fundamental reason why Britain has been perceived to be out of touch with Europe, always dragging her heels, always throwing cold water on ideas, always negative, carping and petty: she is a stable society which feels no need for a protector. There is no other country in Europe that does not have cause for shame in its recent history or have a memory of invasion, civil war or some other major disruption of one kind or another. Tristan Garel-Jones:

All the other eleven member states, in one way or another, are burying a ghost in the Community. So the Germans are burying the Nazis; the French are burying collaboration; the Spanish are burying Franco, and so on. And even the little countries who didn't commit mortal sin, were ravished by the sinner – Belgium, Holland. . . . And therefore, what actually happens with most European countries other than Britain, is that the Community means something to them that it doesn't mean to us. . . . They all look at the Community and find something there that endorses their own democracy in some way or another, after having been ravished in the Second World War.*

So Britain does not 'look to the Community to endorse our democracy. We're quite proud of our democracy and we think it works.'

If that is the great divide, there are other smaller ones. The visceral British commitment to free trade – the inborn conviction of a country which was once the greatest trading nation of the world – is deeply resented by – among others – French and Irish farmers. Like France, Britain is out of step with most other countries in the Community in being both administratively and politically highly centralised and is therefore resistant to attempts to push the rights and privileges of regions. Then too, Britain is promiscuous, wishing to keep a major role in the Commonwealth as well as to maintain a special relationship with the United States. Having one's eggs spread around a number of baskets makes one less protective of any individual one.

There is therefore no danger that Britain might become Euro-romantic. What it should do, said the pro-Europe Garel-Jones, 'is stop arguing about whether we belong to it. We should regard it as we do Whitehall, the popular press, Radio Three or the Welsh Rugby Union. The European Community is an organisation we are an integral part of, and we should make it work.'

That is not the way it is seen from Brussels, where various European leaders want to dream dreams and talk visions and Monsieur Delors wants to take leaps of the imagination in directions where Britain is temperamentally incapable of going. From the perspective of the European-minded, the British presence in Brussels is a superb machine efficiently devoted to retarding progress. 'It is a Rolls-Royce', observed an *Economist* journalist in Brussels, 'which is just driven in and out of the garage and up and down the drive but has never been allowed on to the motorway. It would be nice if the British, just 5 per cent of the time, could say they're doing something for the sake of Europe rather than for the sake of British interests.' 'It would be so marvellous', said an Irish Eurocrat, 'if this machine could be harnessed to taking the European ideal further rather than holding it back.'

But that is not the English way, and in any case, apart from taking no account of the Anglo-Saxon character – solid, prosaic and conservative – it does not consider the parliamentary constraints under which British policy in Europe operates, because of the deep ambivalence about Europe within the current Conservative party and the country as a whole. Few Europeans have any appreciation of the hideously difficult footwork that was necessary to carry most of the Tories into the yes lobby over Maastricht. To get the Bill through Parliament at all was a near-miracle, but all that Europeans could see was British procrastination and parochialism.

The Foreign Office has been accused over the years of being dominated by many groups – Freemasons, Jews, Catholics, anti-Semites, Arabists, appeasers, wimps, and so

---

* Ireland is an exception, but it lives with the fear of destabilisation from across the border with Northern Ireland.

on. Most recently the finger has been pointed at Euro-fanatics. There was some truth in this in the 1960s, when Britain was desperately seeking – late in the day – to be allowed to join the European club, but those days are long gone. The Foreign Office confines itself to representing British interests in Europe as effectively as possible, having regard to the political realities at home and in Brussels. Its guiding principle – as laid down by Mrs Thatcher in her Bruges speech (the positive part of which was drafted by Sir John Kerr) – is to oppose integration but encourage practical cooperation. 'We're all pretty pragmatic people,' said Tim Hitchens.

You very rarely find a Foreign Office person who would be passionately for Maastricht or passionately against. We're mostly fascinated by the tactics of it, fascinated by trying to work out how to square what the realities are with what the politicians want. But often if you ask us what we really feel about something like this, it's often a question we haven't posed ourselves.

During Britain's European Presidency in the second half of 1992, the job was to try to rescue the Community from potential disaster by finding a formula that meant the Danish people, who had rejected the Maastricht Treaty, would vote for it, in a second referendum, on terms acceptable to the rest of the Community. From the British point of view there was also the desire to push up the agenda subsidiarity – the principle that the Commission should do nothing that was better done at national level – and enlargement, for Britain is committed to a European Community that eventually encompasses the whole of Europe in a structure enabling individual nations to operate in the way that best suits their traditions. In the Autumn of 1993 the prime minister wrote:

It is for nations to build Europe not for Europe to attempt to supersede nations. I want to see the Community become a wide union, embracing the whole of democratic Europe, in a single market and with common security relations firmly linked to NATO. I want to see a competitive and confident Europe generating jobs for its citizens and choice for its consumers. A Community which ceases to nibble at national freedoms, and so commands the enthusiasm of its member nations.

In other words, Britain is diametrically opposed to the federalists in its vision. The federalists want more control for the Commission. For the politicians to work harmoni-ously within Europe – 'at the heart of Europe' as Geoffrey Howe wanted – against a background of public perception which has the largest-selling newspaper in Britain running headlines like 'UP YOURS DELORS', is a hard row to hoe. The British public was conditioned by Mrs Thatcher's approach to think that Britain winning was 'MAGGIE TRIUMPHS UBER ALLES' or 'MAGGIE STANDS ALONE AND DEFIANT'. The noisy arguments of the Thatcher years bore some bitter fruit in Brussels. She might – like her European colleagues – have gone in for rhetoric, but they disliked the rhetoric she went in for. But, although they are happy to have less noisy confrontations these days, every time another flat, sceptical, dull statement emanates from the uncharismatic prime minister or foreign secretary, damping down European enthusiasm, the partnership becomes more strained.

The Foreign Office has essentially been told that its job is to try to keep the Commission's nose out of British business, encourage free trade, encourage enlargement, try to contain massive public spending in Europe and huge handouts to the 'cohesion' countries – the net gainers from the European budget – and to attack waste. So among their tasks is urging the application of fiscal rectitude to a group, many of whose component parts benefit greatly from fiscal irresponsibility. The British are forever coming across as tightwads and spoilsports.

Talleyrand, who succeeded in dominating French foreign policy before, during and after Napoleon, once wrote: 'To engage, or at least to persist, in a struggle in which you may find everybody interested on the other side, is a mistake.' Yet that is often what the British Government does in Brussels and it is the job of Sir John Kerr, the UK permanent representative to the European Community (UKREP) and his team, to follow orders from London and cut what deals he can. Kerr has had a unique career, having been both private secretary to the permanent under secretary of the Foreign Office and private secretary to the chancellor of the exchequer. Widely regarded in Brussels as the best of the twelve permanent representatives, Kerr is unassuming, very able, amusing and astute. 'But', said one European observer, 'you have no idea what he's really thinking. I've met him at several parties and I still don't know him any better.'

'John is . . . in jest I always say the cleverest man in the Northern Hemisphere,' said Tristan Garel-Jones. 'He's certainly one of the cleverest, quickest people I've ever worked with in my life – amazing.' He would need to be, for his is a job requiring an extraordinary mixture of skills. As Michael Jay, the assistant under secretary in London in charge of the European Community, put it. 'The attraction of all Civil Service or diplomatic jobs is the mixture of the technical knowledge and understanding of highly complex issues, mixed with their political importance. . . . The European Community is perhaps the best example of the fusion of those two things.'

Sir John Kerr is also the UK representative on the twelve-man Committee of Permanent Representatives (COREPER), the EC powerhouse. He heads a large team of negotiators in Brussels which is fifty:fifty Foreign Office and other Whitehall departments: they cover everything from agriculture to transport. Kerr does not have to worry about motivating them: they are young, clever, ambitious, the experience is extremely valuable in career terms (in the case of the Foreign Office, it is now essential for a serious high flyer), Brussels is an agreeable place to be, spouses can usually get jobs, and though the hours are very long they are bearably so. Kerr is a negotiations junkie and the young ones learn from him the skills that are coming to dominate international relations.

Domestic critics say that there is no need for Foreign Office involvement – either bilaterally or multilaterally – in most aspects of European Community negotiation in Brussels. On matters environmental, for instance, they say, UKREP delegates should be from the Department of the Environment and colleagues in London would conduct back-up negotiations and lobbying simply by ringing up their opposite numbers in the capitals of Europe. That is an argument which starts from the premise that classical diplomacy in this technological age is an irrelevance. Sir Ewen Fergusson, ambassador to France for five years from 1987, attacked that view stoutly.

There is an enormously important role in the interpretation of one country to another. No one but a fool thinks that the French are like us, and yet it's astonishing how often unguided people from within our administration, in the broadest sense, will fall into the trap of making the assumption that we are very like each other. The administrators aren't the same, the ministerial responsibilities are different, the relationship of ministers to their officials and administrators . . . are very different from the relationships that you have in London and they aren't relationships that you can absorb by reading three pages of a book summary. They are relationships that you've got to feel. You've got to know how to handle people, you've got to know how to tackle people. . . . Without an organisation like ours you'd not only have an awful lot of time wasted by people in London but you'd find people falling into avoidable traps.

For a classical diplomatist, it is vital to understand not only the relevant culture, but the constraints on your opposite number and the limitations on his power, as well as assessing realistically where and what he might yield: the object is to reach an agreement without causing resentments which might jeopardise the next set of negotiations. To do that you need to have time to form relationships. As David Gore-Booth put it: 'Diplomacy consists of a lot of actual eye contact followed by telephone contact.' An official in London in the Department of the Environment cannot form relationships and keep in touch with frequently-changing opposite numbers in eleven European capitals without spending most of his life in shuttle diplomacy. And while the UKREP representative in Brussels will be on terms with his colleagues from other European countries, he cannot know their backroom boys who direct them from the specialist departments at home. That is the job of the relevant diplomat in the British Embassy, who also plays a part in trying to educate home departments to the realities of negotiating in Europe.

When the Eurocrats talk about the failings of UKREP in Brussels, when they have finished anathematising its perceived anti-Europeanness and its relentless harping on British interests, they complain about the unrealistic expectations of many of the specialist departments – which come about precisely because they do not understand Europe. A British Eurocrat observed that in the area where he was supremo, nobody now bothered to listen to the British delegates, bright though they were, since they were always being instructed by their parochial home department to stick out for the impossible. Whereas the Foreign Office is always of the same mind as its negotiators overseas, home departments – both at official and ministerial level – get suspicious that their men have gone native in Brussels.

One of Kerr's staff compared UKREP to a symphony orchestra in which the individual instruments included both representatives of Whitehall interests and embassies throughout the Community. The conductor and the leaders of the orchestra had to be diplomats because they understood the role of each instrument and where it fitted into the whole symphony. It is necessary to know that issue A impinges on issue G and may scupper negotiation Z and to decide on what has priority. It is Kerr's job to try to coordinate all the instruments and to that end he returns to London every Friday to talk through that week's, and the next week's, business with his headquarters, with the Cabinet Office, with Number 10 and where necessary, with ministers.

Needless to say, the French have no domestic threats to the supremacy of the Quai d'Orsay. It was Richelieu who insisted on centralising France's foreign affairs in one ministry and 'ruthlessly saw to it that other departments kept their fingers out of the pie.' Nothing has changed. Kerr's French equivalent and his staff have tremendous prestige and France's diplomats are in the lead on all fronts of Commission activity. Less apologetically than the British, the French hold the view that generalists can be trans-formed where necessary into economists, accountants, lawyers and administrators much more successfully than specialists can become generalists. The French Foreign Ministry takes precedence over all other French ministries, so the French delegation has more autonomy than the British. The Germans have the opposite approach; their delegation is full of secondees from all relevant departments and the result is a chaotic lack of coordination.

Apart from the French the competition in Europe – although it can be disruptive – is unevenly spread. The small states have to specialise in the areas that concern them most directly, so the Irish, for instance, will fight their corner effectively and savagely on farm protection. Some of them, like the Greeks, just about turn up to meetings. (One measure of Europeanness is the reaction in Brussels to the Greeks. UKREP Anglo-Saxons are horrified by their irresponsibility: Eurocrats shrug their shoulders and say 'So what? That's their way.')

The British work very well with the Dutch, although the Dutch are federalists, because they have the same confident approach and share a sense of humour. In fact one of the odd aspects of the European Community is that whereas the British are always drawn to people more lively than themselves – Latins, Irish and so on – they do business much better with Northern people, whom they find tidy and sensible. It is no wonder that they are more keen than many of their partners to encourage the Scandinavians to join the Community.

The television series showed Michael Jay, Tristan Garel-Jones and at times Douglas Hurd and John Major, lobbying Europe in a classic British diplomatic campaign of meticulous planning, follow-through, keeping colleagues up-to-date after each phase, followed by further contingency planning. The object was to find a formula to save the Maastricht Treaty in circumstances where the Danes demanded its amendment and most other countries refused to contemplate any changes whatever. Michael Jay played the primary role in finding out exactly what each member state would accept. He was, said Hitchens, 'scurrying to and fro round the Community' visiting countries two or three times in an effort to discover exactly what it was they objected to in the Danish proposals. Meanwhile, the British ambassador in Denmark had been sending telegrams to London daily, passing on the thoughts of individual politicians in Copenhagen. Then there was, said Hitchens, our legal advisor who was the one who came up with the technical wizardry, and then on top of that official base, the prime minister and my minister, Mr Garel-Jones, and the secretary of state just day in, day out, phoning their Danish opposite numbers, phoning their French and German opposite numbers and saying 'What are your real problems? Where is your bottom line?' It's classic diplomacy.

As with all classic diplomacy, the procedure is to find and concentrate on the substantial areas on which you and each colleague agree and build on them. By knowing the maximum about the position of each player and doing every last piece of groundwork in advance to minimise the causes for disagreement, unpleasant surprises at a summit are kept to the minimum.

Multilateral negotiations, therefore, can involve establishing bilaterally what the eleven other members think, establishing their core position and the areas for negotiation, and dealing on the basis of personal relationships with each of them, to try and bring all of them towards a common position. The permutations with twelve partners are enormous, especially since this approach also involves bringing others in from outside the Community if they can bring any useful pressure to bear.

Making sure that all negotiators are working on exactly the same lines is an essential part of this process, as is the remorselessly efficient reporting-back at every stage of the game. At the end of the process comes the detailed briefing of ministers, who will do the final and public part of the negotiation, which, if all goes well, will finally produce the deal. The officials are on hand to help. Garel-Jones gave an example after one difficult international meeting:

If I say – as I had to do to Michael Jay today – what does the Oslo text say about this, he knows the answer to that straight away and can put his finger on a piece of paper and hand me the relevant piece of text and I actually have it in my hand within ten seconds of the question being raised.

At the end of certain summit meetings – the European Council of Ministers, for instance – what is frequently a long and complicated document has to be finally agreed. Here the British Foreign Office briefing technique can be properly described as pyrotechnical. The minister is given briefing with the full text of the latest draft on the right-hand side of the page. On the left-hand side is a line-by-line commentary, telling him where the problems are, where opposition will come from, where he will have to fight a battle, who will back him up and offering various words and phrases which the others may accept. It will show where – should something be debated – there is an opportunity to retrieve a form of words more suitable to Britain, that might have been lost in an earlier round. 'So you try and pick up as many tricks as you can in that crucial little session, when none of the heads of government have any advisers there to help them,' explained Michael Jay, a master of the art.

You try to pick out these little bits of language and reset them to suit our specific policy. . . . The prime minister comes out of a lunch and he's got five minutes, perhaps ten minutes, to prepare himself for this hour's discussion, so this is made user-friendly. At a glance he can see where he's got to go and what he's got to do.

The long-term objective – for the British are good at thinking such matters through – is to make the Community more answerable to its own parliamentary systems, less centralised and more geared to individual national interests. An important part of the British technique in Europe is to try to drive a wedge between the two key Community allies, France and Germany, by playing up such differences as Germany's affection for its own currency and France's preoccupation with the preservation of its food and style of life.

Here Britain's primary objective is to hold the European Commission back from silly meddling with day-to-day life, something she feels particularly strongly about because of her inability to act like other countries and ignore objectionable rules. The British are the only member-state who start the legislative process well in advance, so that on the day a directive is supposed to come into operation, the legal system is geared up to it. So when the Commission decrees that pork chops should no longer be sold with attached kidneys, they disappear from Britain but are available in butcher's shops on the Continent. While Eurosceptics believe that Britain is selling out, UKREP continues painstakingly scoring small victories which cumulatively become big ones, chipping away at the Commission's pretensions, but permanently under the handicap that if for one moment it is alleged to have failed to put Britain before the greater good, if one of its number ever offers one incautiously pro-European sentiment, knives will come winging towards their backs from Westminster, the tabloid press and their many other enemies.

The UN and the European Community impinge in many ways, for the British are to the forefront in trying to persuade Europe to take a common view on foreign policy – not, that is, to adopt a joint foreign policy – but where possible to react as a unit to the relentless series of crises that arise in these newly unstable times. The policy is what Hurd describes as building up 'the place and the role of the Community and its member states in world affairs. . . . We intend to work together for the better world order in which we all believe, and we intend to carry that work forward with greater impetus and greater effectiveness.' With the European Community contributing more than one-third of the cost of UN peace-keeping operations, and the British and the French substantial providers of troops, the European relationship with the UN is indeed a key area of concern. The British are anxious to reduce messiness by delivering the European Community en bloc to the UN whenever possible, a process fraught with the dangers that attend the development of an immature institution, most graphically shown in the fiasco over Bosnia.

OVERLEAF Glynne Evans, head of the United Nations department, travelling
to Bosnia in the belly of an RAF Hercules, discusses plans with Jeremy Braid,
Lord Owen's representative in Sarajevo.

The United Nations

The UK Mission to the United Nations was always a tough posting: now it is almost impossible.

The British view is that while the UN may be a deeply imperfect organisation for bringing about a sane new world order, it is the only one we have. Predictably, the great British contribution is towards making it work more efficiently and rationally than it otherwise might. If the European Community Foreign Office machine is impressive, the UN machine is more so.

Sir David Hannay, the UK permanent representative, is an extremely powerful presence on the Security Council. 'When anything tricky comes up,' said a colleague, 'he can be observed nudging the Americans in the ribs to point out to them things they've missed or things they should say. Everybody looks to him for an opinion.' Hannay is authoritarian, demanding and no man-manager, but he commands tremendous respect from his staff. 'Hannay takes no prisoners at the morning meeting,' said one of them, 'but he *can* lead.' 'It does very good things for my morale,' said Bob Peirce, the first secretary covering UN policy on Yugoslavia, 'to know that . . . the cleverest chap on the Security Council is our man and we work for him and we generally get what we want done. That is very inspiring and he always knows where he's going which means we don't waste time going up any branch lines and getting lost.'

Hannay was a 'terrific' permanent representative to the European Community from 1985–90, observed one British Eurocrat, 'although difficult to work with – he is just the man to deal with Saddam Hussein.' His European Community experience is invaluable. Multilateral diplomacy in the UN requires an astonishing grasp of detail, speed of movement and ability to capitalise on one's gains.

There are five permanent members of the Security Council: Britain, France, China, Russia and the United States. Britain and France are the most effective members. China is interested only in what impinges directly upon her interests, and Russia is trying to come to terms with its cataclysmic upheaval and with a complete change in the diplomatic requirements facing it.

Before the collapse of Communism, a Soviet spokesman knew exactly what to say – yes or (mostly) no. The line from Moscow was absolutely clear and there was not the faintest room for manoeuvre: it was a simple, if frustrating, fact of life. Russian diplomats now have to learn new tricks. One of the most remarkable and encouraging developments on the diplomatic scene is to meet diplomats from the former Soviet Union and from Eastern Europe who have a subtle and humorous approach to the hideous problems they face. They are learning fast, but they have enough problems on their own doorstep without looking for extra responsibilities on the Security Council.

The United States, well-meaning, rather gauche and sometimes querulous, is burdened by an internal political structure too democratic to allow spokesmen to do their job properly. Institutional rivalry ensures long consultations, so the United States frequently misses the bus because the State Department, the National Security Agency and the White House cannot work out a joint position in time to catch it.

Over-burdened, under-financed, structurally inefficient and often corrupt, all the UN can realistically do is limit the damage of the new world disorder. As Janet Douglas, a desk officer in the UN department, visiting the Kurdish-controlled areas of northern Iraq, put it:

The UN is being pressed, stretched more and more, because we are talking not just about existing problems here, [or in] former Yugoslavia, [or in] Somalia where there are enormous strains on the UN system. But we've got potential problems coming up like Mozambique, Angola, Afghanistan, possibly the former Soviet Republics all beginning to fall apart. The demands are increasing and almost endless: the prospects are dreadful.

The simple truth is that since the collapse of Communism the complexities of the ensuing crises are far beyond the ability of the world's institutions to solve. The United Nations was a name adopted by the twenty-six states that by 1942 had joined the international alliance to defeat Nazi Germany and Imperial Japan. It emerged three years later as a club of victors which others – including the vanquished – were subsequently invited to join. Some saw it as the forum from which world government would emerge, but its charter, drawn up at San Francisco in 1945, had a more pragmatic purpose: to deter large and aggressive powers (they were thinking of Germany and Japan) from invading weaker neighbours.

The United Nations now has 184 members, of which the United States is the biggest contributor, providing – when it pays up – nearly a third of UN funds. World-wide contributions to the UN are constantly and shamefully in arrears: Britain, France and New Zealand are the only countries that always pay on time. And the work increases at a terrifying and completely unpredictable rate. Bob Peirce described his responsibilities.

I came here to do a job covering Africa and Asia. The first thing that I was required to do when I got here was Cyprus, and then Yugoslavia blew up after I'd been here about a year. Now I am dealing with Europe and Asia; the big one is of course Yugoslavia, which is a whole complex of subjects and there is the associated issue of Yugoslavian sanctions. As well as being the political desk officer for Yugoslavia, I am the desk officer for sanctions and the British representative on the Security Council Sanctions Committee, and that, in an ideal world, would be two full-time jobs in themselves and some other Missions in town do indeed treat them as two completely separate jobs.

He also tracked Security Council involvement with both Cambodia and the former Soviet Union. In mid-1993, like his colleagues, he worked a seventy-to-eighty-hour week, arriving at 8.00 am to read telegrams, spending his day at meetings, lobbying, drafting

RIGHT Sir David Hannay is driven through the streets of New York City
to a meeting at the United Nations.

resolutions, briefing journalists and European or Commonwealth diplomats and finally, when released from UN meetings in mid-evening, returning to draft reporting telegrams to London, so that the following morning Foreign Office instructions would be on his desk at 8.00 am.

Many diplomats in other missions also work very hard and are discouraged by the public view that the UN is doing nothing. The UN was not designed as a global firefighter; it has no troops of its own. Yet everyone expects it to put out the fires and, when disappointed, looks around elsewhere for solutions.

NATO cannot help. The UK permanent representative on the North Atlantic Council, Sir John Weston, a subtle and scholarly reflector on international relations, is one of those trying to impose orderly thinking on the disorderly, while the organisation struggles to find a role, disagrees internally about letting in new members, frets at the tension between America and Europe over Bosnia and fears a weakening of the essential American involvement in NATO. America meanwhile, anxious for more gung-ho behaviour by those closest to the conflict, wonders if its allies are going soft. Why is NATO armed if it cannot sort out the Serbs?

The European Community wrings its hands, horrified by an outbreak, terrifyingly close to home, of mediaeval tribal and nationalist passions that optimists had thought permanently buried, while it tries to deal politically with the huge economic problems of a reunited Germany, the pressure for economic migration and the racist upsurge around Europe. The British press and many of the British public long for the days of gun-boat diplomacy and want Britain to march in and sort out Yugoslavia without incurring any casualties or expense along the way.

The British would like a United Nations corps of junior diplomats to roam potential world trouble spots and to try to defuse conflicts before they turn violent and require over-stretched peace-keeping missions: they want preventative diplomacy to help the UN in a world where 'the international task of the decade is managing disorder'.

At the time of upheaval and fear Britain is one of the few countries who are thinking about how to make institutions develop and work better. Douglas Hurd believes that the task is to reform and make better use of international institutions, particularly the UN: peace-keeping missions should be trimmed to those with definable goals.

We need to look at tasks closely, to ensure they are properly defined, and that the resources are available. We may on occasion have to recognise that a mandate should not be given [to send a peace-keeping mission], because in reality it could not be fulfilled . . . what we cannot do we should not pretend to do. If we play a game of bluff we can deceive and disappoint others, and sometimes ourselves.

LEFT Working in the margins: Tom Richardson (centre), deputy permanent representative to the United Nations, meets with a member of the Rwanda Patriotic Front under an Arabic wall decoration in a lobby at the UN.

Even if everyone pays up, the UN will always be short of money and good causes will have to be turned down. 'Without thrift and financial probity, the authority of the UN will weaken and vanish.' It is difficult to get the world stirred up about getting machines to work efficiently.

As if things were not complicated enough, the US backs expansion of the permanent seats on the Security Council to bring in Germany and Japan, while Britain, whose dominant role on the Security Council is its chief source of diplomatic clout in the world today, is extremely reluctant to allow more permanent members, such as the Japanese or the Germans, onto the Council. Britain and France also feel that increasing the permanent membership would make decision-making even more difficult. The argument remains that if it ain't broke, don't fix it.

Britain and France sometimes argue that they have a natural home on the Security Council because of their large constituency in their former colonies – the Commonwealth and the Francophonie (French-speaking countries) – and that in the post-Cold War era these countries rely on their former colonial masters as a conduit. And it is true that representatives of their old colonies routinely come to them for briefing. There would not be the same relationship – aid or no aid – between Third World countries and the Japanese.

The Japanese claim that they have a right to a permanent seat as the world's second largest economy and largest aid donor, as well as being a major contributor to the UN budget. Their political leaders, however, are divided, their constitution renounces the use of force to settle international disputes (which would appear to compromise their participation in UN missions) and domestic opinion is against Japanese citizens being exposed to any dangerous activities overseas: in Cambodia Japan lobbied to have its people sent to the safest part of the country where they were engaged in road-building and engineering. The British and the French gain a great deal of cachet from putting their well-disciplined and experienced troops into the dangerous places.

Surviving the 1990s will require enormous psychological adjustment. In the absence of miracles or political genius, inadequate institutions will have to be improved or replaced. It is slow, frustrating and detailed work, for there are, as civil servants say, 'no quick or easy solutions'. But whatever happens to the world during the 1990s, it is unlikely that diplomats will be phased out. They have become more necessary than ever.

LEFT Bob Peirce, first secretary covering UN policy on the former Yugoslavia.

· 10 ·

WRITING IT

A Word, or Two, about Drafting

Other people write: the Foreign Office drafts. The *Oxford English Dictionary* definition of drafting is 'to draw up in a preliminary form, which may afterwards be perfected.'

In today's Foreign Office there is a subterranean drafting war going on. There are those who believe that drafting must always be first-class, and there are those who say that much time is wasted giving routine briefing the attention one would give to a *communiqué* that follows a summit.

'One can't endorse declining standards,' says one side.

'All that matters is making yourself understood,' says the other.

The best of the former immeasurably improve their subordinates' prose, teach them by example and do not change what is already perfectly good; the worst have their pens hovering as they begin to read and change the first line before they have finished reading the sentence. The best of the critics clamp down on pedantry and pernicketiness; the worst would be lethal if they were given a chance (and of course, with so many long-stops, they are not), for good drafting skills are vital to diplomats.

At the very least, diplomats have to be precise about language. Every so often something major goes wrong in foreign policy and a public investigation follows: every relevant memorandum, letter, despatch and telegram is scrutinised in full public view. The Scott Inquiry into arms exports to Iraq, for instance, featured much stress on the key difference between the phrase 'revised policy' and 'revised interpretation'. One Foreign Office witness described a submission in which the wrong phrase had been used as 'frankly sloppy', and so it probably was. But given half a chance, conspiracy theorists see dark meanings and sinister nuances wherever possible; the Government, the Service and an individual career can be badly damaged by such a slip. Clarity and accuracy are the essential virtues.

LEFT Glynne Evans, head of the UN department, drafting in her office.

More positively, a foreign service needs at least a few people whose skills approach perfection. Even Mrs Thatcher, usually a great enemy of the Foreign Office, appreciated those she described as the 'golden pens', particularly Charles Powell, whom she took to Number 10 and who there went native (he jumped ship and went into business after she resigned), and John Kerr. Kerr, then in Washington, could interpret Mrs Thatcher's mind and put her views in terms acceptable to the Americans. John Dickie describes two occasions, in *Inside the Foreign Office*, when Kerr helped her pull off diplomatic triumphs.

The first related to the Strategic Defence Initiative – Star Wars – which she feared the Russians were intending to copy; this would make the British nuclear deterrent valueless. 'At stake was the entire concept of nuclear deterrence which was the one pillar of British foreign policy which successive governments believed had kept the peace for forty years.' In December 1984, Mrs Thatcher went to negotiate with the Americans at Camp David. After she had been wearing down Reagan, Bush and others for some time, Kerr passed her a note saying there were sufficient points of agreement for a joint statement and offered to draft a *communiqué* covertly. She removed Reagan to lunch and Kerr and Charles Powell, along with someone from the embassy to do the typing, found an empty office. Having learned what Kerr intended to say, Powell left him to it; thirty minutes later, Kerr told Powell he had finished, and secured his blessing for the draft.

At the appropriate moment Mrs Thatcher produced the paper from her handbag: the Americans asked for only two words to be changed. 'This historic agreement,' wrote Dickie, 'compressed into sixty-one words in less time than it takes to have lunch, became a model for diplomats to study. The document was a classic for its simplicity, and its breadth of application:

1. The United States and Western aim is not to achieve superiority but to maintain balance, taking account of Soviet developments.
2. SDI-related deployments would, in view of treaty obligations, have to be a matter of negotiations.
3. The overall aim is to enhance and not undermine deterrence.
4. East–West negotiation should aim to achieve security, with reduced levels of offensive systems on both sides.

Almost two years later, with US security policy in a muddle and much alarm in Europe about the nature of disarmament proposals, Mrs Thatcher again went to Camp David with John Kerr and Charles Powell. This time Kerr negotiated the framework of the *communiqué* with an American counterpart and stayed up much of the night drafting something appropriate. It was approved by Mrs Thatcher and the relevant US assistant secretary of state, Rozanne Ridgway, but the national security adviser, John Poindexter, asked for the insertion of a comma so that a particular sentence read: 'We also agreed on the need to press ahead with the SDI research programme, which is permitted by the ABM [Anti-Ballistic Missile] Treaty [of 1972].' First Kerr and then Thatcher rejected the comma, which would have meant Britain accepting that all SDI research was permissible under the 1972 treaty.

Even if it is only rarely that perfection is needed, politically-sensitive drafting is a central part of negotiating. As Tim Hitchens explained *apropos* the Edinburgh European Council meeting in 1992:

So many heads of mission and heads of state . . . are here . . . [and] you have to make their lives as easy as possible and so the conclusions have to be precooked and written beforehand, so that they can spend their time looking at them and saying 'Let's cut this sentence out,' or 'Let's add that sentence,' rather than writing them themselves, because there's practically no way they [would have time for] that.

So drafting skills do matter. The Foreign Office trains people commonsensically to be good, clear, unpretentious drafters. 'Foreign Office drafting is not a category of its own,' explains the relevant booklet. 'It is more a species of a wide class of prose; informing, discussing or decision-seeking, straightforward with never (or almost never) any literary devices. . . . The fact that a draft is official does not mean that it should not be vigorous and incisive; nor that it cannot be elegant in its simplicity.'

Examples given to study include: Julius Caesar's *Gallic Wars*, Venetian despatches on the Spanish Armada, despatches from the Duke of Wellington in the year of Waterloo and some particularly fine valedictory despatches from ambassadors. All are a model of lucidity.

All significant telegrams go out of the Office signed by the secretary of state, or from abroad signed by the head of mission, so in theory, only they are not drafters; everyone else is submitting everything he writes upwards, everyone drafts.

When Samuel Hoare was ambassador in Madrid, he insisted that all telegrams emanating from his embassy should not only be signed by him, but should be written in the first person. His resentful staff seized their opportunity and sent one of the Foreign Office's favourite telegrams: 'I have fallen down a liftshaft and am unconscious.'

One diplomat recalled his first experience of drafting. He submitted something of which he was proud, and was extremely disconsolate to have it returned to him massively rewritten. Seeing his dejected look, his superior said kindly, 'Oh, don't feel bad. It was quite a good draft. But you must remember that any draft, however good, can be improved by someone else.' The tyro reflected heretically that if the notion was thoroughly prevalent, the entire Office could spend all its time simply passing around the same piece of paper in the pursuit of ultimate perfection.

The following minutes of a real 1937 meeting show what happens when clever people become particularly silly and how an official can get his own back.
Those present were:
Norman Ernest Archer, OBE, assistant secretary, Imperial Conference;
Sir Harry Batterbee, CVO, CMG, KCVO, KCMG, assistant under secretary of state, Dominions Office;
Sir Edward Harding, CMG, CB, KCB, KCMG, permanent under secretary of state, Dominions Office;

Sir Rupert Howorth, KCMG, deputy secretary to the Cabinet;
Roland Venables Vernon, CB, assistant secretary, Colonial Office.

I attended a meeting in the Dominions Office to revise the draft Report of the Imperial Conference. I did not take exact notes at the time and I now give my recollections of the meeting from memory after a night's sleep.

The sentence in the draft Report under discussion was as follows: 'Mr Ormsby Gore [Secretary of State for the Colonies] dwelt upon the strategic and economic importance of the Colonies.'

Sir Edward Harding thought it was very unwise to say anything about the strategic importance of the Colonies. If anyone were to look at a map of the Colonies he might find out where Singapore was, and who could say what that would lead to? He proposed to strike out the word 'strategic'. Mr Vernon agreed.

Sir Harry Batterbee thought that it was very dangerous to refer to the economic importance of the Colonies. Any such reference would direct the mind of the reader to the claims of Germany for the restoration of her past colonial empire upon purely economic grounds. He thought that the words should be omitted. Mr Vernon agreed.

Sir Rupert Howorth did not like emphasis being laid on the importance of the Colonies. We were already to a large extent the object of envy and suspicion of the world on account of our possession of Colonies. The best line for us to take was to minimise their importance, and even to underrate them. He suggested that the word 'importance' should be omitted. Mr Vernon agreed.

The sentence in the draft now read: 'Mr Ormsby Gore dwelt upon the Colonies.' Mr Archer thought that this was a rather unhappy expression and suggested a lingering, continued exposition of the Colonial aspect of inter-Imperial affairs, which might very easily provoke jealousy on the part of the Dominions. Mr Vernon pointed out that the report would probably be read by a large number of agents of foreign Governments who might be imperfectly acquainted with the English language. There was a grave risk that they would interpret the words as 'Mr Ormsby Gore dwelt in the Colonies.' This would not be true. He suggested the substitution of the words 'referred to'. Sir Edward Harding pointed out that these words had already appeared in every sentence of the draft report which had so far been passed, and he thought it would be a good thing to find another expression this time. Sir Harry Batterbee suggested the words 'alluded to'. Mr Vernon agreed.

The sentence thus revised read 'Mr Ormsby Gore alluded to the Colonies.' Sir Rupert Howorth enquired whether it would not really be better to leave the sentence out altogether. If the Report merely stated that Mr Ormsby Gore alluded to the Colonies, it might excite suspicion on the part of foreign readers that the real gist of his remarks had been of a quite different character and this was nothing more than a screen or a disguise. Sir Harry Batterbee pointed out that Mr Ormsby Gore's name would in any case appear as one of those present, and that as he was Secretary of State for the Colonies it might probably arouse some jealousy in the minds of Dominion Statesmen if they considered that he had talked about the Dominions just as if they were Colonies. It therefore seemed wiser to leave the sentence in. Mr Vernon agreed, but suggested that the addition of the word 'furtively' before 'alluded to' might be an improvement. This was negatived without a division.

One difficulty with young drafters can be their insistence on showing-off: trying to make the highly-educated write for their intellectual inferiors is always difficult. According to a Foreign Office guide to speech-writing, the record for classical references in one draft is nine: St Simon Stylites, Virgil, Avernus, the Vestal Virgins, the Sabine Women, Oedipus, Cassandra, Horace and Cassius. The guide suggested more imaginative sources: 'James Bond, Woody Allen and Bob Marley are just as acceptable as Shakespeare or Virgil.'

Also, the needs of foreigners have to be borne in mind.

Hit for six, offside, Pandora's Box, Gadarene swine, lotus-eaters, pound of flesh, wind of change, never had it so good; such phrases as these, for a reader with the necessary background, may be much the best and shortest way of conveying the writer's thought. For readers without this background they may mean literally nothing at all.

Private secretaries aim to become ministers' ghost-writers. Nicholas Lawford was Bevin's. When dictating speech notes to a stenographer, Bevin 'rambled semi-coherently so much that he would eventually catch her look of bewilderment and concern. "Never mind, Missy," he would say on these occasions, "just get it down like I say and Lawford here will try and put it into English for you."' According to Sir Nicholas Henderson, Lawford could preserve Bevin's

idiosyncratic syntax while leaving no doubt about the meaning. . . . He would dash off a Bevin telegram with aplomb, and the other Private Secretaries came to model themselves on his style rather than on the true Bevin, rather as a portrait painter will sometimes prefer to work from a photograph than from real life.

Civil servants – not just diplomats – sometimes complain that their skills are unmarketable, because they are impossible to define. Those seeking to understand this arcane area of Foreign Office expertise might usefully reflect on the following explanation from Alan Judd's novel. The ambassador is reacting to a letter submitted to him by his novice third secretary.

'The essence of good drafting is to be both clear and comprehensive, which is never easy. This isn't bad. The essence of good diplomatic drafting is, where possible, to avoid saying anything that admits of only one meaning. That's why good diplomatic drafting is bad, but you have yet to learn that, fortunately.'

· 11 ·

CONSULAR AND VISA WORK

Distressed British Nationals and Would-be Immigrants

I went to call on the consul in Delhi, and as I sat down, I made an idle joke about the rucksack in the corner of his office. It had belonged, he told me miserably, to a nineteen-year-old English girl who had drowned when a bus had tried to cross a flooded river. He was in the process of doing the job that consuls most hate – dealing with terrible human tragedies. Consular work is about looking after your countrymen when they get into trouble abroad, or, as one main-stream officer who had determinedly avoided it all his life told me, 'it is all about the awful things that can happen: rape, death, muggings, assault, arrests, prisons and grief, which of course is probably why women are particularly good at it. It's all to do with human problems'.

It is consular staff who identify bodies – many of them bloated, some of them badly injured, some of them even decomposing. It is not an aspect of the job that gets a mention in the recruitment literature. Indeed all the recruitment literature has to say about consular work is that it 'involves helping or advising UK nationals abroad'. A Cinderella of the Foreign Office, consular work is insufficiently valued – probably because the people running the Office and speeding up the promotion ladder have never done the actual work. Yet for anyone with an interest in people, it is exceptionally rewarding: aspects of the job are frightful, but you acquire an astonishing understanding of humanity.

In Bangkok, Jean Sharpe runs one of the largest and busiest British consular office outside Western Europe. She and her staff deal with an immense array of consular and visa problems from the usual lost passports to the special difficulties that arise in a country which is not only in the drug-smuggling Golden Triangle, but is a notorious prostitution centre and has a large number of beautiful young women desperately seeking European husbands. 'We're a cross between Marje Proops and a nanny quite often,' said Helen Squires, a vice consul in Bangkok. But they deal with issues that never trouble nanny.

LEFT The visa section of the Bangkok consular department where
the staff process about 500 applications a day.

171

Here Lem Morgan, a vice consul, is the 'Death Man', dealing with an average of six dead British nationals every month – businessmen or tourists who have died of natural causes; victims of accidents, or worse. If there is no one else to identify them, he does his best from photographs among their possessions; through the FCO he liaises with relatives in Britain or wherever they can be found and looks after them when they arrive in Bangkok. Alternatively, he arranges for cremation, burial or for the transporting of the body, or the ashes, back to Britain.

Lem Morgan, a vice consul in Bangkok, overseeing the cremation of a British citizen who died in the city. None of the deceased's relatives was able to attend: the ashes were sent back to England.

There are, of course, even in this kind of work, moments which, in retrospect at least, are blackly comic. One vice-consul who was in the police morgue attending the identification of the bodies of two tourists, 'lost a number of heartbeats when the refrigerated compartment door behind him burst open to release an embalmed oriental, dressed immaculately in suit and tie.' Then there was the case of the relative whose loved one had died on the plane. It was, the vice-consul presumed, the result of shock that she took considerable persuading first that the body could not simply travel on to London as it was and second, that although there were still two tickets, duty free goods could now be purchased for one person only.

Distraught relatives are a part of the job. Where there are no relatives the consular official also has to sort out personal effects, luggage and so on. Two rather grisly precautions that are frequently taken in these days of widespread drug addiction and AIDS, are tipping the contents of a bag out on the floor of the morgue for fear of syringes, and putting on rubber gloves before sorting through the possessions.

The worst cases, of course, are air crashes, when the whole embassy may get involved. One spouse at the Kathmandu embassy wrote in the *BDSA* [British Diplomatic Spouses Association] *Magazine* about what happened in September 1992 when a plane carrying British citizens crashed in Nepal killing everyone instantly.

The Embassy went into top gear. It was a public holiday and we were supposed to be closed for four days, but that never happened. . . . We were assigned names of families to liaise with, we were warned about the effects of bereavement; grief, silence, tears, anger, helplessness, rejection of help.

We saw them all, but I was glad I had been warned. It was all very exhausting. The first sight of the relatives had been at a briefing in the hotel the afternoon they arrived. Seeing the grief and shock on their faces and knowing how tired they were feeling after travelling for twenty-four hours made me realise how difficult the next few days were going to be.

The local community provided transport and practical help; the local hotel managed to produce lunch for ninety on the ambassador's lawn. The following day nine Land Rovers were taken up to the crash site with fifty relatives and helpers and the staff driving.

It has affected the people concerned here. We are suffering from the symptoms of bereavement even though they were not our relatives on that plane. Things that we would normally take in our stride upset us.

Even more ghastly is dealing with someone who is going to be executed. One consul, like most in the Far East, had responsibility for several Hong Kong UK nationals who had been caught smuggling drugs. A Hong Kong Chinese woman with a British passport was condemned to death. The consul was present when her fourteen-year-old daughter came to Malaysia from Hong Kong to visit her and was told during their meeting that there was no hope of a reprieve. 'She was crying, the daughter was crying, the prison wardens were crying, the interpreter was crying.' Before the woman was hanged, her last words to the consul were, 'Please save my life.' As he remarked with admirable Foreign Office understatement: 'That takes it out of you.'

In Bangkok, where there were almost 200 prisoners to deal with when I was there in the summer of 1993, they at least have the advantage that recently no foreigners have actually been executed. But the consular load is very heavy and prison work is one of those areas where there is a tremendous gap between what consular staff are required – indeed permitted – to do and what British nationals – particularly British citizens – expect of them.

'Nannying', observed Helen Squires,

is what a lot of Brits overseas tend to expect. Anything goes wrong and they come bowling down to the Embassy and expect us to be able to put it right at the wave of a magic wand. We can't. My feeling is that when you travel overseas and you arrive in another country, you are automatically undertaking to abide by that country's rules and regulations and laws, so if in the UK you have a few pints too many and you get obnoxious, the cops may sort of warn you and send you on your way. Here it could be a completely different thing. You find yourself in clink . . . and people seem to think that just because they're British, they can ring up the Embassy and we can pull them out of any pickle.

'*If arrested*', explains Bangkok's information package, consular staff can:

Visit you in custody as soon as possible after notification of arrest; provide a list of local lawyers; give advice on local procedures; liaise with local authorities to provide doctors if necessary and notify next-of-kin if wished.

Many of the prisoners and their relatives see it more simply: the job of embassies is to get them released.

Misunderstandings occur from the very beginning. In one corner is the British Foreign Office, whose representatives are required to operate on the principle of do-as-you-would-be-done-by: behave towards the host country as one would wish its representatives to behave in similar circumstances in the UK. Among other things, that means not trying to intervene in judicial procedures or seek preferential treatment. Additionally, the consular department has no money available for anything but the direst of short-term emergencies.

In the other corner are the prisoners/relatives, who revert to Victorian attitudes and believe that Britain can have anyone released simply by kicking up a fuss and making threats, that when help is required a British consul should pop up immediately like a genie from a bottle and that there should be unlimited staff and funds abroad to help distressed British nationals.

In the immigration queue in Riyadh I met a small group of British oil engineers working in Saudi Arabia, who protested loudly that when they had landed up in jail on some alcohol-related offence, the embassy had failed to visit them. It turned out that they had been released after a mere thirty-six hours. The Saudi British expatriate population exceeds 30 000, and many of its members get picked up for various minor offences from time to time. They are usually released either before the embassy has been notified that they are inside, or before the consular staff can secure permission to visit them.

In Bangkok consular staff deal routinely with mules – vulnerable, gullible young people who smuggle the drugs the Mr Bigs would never carry themselves. Typical would be an impoverished single mother from Hong Kong or a nineteen-year-old unemployed youth recruited in a London pub. They, and others like them, are told of a foolproof method, given a ticket to Thailand and promised a wad of money when the drugs are delivered at the other end. As one of the consular staff observed tartly, 'there ought to be a "wet-behind-the-ears-test" at Heathrow before anyone is allowed to leave.'

Having been arrested, and being unable to speak the language, people like these wait for an embassy representative to come galloping to the rescue. They become more and more upset over the several days it may take before the British consul is told they are there. When the embassy does hear and the British prisoner is visited, he is frequently desperately disappointed that he cannot simply be released, or, failing that, be provided with an English-speaking lawyer free. The news that this is impossible frequently provokes an outburst along the lines of 'What do I pay my taxes for?' – a protest, as consular staff note wryly, that tends to emerge most indignantly from people who look as if they never paid taxes in their lives.

But it is not only first-time visitors who get into trouble. In 1993, twenty-five-year-old Kevin James Grant was charged with selling drugs. Grant had lived in Thailand for four years and had a bar/restaurant which began to fail. Following an accident, he went back to the UK and returned to find his partner had sold the establishment from under him. Grant's Thai girlfriend was pregnant and he was short of money. He began to deal in drugs. He was picked up in Bangkok in a restaurant with about 650 grams of heroin in a plastic bag. He claimed he was only passing it on, but he was charged with selling. Having tried to escape, he was handcuffed.

As the television series showed, Jean Sharpe despatched one of her two full-time prison visitors, Joy Bartrup, a British-born Thai resident who is hired locally. Grant, like so many others in such a position, did not want his next-of-kin informed, so Bartrup, like vice consuls everywhere, had the job of convincing him that usually, if next-of-kin are not notified, they will eventually find out about their relative through the newspapers. She had then to offer the limited help available from the embassy, explain the procedures about remanding narcotics offenders, give him the address of Prisoners Abroad, who help with money and general support, answer his questions about the transfer agreement between Thailand and the UK which allows for the possibility of serving a sentence at home, and promise visits in the future from her or her colleague, Rachel Eyres.

From the embassy's point of view Grant was an easy case. He knew his way around, had a local girlfriend and took a realistic attitude. There was no outraged protest either from him or his relatives about trumped-up charges and he was prepared to play the system sensibly in the hope of leniency.

Others take a different approach. In some of the worst cases a parent arrives, and, through shame, their child claims to be innocent. They might see a lawyer from the embassy list who recommends that the prisoner plead guilty and exhibit remorse; that way he might get away with seven years. The outraged parent denounces the pusillanimity of the lawyer and takes on a local charlatan. In such cases a not guilty plea with its implication that the local authorities have been venal can make for a much longer sentence.

During the long remand period and then the prison sentence, consular staff visit every few weeks to make sure that prisoners are being treated properly and to do odds and ends of shopping for them, for conditions are extremely basic. Rachel Eyres and Joy Bartrup will sometimes have to deal with prison authorities when there has been trouble between one of their prisoners and some of the Thais, for it causes much resentment with incarcerated natives that in the men's prisons (unlike the women's), foreign men are not required to work and are allowed to spend most of their time together. So there are occasional fights and sometimes also trouble with the warders. Prisoners are rarely comforted by having it pointed out to them that conditions are no worse than in most British jails.

The majority of the UK nationals in jail in Bangkok receive no media attention. The story of the eighteen-year-old Karyn Smith and the seventeen year-old Patricia Cahill was one of the exceptions. They were picked up at Bangkok airport because of a tip-off from British Customs and Excise. Patricia Cahill pleaded guilty. Karyn Smith said in court that she was innocent. They were jailed for twenty-five and eighteen years respectively. Because they were female, young and pretty, their fate was well-covered in the newspapers, which pleased everyone involved in trying to stamp out drug trafficking. It was hoped that what had happened might serve to deter other young people.

Jean Sharpe, Joy Bartrup and Rachel Eyres looked after the girls as best they could. They cannot afford to become too emotionally involved, but they do care about making the lives of their many charges as bearable as possible and they do get upset about some of the more vulnerable. Consular staff were extremely relieved, for instance, when another of their female charges, who was in the second stage of AIDS and afraid of picking up an infection, was able to go home.

The consular staff not only did shopping for the two girls, followed up their complaints and kept in touch with their relatives, but they tried to help them adjust to the loss of their youth by giving them whatever pastoral care they could. They brought books to Patricia Cahill, who was intelligent and was educating herself and what they hoped for them was what they hope for all the sentenced UK prisoners in their care: that within a few years they would be quietly repatriated to a UK prison, where, after serving the much shorter sentence than they would have received in Thailand, they would be released.

Then a lawyer called Stephen Jakobi came on the scene. His real villains emerged as corrupt Thai police, cynical British customs officials (who had tipped off the wicked Thais) and, of course, the fumbling and uncaring Foreign Office. The pressure grew to demand a pardon. The media made much of the girls' youth and beauty, and eventually persuaded the prime minister to ask King Bhumibol to grant them a royal pardon.

There had always been a chance of a pardon on the grounds of the girls' youth, although they were not the highest priority cases. A more urgent and deserving case was a Hong Kong national who had been a teenager when sentenced, who had smuggled drugs only to get the money to support her baby, who had already been in jail longer than Smith and Cahill and who had had a major operation while inside. But this woman's case was not supported by the tabloid press, an MP and a naive Bishop, and did not have the pulling power exercised by two young white British girls.

The political side of the embassy expended much effort on trying to reduce the potential damage to Anglo-Thai relations done by the Jakobi campaign. As a general rule, embassies abroad believe that operating in partnership with the local authorities, appealing to their compassion and keeping publicity to a minimum is the most effective method of getting prisoners released. The girls had always had the sense to continue to admit their guilt, whatever was being said at home, so the Thais were well-disposed. Keeping the request private was essential: public pressure rarely produces goodwill gestures.

I was visiting the British Embassy at the time Smith and Cahill were released. Because, at the request of ministers, the pardon had been announced prematurely, Jean Sharpe and Joy Bartrup endured a nightmare day. They hung around the prison from 7.30 am until 6.00 pm, keeping the girls calm while they waited for the actual letter of pardon to arrive. Thus the journalists – fifty:fifty British and Thai – had plenty of time to gather, and become intensely frustrated. By the time the girls were released there was a huge crowd. At one stage, with the temperature in the nineties, Jean Sharpe, Joy Bartrup, the two girls, five prison warders and a driver were trapped in a small van without air conditioning, unable to get out because they were surrounded by serried ranks of hacks, who were becoming abusive because the girls would not be interviewed. Suffocation seemed imminent and the girls were terrified.

Complex organisation back in the consular office, and the wooing of Thai officials, allowed the girls to get through the bureaucratic immigration procedures in time to catch a plane home that night, and be saved ending up in an extremely unpleasant immigration unit. Having seen them off, Jean Sharpe then had to meet the incoming Smith parents and their accompanying journalists and shepherd them straight on to another plane back to the UK.

Meanwhile the political side of the embassy was talking to the Thai Ministry of Foreign Affairs, drafting and coordinating statements in conjunction with London to ensure that the pardon improved rather than damaged Anglo-Thai relations, for there was a real fear that this goodwill gesture could go sour, with serious consequences for trade as well as the prospects for the early release of other prisoners.

What struck me most throughout that day was that embassy staff were concerned about three issues simultaneously: servicing their ministers, who during the day were being briefed across the world and time zones for their various statements to the media; the welfare of the girls; and the health of the Anglo-Thai relationship. How the media would treat the Foreign Office seemed to be a question in no one's mind except mine. They were grimly doing their jobs and, in any case, they always expect bad publicity.

Sandra Gregory (right) and Patricia Cahill (centre), both inmates of Klom Prem women's prison in Bangkok, talking to Jean Sharpe, the British consul in Bangkok.

The following afternoon, when it was all over and the girls were back in England and reunited with their relatives, the consular staff and a few others stood (after working hours) in the staff club in Bangkok watching the television coverage. For the first and only time in my many months with the Foreign Office, we were drinking champagne – paid for out of Jean Sharpe's own pocket. I asked for an update on the press coverage and she laughed and said: 'What you'd expect. Half of them blame us for kow-towing to the Thais and letting the innocent victims stay in so long, and the other half blame us for being soft on drug traffickers.'

And so it proved to be. The *Sun* took a high moral line and hoped ministers and the Foreign Office expected no bouquets for going soft on drugs. And its sister-paper, *Today*, hoped

that the Foreign Office resists the urge to pat itself on the back for its part in the royal pardons . . . for their convictions should never have occurred in the first place – and would certainly never have happened in this country [a breathtaking allegation in itself].

Most of the drugs had been planted on them.

Throughout their trial and imprisonment, the two girls were ill-served by the Foreign Office . . . [which] bent over backwards to appease this corrupt regime, right up until the last moment when it sought to play down increasingly strong rumours that a pardon was about to be given, for fear of causing offence.

Today was very keen that henceforward, in similar cases, British lawyers should be sent to represent our citizens abroad. It would be an expensive innovation. In 1992 2396 UK nationals were charged abroad, 665 of them with drug-related offences. And as with the impoverished West African female 'drug mules' in British prisons, one cannot always tell which ones are innocent.

The media, like the British public, are ambivalent about the level of consular service which should be provided. As Jean Sharpe put it:

Obviously if Granny loses her passport and gets into trouble, she should be looked after. So should the young and simple and innocent who are taken advantage of. But what about the irresponsible, the backpackers who forget to phone home and whose frantic parents want them traced, the people who just don't bring enough money and who get into trouble through their own fault? How much of a service should be provided?

Although it is all about human beings, consular work is immensely technical and requires a vast range of knowledge of all sorts of rules and regulations. The basic three-week consular course for Grades 5 to 10 covers:

The British Nationality Acts, The Immigration Act 1971, Passport matters, Protection, Assistance, including financial Assistance, and the Repatriation of British Nationals. Other aspects of the course include Registration of Births and Deaths, Administration of Estates, Notarial Acts, Service of

Documents, Customer Relations and the need to maintain good relations with the British community and local authority.

DBNs (distressed British nationals) are no longer the uncomplaining stoics of yore. It is a sign of the times, Jean Sharpe said,

that we now have to work behind glass windows, that we have a separate interview booth and that we don't actually meet our customers face to face any more because many of them have drug problems, drink problems and other problems, and we are at physical risk.

Expectations have risen. People expect solutions and complain loudly if they are not forthcoming. Yet staff numbers and financial resources have gone down. The Citizens' Charter, which the Foreign Office takes with deadly seriousness, is adhered to rigorously, yet customers are increasingly frustrated because the consular staff operate under such financial constraints that they have to behave more like pawnbrokers than Good Samaritans.

Consuls swap stories about the demands of the travelling British public, which become increasingly peculiar as the night wears on. Several urgent late-night phone-calls to duty officers have been along these lines:

CALLER: I am a bit concerned about my brother (uncle/sister/cousin) because he hasn't been in touch for a while and I wondered if you could contact him for me.
DUTY OFFICER: OK. When exactly were you last in contact with your brother?
CALLER: Oh, around 1981.

British faith in the versatility of their consuls knows no bounds. There was the woman who telephoned the Florence consulate in the middle of the night because her cat was on the roof and she feared it could not get down; another telephoned at 2 am – 'desperate' to acquire an au pair girl. But the winner from the stories I heard was

a lady of mature years who wished to have some advice on marriage in Nepal. She had, while trekking on her last visit to the country, become friendly with two sherpas. She had wished to marry one of them and had therefore been disappointed to discover that he already had a wife. Unabashed she proposed to the second sherpa and had returned to Nepal to get married. However, in the intervening months the first sherpa had been divorced and was available to marry; she asked which one we thought she should choose.

Despite the ghastliness of quite a lot of consular work – and many main-stream people get out of it as fast as possible – it is rewarding if you enjoy the unexpected and get satisfaction from being useful. One consul told me of a case which still delighted him many years later. A woman travelling from Australia with her five-year old daughter was put off her plane at Kuala Lumpur because she was seen to be miscarrying. He visited her in hospital where she was found to need a minor operation and she was terribly upset about what would happen to her daughter. The official took them home for the night to give the child the opportunity to get to know his family, and they looked after her while the mother was in hospital: ten years later he was still getting grateful letters and Christmas cards.

Then there is the enjoyment that comes from solving esoteric problems and being simultaneously ingenious and helpful. As for instance in the case of the consular official in Saudi Arabia who was asked to provide a form of death certificate for a British couple's labrador so that its body could be returned to the UK for burial, for without it, the airline refused to transport the body. 'In view of the couple's distress, our man in Al Khubar concocted a suitably official-looking form which did the trick.'

There was an excellent precedent for this in the favourite consular story of the British travelling circus that went bankrupt many years ago in France. Its human performers had to be repatriated, but they refused to leave without their elephant and could prove that it was British-born. Ultimately, the consul declared it a 'distressed British elephant' and repatriated it along with its owners.

But the jolly moments are infrequent. Most of the work is routine, and much of it involves dealing with people at their most vulnerable or their worst. Consular staff face people who are bereaved, desperate, drug-crazed, drunk, broken-hearted and mad. The consular staff are generally polite, helpful, patient, sympathetic and unshockable. Often, they defuse problems that might otherwise wreak havoc in international relations. Yet they stay consistently undervalued within the service. The Foreign Office belief that consular work is just common sense and therefore should not have fine brains wasted upon it, comes about, said Jean Sharpe forcibly, speaking for many of her colleagues, because

they have never done consular work, don't know what it's about, don't know how difficult it can be, don't know that common sense is not common, [don't know] that dealing with people takes a certain expertise [that] they may not always have. People in political work are dealing with people of their own intellectual ability and arguing matters of state and fine print. They are not being told that the person facing them is a taxpayer and wants advice, so why can't you help. They are not used to being sworn at and spat at.

As far as most British people are concerned, the Foreign Office *is* the Consular Service. Yet there are still ambassadors who merely visit their consular section annually, and new fast streamers who regard it as something which will never have any relevance to their career. I have heard of one or two who, in a two-year posting abroad, never set foot in the consular offices which were only one minute's walk away from the main entrance. The surprise is that the staff stay as committed and effective as they do, cheering themselves up with occasional letters of gratitude and seeing the joke in the bleakest of circumstances.

Here is a classic consular story. Of all those told or sent to me while researching this book, this is my favourite, for it illustrates not just the splendidly practical approach of the consular service but it is also quintessentially English. My source feared it might be apocryphal, but it had been told to him as a true story.

My tale concerns certain medical problems of a social nature contracted by young Royal Navy (RN) sailors when their ships put in to port at Freetown, Sierra Leone. Apparently, RN doctors noticed an alarming increase in infections in these young men when they returned to Portsmouth, after a night out in Freetown. The RN sought the High Commission's advice and in the best traditions of the Service, the consul took a very pragmatic approach. He visited, for purely official reasons, of course, a number of establishments and spoke to the Madams. He undertook to direct the trade to them alone with the proviso that the girls remained healthy and clean. The Madams readily agreed and the result was a great reduction in infections. Some time later the RN sent their thanks to the High Commission and the consul decided to visit the Madams to congratulate them and to encourage them to keep up the good work. Imagine his surprise when he saw the sign above the door of the first brothel which read: 'By appointment to Her Majesty the Queen'!

Entry Clearance and Visa Work

[The consular department is] the shop window . . . of the Foreign Service overseas. We're the people who are seen by the general public [in each country]. The Thais see our visa section – that's really all the majority of them know [about] the British Embassy.

Equally most British citizens . . . don't see the ambassador and the political staff at work . . . they probably have as little idea of what they do as most people in the UK. If you asked anyone in the UK what an embassy does, I think they could come up with passports and visas.

So said Jean Sharpe in Bangkok.

The job of the Foreign Office's entry clearance work is twofold: to ensure that the right applicants are allowed into Britain, and the wrong ones are not. The Foreign Office runs visa sections in over 150 posts. The entry clearance officers (ECOs) who work there are drawn from both Foreign and Home Office staff and some are hired locally.

The Home Office's job is to control immigration. Its secondees are professional immigration officers who understand all the small print of the work, as well as its implications at home. They have spent time on immigration control desks at ports and airports; they have sent people back home without letting them in; many of them have been involved in the pursuit and expulsion of people who have overstayed their official welcome. Their experiences of foreigners will have tended to be negative.

The Foreign Office ECOs are main streamers who have a broader view of foreign cultures, and a less jaundiced view of their clients. They will also be rather more aware that good international relations are to some extent dependent on the experience of individuals in dealing with the 'shop window' of a foreign power. And the locally-engaged know the language and the culture in depth.

'My Home Office colleagues,' laughed Marie-Louise Childs, a Grade 9 ECO in Bangkok, 'joke about the Foreign Office pussy-footing around, hiding behind smokescreens of words, whereas they are the bovver boys who go round, smash the door in first and ask questions later. We tease each other about that.'

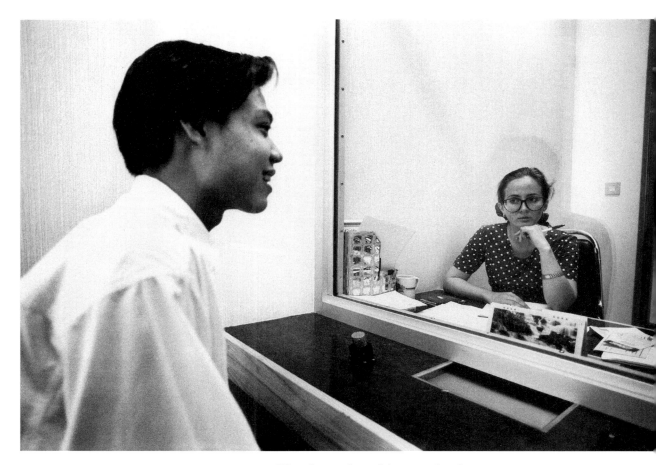

ABOVE AND RIGHT The visa section of the consular department
in Bangkok: Marie-Louise Childs (above) and Claire Sakornpant (right),
entry clearance officers, interrogate visa applicants.

When I suggested, provocatively, to a fast streamer that she should spend some time on entry clearance work, she replied 'perhaps about five minutes'. This young woman is clever and industrious, but her reaction sums up why I became convinced that her kind should spend time at the Foreign Office coal-face, meeting DBNs and deciding on the fate of those wishing to emigrate to the UK. It was clear that this fast streamer neither understood what this work was, nor thought there was anything valuable to be learned from doing it. Yet she is precisely the kind of person who most needs contact with the reality of so much of the Foreign Office's work. She and her kind end up running embassies with no knowledge of this, vital, work.

And entry clearance work is psychologically the most educational as well as the roughest. With a consular case, if you make a bad judgement you may temporarily upset an individual. Make the wrong decision about a visa application, and you may permanently damage the lives of several people.

Kevin Fuller, the entry certificate manager and chief immigration officer in Bangkok, on secondment from the Home Office, said that he was often under strain because he found himself making 'decisions about people's lives which I wouldn't like made about mine [by somebody else]. It's very stressful [to be] dealing with [the future of] someone's whole life. You can't possibly say "I'm not sure about this, so just to be on the safe side I'll ruin the rest of your life."'

The new world disorder increases the number of visa applications inexorably. Over a million visa applications were processed in 1991, and the estimated annual growth over the next few years is about 5 per cent. But that is only an educated guess. Who, five years ago, would have anticipated the huge demand from Eastern Europe and the Soviet Union?

In Bangkok they process about 500 visa applications a day, and they receive around 700 settlement applications a year. And the number is growing. Kevin Fuller again:

Settlement applications really only account for 2 per cent of our work . . . but a lot more effort and time is involved in dealing with them because of the complexity of the applications and because of the actual effect that we create by refusing them. About 20 per cent of [annual settlement applications] will probably be refused.

All ECOs are enjoined 'to treat applications with respect, sensitivity and consideration,' and to issue visit visas within twenty-four hours, and settlement visas within three months.

Periodically, frightful storms blow up about the heartless treatment of wives and children seeking to join husbands and fathers in the UK, and there have, of course, been many injustices along the way. But the judgements that have to be made in the difficult cases are very difficult indeed. The wonder is that these youngsters – for most of the junior ranks are in their twenties and (in the case of the Foreign Office people) have just three weeks of formal training – bear the responsibility as well as they do.

Some of the most exacting entry clearance problems concern newlyweds. First it has to be determined whether a valid marriage has taken place at all, and that requires the application of different criteria of proof, depending on which region of what country and which religion is in question. In Delhi I saw one interview where the proof was a photograph album of a Sikh ceremony that showed unquestionably that the bridal pair had circled the fire the requisite number of times. In Bangkok this stage of the proceedings is usually simpler: there will be a proper marriage certificate. The tricky part in both places is usually the next part of the business, where ECOs are required to divine the reason why the visa applicant married the UK citizen. The rules, observed one high commissioner, are 'very angular'.

What the ECOs have to determine is if the 'primary purpose' of the visa applicant, in contracting the marriage, was to live in the UK; if so the visa will be refused. This criterion was introduced to control the numbers entering the UK, and it is a British yardstick which is supposed to determine whether a marriage is real or not. Unfortunately it has little meaning for people in cultures where women get married mainly for economic reasons, and the UK is seen as the passport to riches. In Thailand, for instance, some women are happy to get divorced in order to acquire a British husband and the money that they hope goes with that. Later they will rejoin their Thai husbands. To Western eyes this seems a touch cynical, but it is sheer pragmatism in Bangkok. There are usually children to be supported, and, as with prostitution, duty drives the mothers to desperate measures.

Kevin Fuller described a typical case in Thailand:

The classic one-off meeting somewhere. She says they met by chance at Singapore airport as she was coming back from working there. He was passing through on holiday and they exchanged addresses. They corresponded for twelve months, but never met again. He proposed, she accepted. He's arrived here, and they married within five days. There is a twenty-year-age gap. He's never married before; he's in his mid-forties. She's worked abroad in Singapore; she's applied to go and work in Hong Kong.

LEFT Kevin Fuller, the entry certificate manager and chief immigration officer in Bangkok, oversees a visa application interview.
OVERLEAF The long queues for visas at the Bangkok Embassy.

So the ECOs have to find out if the woman has deliberately set out to use the man to get her to a more prosperous country than Thailand. Is she even being organised by an agency who will use her as a prostitute in Britain, if she gets there? Is she likely, once settled in the UK, to want to bring in children, parents and siblings?

The Bangkok visa section deals with a steady procession of naive British men who have fallen madly in love with a pretty and apparently accommodating girl, and who are loathe to believe that her motives are anything other than romantic. All that the ECOs can realistically do is try to determine if she likes him and intends to be a wife rather than an exploiter.

In Delhi, on the other hand, romantic love is rarely involved. The ECOs will be trying to decide if the Indian woman or man would have been content to marry the UK citizen even if he or she lived in India.

The ECOs are well aware that when they look an applicant squarely in the eye and ask the key question, an innocent applicant in either country may well say the wrong thing, whereas one whose primary motivation is to get to the UK at all costs, may well have been set up and coached by – in Bangkok – an agency and in India, knowing relatives. What is particularly hard is the sheer arbitrariness of some of the decisions they have to take. They have to stay strictly within the rules and write a report explaining why any visa has been turned down.

Yet, though the law, as ever, is in certain respects an ass, there can be no foolproof way of separating the deserving from the undeserving would-be settler. The world is full of ever larger numbers of desperate people trying to reach the West, and if marriage is the only route, then many of them will take it. Yet to refuse British citizens the right to marry foreigners would be an invasion of liberty.

In order to cut down on the number of immigrant males, the British Government decreed that British women could not automatically bring foreign husbands into the UK. This sexual discrimination caused outrage and British women were granted the same rights under the law as British men, ie, they may bring their spouses into the UK. But this has led to other problems. Now, some British-born Asian girls who do not wish to marry a man from India are under pressure to do so. When I was in Delhi I was told about one such case.

A British girl smuggled letters from a remote village in the Punjab to both the prime minister and her boyfriend in London, saying that she was being forced into an arranged marriage. Her family had taken her from the UK to visit her grandmother and had asked her to stay to look after the grandmother when she had her eye operation. She was being held prisoner.

The prime minister wrote to the high commissioner, who summoned the consul, who placed the matter in the hands of H. B. Singh, for more than fifteen years the locally-engaged linchpin of the consular department in Delhi. Singh set off on his lengthy journey, taking his wife with him in order to forestall the argument that he could not see an unmarried girl alone. Having faced down 400 angry villagers armed with staves, he succeeded in getting his wife a private interview with the girl, who told her that she wanted to go back to London, would commit suicide rather than marry the local chosen for her, but would not say that publicly because she was too terrified. Her fear was well-founded, since the prospective bridegroom was the son of the local police superintendent who had sworn to kill her entire family if she refused to go through with the marriage. By a succession of miracles of diplomacy, and in the end the bringing in of a force of female constabulary, Singh, after several days, succeeded in rescuing the woman.

The Consular Service are seeing an increasing number of such cases. They also have British nationals, who married Indians and did not return to the UK, coming in and saying: 'I'm afraid that my husband's family are going to burn me to death because I won't do everything they tell me to do.'

ECOS see the indigenous population at their worst. One consequence of spending a large part of every day being lied to is that it induces a certain cynicism. 'They're all racists [in the consular department],' said a worried fast streamer. 'You wouldn't believe how they refer to the locals.' But as a fast streamer he can have no idea what xenophobia might be produced in him if he were doing consular and visa work. He will never gaze into the limpid eyes of a Thai girl to try to gauge her feelings for the fat, middle-aged man beside her. And he will never have to make a judgement about whether the twenty-nine-year-old Arab truly wants to go to London to learn about marketing, or whether he wants to kill Salman Rushdie. It is a pity, he could only benefit.

Consular Statistics

	1989	1990	1991	1992
Visits abroad by UK residents (millions)	31.2	31.1	30.5	*31.5
Prisoners: British and others for whom we are responsible	3377	3472	3196	3821
Number of British citizens given financial assistance (including advances against both deposits and undertakings to repay)	1853	1872	1055	1841
Number of repatriations carried out (against undertakings to repay)	137	91	157	83
Number of reported deaths overseas of British nationals and others for whom we are responsible	868	834	782	1261
Number of passports issued overseas (thousands)	271	281	293	*285
Number of Registrations of Births and Deaths overseas (thousands)	11	11	10.5	*10
UK-based staff years employed on consular work overseas	108	106	104	*103

* Estimated

OVERLEAF A waiting area in the visa section of the consular department of the Bangkok Embassy.

· 12 ·

PROPAGANDA AND PROFITS

Selling Britain

Those employed in information or commercial work sell British values and British goods; indeed like many of their other colleagues, they talk of marketing 'Britain plc', the 'UK plc' or 'Great Britain Ltd'. The job of those in information work is to project a positive image of the United Kingdom abroad; the job of the commercial side is to make it easier for UK goods to be sold in foreign markets.

The most straightforward – if often wearing – part of information work is the answering of vast numbers of questions from the public, which will vary from 'Is Scotland in England?' to 'When did Parliament begin?' to 'Why won't you guys sort out Bosnia?' But the underlying purpose of the job is to project the best image of this country. 'Propaganda', said the American diplomat, Charles Thayer, 'is the cowcatcher of diplomacy, attached integrally to it and designed essentially to sweep the impediments from the path of the man who is implementing policy – the diplomat.'

Information work used to rely heavily on routine distribution of ministerial speeches, the organisation of visits of foreign journalists and so on, but gradually its methods have become more sophisticated and complex. Among recent innovations is British Satellite News (BSN), a London-based television service set up in May 1992 to transmit news items five days a week, by satellite, to TV stations overseas for inclusion in their own news broadcasts. BSN's object is to gain influential audiences for a British view of international events by providing interviews and topical material of interest to the target areas, initially the former Soviet Union, Eastern Europe and the Middle East. Run by a private sector contractor for the Foreign Office, BSN cost £1.6 million in its first year; within six months, sixteen countries were taking the service regularly and the London correspondents of seventeen television stations were using it habitually. Being a propaganda vehicle, it complements the BBC World Service, for although the Foreign

LEFT John Thomson, director of export promotion at the British Trade and Investment Office in New York.

Office administers the public funds which finance the World Service and although it determines in which languages and for how many hours it broadcasts, the BBC has editorial independence.

The paradox about propaganda and the British is that they excel at it, yet feel ashamed of it. Propaganda, cultural or otherwise, always seems to conjure up images of Dr Goebbels in the British mind, yet what works in the long term overseas is the low-key, slightly self-deprecating soft-sell that the British do well. It is the very British qualities of honesty and absence of bombast that have helped make the BBC World Service, and the British Council, assets which are envied by all the United Kingdom's high-spending competitors, yet they are under-funded. The World Service has an estimated audience of 120 million regular listeners. In September 1992 its audience was reckoned at 2586 listeners annually per output hour, compared to 776 for the Voice of America. The British Council struggles financially to meet an almost insatiable worldwide demand for British culture and British English, knowing that if British, rather than American, English can become the language spoken in the ex-Communist world, the political and financial benefits to the United Kingdom will be enormous.

The best investigation of the Foreign Office, that by the Plowden Committee in 1964*, commented:

The Information Services must not come to regard themselves as purveyors of information as an end in itself. . . . The more closely the information effort can be related in the mind of each Information Officer to the pursuit of a conscious British interest, the greater his worth is likely to be. . . . Sometimes effective propaganda can make the vital margin of difference between the success and failure of a policy. . . . We should strive relentlessly to make our views heard. The aim should be to be selective and realistic.

Sir Douglas Busk defined the three qualities he believed a good information officer should possess. First,

he must accept wholeheartedly that, while he is endeavouring to win respect for his country, it is futile to expect that his hosts manifest affection for or even gratitude to his homeland on a national scale. . . . Secondly and more actively, the good Information Officer must have the necessary 'feel' to know how best to put over publicity for his country. . . . Thirdly, the Information Officer must realize that he is working with and for policy makers at home and that his eyes should therefore be fixed on their counterparts in the country in which he is posted.

---

* During the last fifty years the Diplomatic Service has had little rest from official scrutiny: the proposals for internal reform that became known as the Eden–Bevin reforms were announced in 1943; in 1954 the Drogheda Committee reported on British information work overseas; in 1964 the Plowden Committee examined changing priorities and was instrumental in hastening the mergers of the Colonial Office, the Commonwealth Relations Office and the Foreign Office; the Duncan Committee, set up to find ways of saving money on overseas representation, got nowhere in 1969 with its recommendation that there be a two-tier diplomatic operation – an Area of Concentration (Europe and North America) and an Outer Area; the government think-tank, the Central Policy Review Staff, produced a report in 1977 that 'reeked of misapplied egalitarianism' and died the death.

For Nick Browne, information counsellor in Washington in 1993,

the central question that you ask yourself when you come in in the morning is, what do people want to know about what messages we are trying to get across? There'll be a sense of priorities in your mind: sometimes you'd be reactive, you'd be answering questions; sometimes you'd be proactive and you'd go out and try and sell a message.

Northern Ireland is a key issue in information work in the United States, where Irish-American passions run high and British diplomats (Foreign Office and Northern Ireland Office secondees) struggle to counter the view that the British are in illegal occupation of a part of Ireland; in the course of this work they frequently attract a great deal of aggression and abuse. Indeed until recently, the lives of the staff of British Information Services in New York were enriched by the presence outside their office of an enthusiastic Irish Northern Aid Committee (NORAID) picketer whom they nicknamed 'Screaming Sheila'. Information officers disseminate relevant material, brief journalists, and at meetings, socially, on radio and on television, they slug the issue out with supporters of Irish republicanism. In combination with their colleagues on the political side, the information services have done much to shift the perceptions of US politicians away from the traditional cherished image of Britain as a brutal colonial power.

In 1954 information work, hitherto looked-down on, became briefly fashionable, after a committee under the aristocrat-cum-newspaper manager, Lord Drogheda, recommended massively up-grading propaganda work overseas as a means of spreading British influence. For a few years, fast streamers sought information posts, then other gods beckoned and enthusiasm waned. So most information jobs continued to go to main streamers, though fast streamers are usually appointed to the senior jobs.

Information is an area which has suffered in the past from the traditional Foreign Office fear of specialisation. A main streamer who was brilliant in dealing with the press would be sent elsewhere, after his four years were up, rather than be given a promotion before his turn came up; while a fast streamer, whose gifts were political or representational, was pushed into an information job on the grounds that it required only intelligence.

In an age of instant communications and itinerant politicians and journalists, information staff come increasingly under the spotlight and they require a sensitive nose for what will interest the press as well as the confidence to deal positively with ravening hacks in search of victims. It can be a very difficult and stressful job and in places where aspects of British policy are under the spotlight it requires particular skills. The Foreign Office has among its staff the occasional officer who is in his element with the press, and who gets tremendous enjoyment from the game of getting them on-side. Increasingly, the Office is recognising that these gifts are exceptional. Christopher Osborne, for instance, went from information work in London to the hot information seat in Hong Kong. But others with a particular taste for the work are languishing in inappropriate jobs, wistfully reminiscing. The bureaucracy should find some way of rewarding them appropriately and keeping them in the line of battle while they are still fighting-fit.

As with information work, the importance of commercial work to the Foreign Office can be calculated by the number of fast streamers who are given commercial jobs. Those main streamers who particularly enjoy this area keep a suspicious eye on changes in its staffing, for this is an area more afflicted than most by the vagaries of political fashion, and by intellectual confusion, in the Foreign Office and in the country as a whole.

Britain's ambivalent feelings about trade have been clearly visible in the Foreign Office's attitude to commercial work since the last century. It fought for free trade, but it felt that on the whole the vulgarity of selling should be left to businessmen. Although a Commercial Department was established in the Office in 1866, it was regarded with disdain, and when, in the 1880s, embassies began to be sent commercial attachés, they were treated like tradesmen.

For years (as they still do) businessmen exercised pressure on the government to step up its commercial activities, complaining justifiably that the UK was lagging behind other major countries in putting significant resources into export promotion. At the end of the First World War, therefore, a Commercial Diplomatic Service was formed. Nominally under the control of the foreign secretary, it operated under the supervision of a Department of Overseas Trade, and was described decades later by a diplomat as 'the unloved bastard of a socially startling union between the Foreign Office and the Board of Trade.' Commercial diplomats were regarded at home with the envy that is attracted by all those who work overseas, while in the embassies where they served, their political colleagues remained aloof. In the Foreign Office – as in British society as a whole – trade was for commercial travellers. In 1943 the Commercial Diplomatic Service was abolished and its staff, along with the Consular Services and the Diplomatic Service, were – in theory, at least – amalgamated into the Foreign Office.

Anthony Eden's object in integrating the various services was to raise the status of all of them, but Foreign Office staff continued to believe that the path to glory lay in political work. In 1964, Plowden tried again. Commercial work 'must be regarded as a first charge on the resources of the overseas services.' Britain could not afford

to entrust commercial work to any but the best. . . . We look forward to the day, in the not too distant future, when every Ambassador and High Commissioner will have served in a commercial capacity and have acquired at first hand a detailed knowledge of export promotion and what it entails. Each Ambassador and High Commissioner must regard commercial work as a prime function of his Mission and its subordinate posts.

Fast streamers read and inwardly digested this, squared their shoulders and accepted the burden, their sinews stiffened five years later by the injunction of the Duncan Committee to make commercial work a major priority. Jean Sharpe spoke for many disgruntled main streamers when she observed that in the 1970s commercial work

suddenly became the in-thing . . . ambassadors and counsellors had to have commercial work under their belt, so suddenly . . . the best brains [went] into commercial work . . . [it became] part of their career structure [and pushed] all of us E streamers into something else. . . . We were finding it difficult to get commercial jobs because the A streamers wanted [them] suddenly. Very annoying, you know, when . . . it becomes flavour of the month and we [are pushed sideways].

One of those who threw himself enthusiastically into this new approach was Anthony Parsons, who showed, in Tehran in the mid-1970s, how a truly commercially-dominated embassy could make a vast contribution to British industry. Oil-price rises had turned Iran into a booming economy with an enormous appetite for arms, industrial equipment and consumer goods. In a country where major purchasing decisions were made at the centre, the British Embassy could unlock the key doors for the right salesmen, and the diplomats addressed themselves to seeking out opportunities for British business as well as easing its access to government. The only problem was that with political work taking second place to commercial, the embassy failed to appreciate the level of opposition to the Shah, whose overthrow came as a complete surprise.

Parsons was more humble than many of his peers, and he talked and wrote openly about where he had gone wrong: he had lost sight of the fact that the primary job of Foreign Office staff – whether diplomats or spies – is the collection and analysis of political information of importance to Britain: all other activities must be secondary. And that is true. If an embassy does not have an accurate grasp of what is going on in the country in which it operates, all its activities are threatened.

The Iranian episode caused the pendulum to swing back somewhat; the eagerness of fast streamers to take commercial jobs lessened and the main streamers sighed with relief. Almost thirty years after Plowden, there are still a few heads of mission today with no previous commercial experience. In the 1980s, however, the Foreign Office once again reassessed its priorities and it was made clear to fast streamers that they would henceforward all be required to do time on the commercial side, usually in mid-career. For a main streamer with extensive commercial experience, hoping to end his career as a Grade 4 commercial counsellor, it was hard to see such jobs going to a thirty-eight-year-old fast streamer with an exclusively political background. But personnel policy is shifting here again. Fast streamers in their mid- and late-twenties are now being put into commercial work, and many of them are coming to enjoy it hugely.

There is a place in commercial work for many different kinds of talent, from the locally-engaged who understand a particular market well, to experienced commercial officers who understand what kind of help British businessmen abroad most need: commercial work involves people at all levels. David Hawkes, for instance, a main-stream (or slow-stream as he describes it) first secretary in his fifties now, is in a rare and comfortable posting in Thailand. Having managed, by a mixture of accident and design, to specialise more than most, what he has particularly enjoyed in his career is commercial work in hardship posts. He speaks Arabic and has served in Kuwait, Iran, Iraq and Jordan and feels that he makes a major contribution to British businessmen in areas where public information is very limited and the culture is very foreign. He has relationships with businessmen and locals going back over twenty-five years in the Middle East. People like him, in difficult markets, are a source of disinterested advice, the value of which is obvious but unquantifiable.

There is no doubt at all these days about the commitment to commercial work of those at the top of the Foreign Office; it was an aspect of his work as high commissioner to Malaysia that Sir David Gillmore found particularly rewarding. And increasingly, there are many heads of mission who delight in the work and thereby raise its status. Heads of mission on the Pacific Rim have proved highly effective allies for businessmen. Duncan Slater, in Kuala Lumpur, although he had no commercial experience when he became high commissioner, is fascinated by the intricacies of relating politics to commerce. The ambassador in Indonesia, Roger Carrick, who came up through the main stream and made his reputation in commercial work, is able to put his innovative ideas into practice in a rapidly developing market.

Periodically, old arguments resurface among politicians and in the media about whether the Foreign Office should be dealing with commercial matters at all. Why not leave it to Chambers of Commerce, like the Germans do? But until British businesses are legally required – like their German counterparts – to contribute financially to Chambers of Commerce, the idea is a non-starter. British Chambers of Commerce are notoriously ineffectual. Should we not have a completely separate service, like the French? But it was because that did not work that the Department of Overseas Trade was abolished.

What exists at the moment is a slightly uneasy relationship with the home-based Department of Trade and Industry which suffers from being reformed every few years by gung-ho secretaries of state. These days there is more emphasis on cross-fertilisation, with 'Overseas Trade Services', a Foreign Office/Department of Trade and Industry (DTI) Joint Directorate, and some DTI officials in key commercial jobs in embassies overseas. The DTI is supplementing Foreign Office work by providing back-up from experienced exporters. The continuous steady background work in London, and in the 196 posts where there are commercial staff, includes organising exporters' missions overseas, encouraging inward and outward investment, rationalising trade policy and pursuing British interests by, for example, lobbying in the United States against legislation which would damage British investors, securing bilateral trade agreements, preventing the European Commission from outlawing, on ideological grounds, products that make money for the UK, and putting pressure on the Japanese to open up their markets. An independent market research company measures the satisfaction levels (high) of exporters who use the services for which the Foreign Office now charges modestly.

Few Foreign Office people question the need for commercial activity in immature markets: indeed staff are under tremendous pressure in Asia. The Office is turning out Chinese speakers as fast as it can and has placed several in the commercial section in Peking. Many Foreign Office people believe resources should be switched to Asia, and other immature markets, away from the United States and Europe. 'Anyone who is unable to do business in Holland doesn't deserve help,' said one critic.

Yet so much of British business is intensely parochial that hand-holding is still needed. The higher echelons of industry have become bolder and more sophisticated, but at the level of the middle and small, there is still much ignorance: it is ignorance and fear that the commercial sections try to overcome. They seek to encourage enterprise through providing detailed and relevant information for those contemplating a venture into Darkest Europe, Africa, Asia or America; they reply diligently and with exemplary patience to specific enquiries, some of which display a complete failure to do any homework and unrivalled stupidity about local conditions, such as asking a tropical post about the prospects of selling electric blankets (an actual case). Businessmen still arrive on embassy doorsteps having failed to do the most elementary research. One businessman wrote furiously to complain that the British Embassy in Saudi Arabia shut on a Thursday; he had not grasped that the Saudi weekend is Thursday and Friday.

Buffeted by criticism about doing too much or too little, the Foreign Office ploughs on trying to respond to the demands of politicians and businessmen. In the end, as in many such areas, the test is what the opposition are doing. Excluding the Germans and their Chambers of Commerce, the others – the French, the Japanese and the Americans – are doing more and continue to step up their efforts. The British try desperately to target their shrinking resources towards the parts of the world where they will do most good.

When it comes to major projects abroad, what senior and experienced businessmen mainly want from the Foreign Office is reliable political intelligence and the judicious use of influence in those countries where the government decides who wins which contracts. Key questions are: Is the country stable? To whom does the king/president/prime minister listen? Who will decide on how this particular contract is awarded?

A word at the right time in the ear of the right person by an ambassador who is liked and trusted, can be decisive. So too, can ambassadorial support for a bid by a particular company, which is seen as endorsement by the British Government. Vital help can also come from a prime ministerial or a royal visit in either direction, a friendly letter from the UK prime minister promising to address himself to whatever is bugging his opposite number, persuading the Export Credit Guarantee Board to be less pusillanimous, or tying in the right aid-package from the Overseas Development Administration, the aid wing of the Foreign Office.

Damage limitation is a key part of the work. It was disastrous for relations with Malaysia when the British Government decided in November 1979 to charge overseas students full fees from the following academic year. Malaysia, a growing British market, denounced this as racism and stopped doing business with Britain. Similarly, when ITV showed 'The Death of a Princess', their documentary about the execution of an adulterous member of the Saudi Royal family, it was calamitous for the British defence industry. Recently I was in Bangkok during a crisis with the Thai Government over the definition of prostitution in Longmans' new dictionary, which cited Bangkok as a prostitution centre. There were demonstrations outside the embassy and desperate attempts by Longmans to find a way to salvage their substantial local business.

Sir Brian Fall greeting the Princess Royal and Commander Tim Laurence on their arrival at Moscow airport for the first leg of their Russian tour in July 1993.

After all such incidents, it is the job of diplomats patiently to restore good relations, as during the normal times they seek to make countries more pro-British. 'Obviously part of our whole purpose here,' said David Gore-Booth in Saudi Arabia, 'is precisely to create the environment that British business will need to be able to succeed abroad and produce jobs at home: that's one of our absolutely key functions.' To the end of trying to increase British exports to Saudi ($£2$ billion annually) he is seeking to broaden out the relationship away from the purely military, shift back to the civil side and organise joint ventures and cultural exchanges to show that the relationship is based on more than hardware.

Yet, as David Gore-Booth knows all too well, commercial and political considerations can collide. Throughout 1992, his last year as assistant under secretary in charge of the Middle East, he had to deal with demands from Salman Rushdie that the British Government should take a much harder line than hitherto on the Iranian *fatwa*, while industry was pressing for the normalisation of diplomatic relations. As Gore-Booth put it:

On the one hand you've got a guy who's under threat of his life . . . on the other you've got this huge country in which we have a political and strategic interest because of our concerns in the Gulf and in which we have a commercial interest. And it is a question all the time of trying to balance the last two interests against the interest of a British citizen and it's an extremely difficult balance to draw.

As both British business and the Foreign Office together seek to penetrate new markets in Asia and in the former Soviet Union, the interlinkage of politics and commerce become ever more obvious. 'By the time you get to be a senior officer,' said Sir Brian Fall at the end of a tour of several of the new republics in the former Soviet Union,

particularly in a bilateral Embassy – I found this particularly as high commissioner in Canada and I find it as ambassador here – I'm not sure when I'm doing commercial work and when I'm doing political work. The major contracts here will either be signed by or approved by the government. When I go and talk to the president or the vice president or the ministry of economy, that's important commercially as well as important politically. . . . I hate it when I have to fill in the form once a year, where I have to say how much political work, how much information work, how much economic work, how much commercial work I do, because this [job] has been a sort of wonderful mixture of all four.

In March 1993 Sir David Gillmore summed up for the Foreign Affairs Committee how he saw the work of the Foreign Office:

The totality of British diplomatic effort is, in my view, what Dr Kissinger used to call a ball of wax. The embassy provides a platform, a central platform, around which we can assist industry and business, where we can protect our investments, where the greatly added value which comes from the British Council, the BBC World Service, is part of a totality of British presence – and the aid programme of course is a key component too – for which the embassy itself, the mission itself, and the ambassador is the central focal point. I would like to think, perhaps it is a slightly vain notion, that the totality is greater than the sum of the parts.

· 13 ·

CAMPFOLLOWERS

Accompanying Baggage

Warning

When I am an old woman I shall wear purple
With a red hat which doesn't go, and doesn't suit me.
And I shall spend my pension on brandy and summer gloves and satin sandals,
And say there is no money for butter.

I shall sit down on the pavement when I'm tired,
And gobble up samples in shops and press alarm bells,
And run my stick along the public railings to make up for the sobriety of my youth.

I shall go out in my slippers in the rain and pick the flowers in other peoples' gardens.
And learn to spit.

I can wear terrible shirts
And grow more fat and eat three pounds of sausages at a go –
Or only bread and pickle for a week.
And hoard pens and pencils and beer mats and things in boxes.

But now we must have clothes that keep us dry;
And pay our rent and not swear in the street and set a good example for the children.
We will have friends to dinner and read the papers.

But maybe I ought to practise a little now
So people who know me are not too shocked and surprised
When suddenly I am old
And start to wear purple.

Jenny Joseph

LEFT Alastair Sparkes, first secretary (political),
and family at a bus stop in Bangkok.

This poem was quoted by a member of the British Diplomatic Spouses Association (BDSA) in its magazine. It could have been written for all those women who married diplomats and unwillingly spent their lives behaving properly. Many of the Embassy wives who smile politely and make small talk have a tremendous longing for a life where they do not continually have to be on public show. Often they may be seething at the loss of their careers, the sacrifice of a normal family life, or at the way in which their sacrifices were taken for granted by the Foreign Office and the public.

Traditionally, the wife of the head of mission (whom, for the sake of simplicity, I shall call the ambassadress) set the tone, and was seen – at least in the mythology of the Foreign Office – as a dragon. Stories abound about wives of junior diplomats being lined up in hats and gloves and inspected before the Queen's birthday party, instructed rigidly on how to behave, and required to perform not only as ancillary hostesses, but, where required, as domestic servants. There is a cherished story of the third secretary who was ordered home instantly when his wife refused to make a hundred strawberry tartlets for an embassy function. And one diplomat told me of an early posting where his, and all the other junior wives, were ordered to pick up the rubbish from the lawn at the end of a Queen's birthday party.

Like most stereotypes, there was some truth in the dragon. Such women existed, and given half a chance, there are a few who would probably still behave in this way. An anthropologist brought in by the Diplomatic Service Wives Association (DSWA, the former name of the BDSA) in the late 1970s to consider the malaise experienced by many of the wives, found that negative memories of ambassadresses outweighed the positive: the more common adjectives applied included: 'imperious', 'autocratic', 'patronising', 'difficult', 'remote' and 'interfering'. The prevalence of those last two suggested to him that it was almost impossible for the ambassadress to get the 'distance' right. Some wives spoke with love and admiration of paragons, who cared for the spouses, families, servants, and everyone within their ambit, with grace and selflessness. Dragons outweighed saints, but then, as he remarked, dragon-stories are much more interesting and tellable. There seemed to be few memories of people in between the two extremes, trying to do their best in difficult circumstances with variable results.

The anthropologist's conclusion was that it was an impossible role. Everyone, inside and outside the mission, judged the ambassadress by the highest standards and allowed for no mediocrity. Either she was 'very, very nice' or 'ghastly'. Wives studied her to learn how not to behave: 'one is learning what one would wish not to do'. The ambassadresses who evaded their responsibilities by doing the minimum, or who drank too much or had an affair were condemned; so were those who developed *folie de grandeur*. 'Her status goes to her head; she is imperious; she issues orders to other wives, accompanied by the explicit or implicit threat: "I'll tell my husband".'

Yet it would be a paragon indeed who could do the job perfectly. For ambassadresses are very isolated and often desperate for informality and friendship. Junior wives fear being relaxed or open, lest it somehow rebound on their husband's career. Few wives behave naturally with ambassadresses: their husbands' work relationships place invisible barriers between them. And increasingly, senior wives, who have given up careers and slogged as unpaid hostesses all their lives, resent the younger women who seem to be able to do what they like, and who demand freedom but complain if they are not given the option of being brought in on embassy activities.

The dragon wives, after all, were schooled in a culture in which the stiff upper lip dominated. They reflected the overwhelmingly male public-school ethos of the public services. One did not admit to problems, one overcame them. Coping was all. The electricity might have fused, the cook might have got drunk, essential supplies might have dried up, one might have just heard that one's mother – two-thousand miles away – was terminally ill, or one might just have waved one's children off to boarding school. But there one was, impeccably turned out, smiling graciously and making stilted small talk with a Ruritanian diplomat with seventy-three words of English, most of them incomprehensible.

If sometimes they were rigid and glacial, they had tremendous courage and the status they acquired was earned. In the bad old days, before the British Diplomatic Spouses Association had wrung concessions out of the Office, they might have seen their children only once a year, for the Office paid for only one return trip and a child might be thousands of miles away, with a second air ticket beyond the pocket of a junior diplomat. 'Nothing', wrote Sir Geoffrey Jackson,

will ever convey the stoical anguish of the exiled mother, watching that twice-yearly charter-flight hoist itself from some tropical runway, bearing back to school – or, surely, to the nightmare of some unimaginable aeronautical catastrophe – the small, subdued, slightly sweating tweed-jacketed figure she loves best of its kind in the world.

There were few countries in which those wives could have worked, even if they had been qualified or experienced enough to get jobs. And before cheap air travel, there was little chance of seeing friends from home, and visitors came only to the most accessible and glamorous places.

The wives battled on, representing Britain, organising coffee mornings and prevailing on other wives to knit and sew and tat to raise funds for local hospitals or schools for the disabled. Annually, they, as well as their husbands, were assessed on their performance. They worked hard, showed willing, stayed cheerful, and never complained. Except of course for the few who would not, or could not, play the game and who through frustration sank themselves in lassitude, cynicism or worse.

What drove them – and still drives the newer, more relaxed breed – crazy, is the public perception of an ambassadress as somebody on Easy Street, lying by a swimming pool, sipping gin and tonic, having a dashing and glamorous social life, and living in luxurious circumstances with all the work done by invisible servants. Even at the top of the tree, where there are relatively generous allowances and usually a great deal of skilled help, there are heavy duties of entertaining and socialising – what Mary Gore-Booth, a modern ambassadress, described as 'hotel management, restaurant catering' and 'public relations'.

The British Diplomatic Spouses Association

In 1965 the Foreign Office helped with the setting up of the Diplomatic Service Wives Association (DSWA) – an amalgamation of the Foreign Service Wives Association and the Commonwealth Relations Office Wives Society (CROWS). In 1991 it changed its title to the British Diplomatic Spouses Association (BDSA).

The BDSA is funded by members' donations and by the Foreign Office, who provide offices and equipment in London, pay for a Grade 9 and for part-time secretarial assistance and contribute three-quarters of the Chairman's honorarium. The portfolios of the committee of volunteers include liaison officers (voluntary welfare officers at post), education, foreign-born spouses, spouse employment, training, welfare, accommodation, widows, retired members and diplomatic neighbours (spouses of foreign diplomats based in London) as well as the twice-yearly magazine and distribution.

The BDSA has developed considerably in the last couple of decades. In 1981, Sir Geoffrey Jackson, wrote of it with some bitterness.

My wife is, as it happens, an expert in the keener hazards of professional separation. While I was kidnapped by urban guerrillas, and she usually presumed she was a widow, she had sensibly suggested, for the comfort and reassurance of other wives conceivably exposed to comparable circumstances, an instant roster of Foreign Office wives who would daily get in touch with them and keep an eye on their well-being. When first she pointed out this special loneliness of a wife desperately awaiting news of a husband missing or endangered overseas, the immensely 'senior wife' present interjected 'But wives at home aren't expected to be social!'

It was the Association's urgent job, Jackson felt, to introduce more compassion into the Foreign Office.

This is an uphill struggle. The old image of the welfare branch was that of a particularly cross school matron. One diplomat was badly injured in Iraq by a bomb early in his career. He was brought home and treated in hospital. When he finally dragged his bandaged body to the office of the appropriate welfare officer, he enquired tentatively if there was any possibility of some compensation for his suffering. 'Surely', she said, 'it is compensation enough that you are alive.'

Pushed by the BDSA as well as by changing social expectations, the Foreign Office has improved its welfare services, for instance, by appointing paid community liaison officers at major posts. The few doctors and nurses also contribute a great deal to spotting the development of psychological problems in over-worked and lonely people.

Depending on where the mission is, the responsibilities of ambassadresses vary between hard manual labour and demanding management and supervisory functions. One wrote about Ulan Bator, where like her predecessors, she had to do all the cooking, for domestic service was not the Mongolians' strongest point.

I recently timed the preparation of a formal four-course dinner for eight and it came to sixteen hours' work (not including earlier hours spent making bread rolls and basic sauces for the freezer, or the usual chores of table laying, tidying, etc.). At the most conservative estimate, I cannot have spent less than 1000 hours a year cooking solely for guests – in fact, the equivalent of a half-time job.

Representational duties and other work took up all the rest of her time.

At the other end of the scale, at an embassy in the centre of things, like the Brussels residence of the UK permanent representative, or the glamorous embassies of Paris, Rome or Washington, the tramp of visitors echoes through the fine halls almost every day. The wife manages her five-star hotel, hiring, firing and motivating staff, choosing menus, overseeing expenditure and keeping an elaborate record for Treasury purposes, exercising economy, keeping the place looking perfect and on top of that acting as a skilled and politically sensitive hostess. I have been at such a residence where the ambassadress had spent most of the morning resolving a dispute between two chefs. And if two chefs seems excessive, this is a residence so busy that she has been known to hold two consecutive formal dinners in an evening. In 1992, at the Paris residence, the Fergussons officially entertained 238 house guests. They gave lunch or dinner to 3492 people, had 3447 to drinks or receptions and gave tea or coffee to 593. The numbers for receptions were down by more than a thousand on the previous year, since in 1992, because of the Queen's state visit in June, they did not hold the usual Queen's birthday party.

It does not take much imagination to grasp that this kind of entertaining is extremely hard work, not just in its organisation, but because the host and hostess have to be continually on duty. They are expected to remember vast numbers of people they have met only once. Some have a genius for this; for others, it is torture. The late Jane Ewart-Biggs was highly entertaining in her memoirs about how she spent much of her life as a diplomat's consort trying to find ways of covering up her husband's hopeless memory for faces.

It will be the ambassadress's fault if the table arrangements do not reflect the correct order of precedence, a nightmare challenge in itself. She must ensure that the bedroom arrangements for the ministerial team still work despite the last-minute addition of another private secretary. If some Royals on a semi-private visit are unable to make up their minds in the morning if they will all, any, or only some, be in for dinner, and if they will wish to eat with the ambassador or in their rooms, the ambassadress must smile and make preparations for every contingency. Many of her guests will be used to having absolutely everything practical done for them at all times. Like members of the Royal Family, ministers are not used to anything going wrong.

Ambassadors still suffer from critical and dismissive visitors. 'I suppose the poor old British taxpayer had to cough up to transport these books,' observed one MP to a senior diplomatic couple with whom he was staying. Of all the British visitors – royals, politicians, diplomats, journalists, businessmen – the ones who arouse most fear and anger are the ordinary MPs. Again and again one hears the cry that it is impossible to get it right. Put yourself out, devote your time to them, mollycoddle them, give them the best bedroom, the best welcome, the best food and refill their glasses constantly, and word will come back later of a speech denouncing the grotesque extravagance and wasteful luxury of the lifestyle of our representatives abroad. Be low-key, scale down the entertainment, give them what you would normally eat yourself and you are denounced for failing to look after a representative of the great institution of Parliament properly and accused of devoting yourself exclusively to the well-being of foreigners.

'I just wish,' observed one wistful senior wife who had had some bad experiences early in her career, 'that people had some understanding of the bad times many of us have had before arriving in circumstances like this.' She hesitantly suggested that perhaps the British Diplomatic Spouses Association might think of publishing a book with some stories of particular hardship. Her husband looked concerned. He shook his head and said: 'One doesn't wish to be seen to whinge.' Certainly whingeing is the last thing they do. 'No grousing!' was one instruction from an ambassadress to wives before the inspection of a mission.

At least the *BDSA Magazine* permits spouses to air their grievances and tell the horror stories that their non-diplomatic friends do not understand, the media mostly ignore and the Foreign Office plays down for reasons of diplomacy and pride. One profile during the Gulf War was of a wife who had been 'bombed out of Damascus, evacuated under fire from Beirut and now exiled from Kuwait.' By the time I met her husband on my travels, a long saga involving lost treasures was nearing its end. The baggage of the British Embassy staff had gone from Kuwait to Baghdad, been looted, saturated and much of it lost permanently on its slow trek back to Britain, including, in their case, family silver and jewellery, a lifetime's collection of oriental art and all the normal sentimental items like photograph albums.

The couple had broken a cardinal rule of diplomatic life: do not take abroad with you what you cannot bear to lose. Yet many people cannot stand the anonymity of furnished accommodation and have to bring loved possessions with them. The single, unable to face the hideous burden of packing, unpacking, nagging transport companies, arguing over breakages and so on, sometimes take the minimum with them, thus, as they progress up the ladder, living in chillingly impersonal surroundings. Families, on the whole, want to create at least an illusion of home.

But possessions are the least of it. These calm, contained women tell the most incredible tales of unimaginable happenings. One described how a few days before their wedding, her fiancé, a second secretary, was told he was being posted to Peking in five days' time. The honeymoon had to be cancelled in favour of setting out immediately for China.

It was 1967, so her first taste of being married to the service was the Cultural Revolution. Apart from being frequently threatened and besieged in their compound, for fifteen months the embassy staff were hostages. One of the wives actually went mad and two diplomats developed cancerous tumours which the Chinese refused to treat. This particular woman lost her first baby because she was given toxic drugs in hospital.

Another memorable story told to me was of the family of five posted to Dacca in Bangladesh with a six-week-old baby; there were no proper medical facilities for hundreds of miles. There was no air conditioning in the kitchen because the Foreign Office had thought it unnecessary. So every night, with the temperature at over 100°F (38°C), the diplomat's wife stood in the kitchen, dripping with sweat, clad only in her knickers, boiling all the water for the next day in great vats. Every six months, when the cockroaches began to walk over their faces, the mattresses were burned. There was nothing to do and nowhere to go and around them was only abject, ghastly poverty. Her main role outside the family was to act as unpaid, unofficial welfare officer to the junior wives, particularly of the Home Office entry clearance secondees, who had absolutely no experience of being abroad and could not believe what was happening to them.

The stoicism of some of these women is extraordinary. Imelda Miers, for instance, opened her article, 'Life in the Embassy in Tehran, 1979' with 'Coming back for a second tour to Tehran after a troubled first one, we had hoped to have a rather more peaceful time than during the long months leading up to the Revolution.' Matters began to deteriorate, but 'despite acute shortages of ordinary commodities, we all made do.'

Frivolously, some of them planned a celebration bonfire 'to commemorate both Guy Fawkes night and last year's attack and burning of the Embassy.' They were put off doing this by the rise in anti-British and anti-American press propaganda. On 4 November the American Embassy was stormed, occupied and its inhabitants held hostage.

We were warned in messages and telephone calls that the same was going to happen to us. Those of us living in the Ferdowsi compound in downtown Tehran, having been faced with a number of emergencies before and used to trouble on our doorsteps, prepared a little bag ready for escape through a back exit, supposing that that would be possible and that the attack would come from the front.

The following day the rumour spread through the town 'that the day of reckoning for the British imperialists had come again.' Revolutionary guards with guns were stationed on the pavement outside the embassy, while most of the police inside 'were surprisingly unarmed.' It was an edgy day, but by dusk they thought it had been a false alarm.

Some of us went out shopping, and I asked one of the wives, with whom I had been pacing up and down the compound, back to the house for tea, urging our youngest, at post with us, not to go away from the house. We sat peacefully for a while and suddenly there it was, unmistakable, the noise of shouting angry people mixed with rattling noises coming from the front gates. My tea companion ran back to her house. I myself started rushing through the downstairs rooms to turn off lights and shut doors but even before I had finished completely the voices were all around the house. I grabbed my son and we ran as fast as we could upstairs, our legs almost refusing to make the long flight of stairs.

She thought they should grab a few essentials and escape in case the house was set on fire. Thomas was frightened and began to cry.

As we emerged on the upstairs landing there they were: the angry youths with the guns, very young, all dark, bearded, with burning eyes, full of zeal, some of them not older than fifteen. In my anger I asked one of them if his mother knew what he was doing. He looked surprised.

It became clear that they had mistaken her house for the embassy itself.

More and more youngsters emerged from everywhere. They had kicked in a door at the garden side and started inspecting all the rooms, expecting maybe to see lots of spies and British plotters creeping out of every corner. I thought of my husband, wondering what had happened to him. He tried to ring from the office where he was trapped, but I was not allowed to speak to him.

The captors kept assuring her 'that they would not harm us, that they were there to protect us against more sinister elements who wanted to kill us.' Along with all the other compound-dwellers, she and Thomas were herded 'in one house, in one room, a group of harmless people surrounded by a myriad guns.' They settled down

waiting to know what was going to happen to us, waiting to know what was happening to the few members of the staff still in the offices. At first we were all rather upset, especially those of us who had already been through the troubled months before the Revolution, but gradually we began to laugh about the situation we found ourselves in. Thomas soon found solace in reading 'Asterix the Gaul'.

After some hours of negotiation, they were all allowed back to their houses.

So we had escaped the fate of our American colleagues. It was with relief that we saw the backs of our 'protectors'. No wonder they had not wanted us to stay in our houses: while we were all huddled together, several of our houses were searched; precious possessions passed without prior agreement into other hands. A very special 'Islamic protection' it had been. We never saw the mob our invaders were supposed to protect us against . . .

Thomas plays endless games with his 'playpeople', the American Marines defending the American Embassy against the rioters, but in his game the marines come out victorious.

We were safe once more, only wondering when we will have to pack our overnight bag next or whether it would be better to leave it packed, ready for the next exit. Will it be through the front gate, the back one, via a ladder, over the wall or through the dustbin hole into the safety and anonymity of the Tehran jungle? Or maybe, like in a dream, an RAF plane will come from the sky and lift us up far away from all this trouble to blessed England.

The Miers family have not had a dull life. David Miers became ambassador to Beirut in 1983. In September 1984 he was visiting the American ambassador when a suicide bomber attacked the embassy; both diplomats were wounded.

All the accounts of material, physical and emotional deprivation, nasty diseases, threatening natives, assaults, terrifying evacuations, accidental deaths and murders are told in person or on paper in the same matter-of-fact and stoical fashion, with every opportunity being taken to look on the bright side or make a gentle joke. Wives understate; they are always conscious that they must not let their husbands down.

Partly because of prompting by the wives, partly because of changing social attitudes and partly because the last two permanent under secretaries have been accessible men who took man-management seriously, the atmosphere is kinder than it used to be. When women, children and most staff were evacuated from Kuwait in August 1990, the consul's wife, Elizabeth Banks, who had been abruptly removed from Libya ten years earlier, was agreeably surprised by the improved professionalism of the Medical and Welfare Unit and the personal concern demonstrated by the most senior members of staff. And when her husband arrived back in London four months later with his ambassador and was asked to go straight to Number 10 Downing Street, she was amazed that the whole family was invited along.

Such extraordinary events, harrowing as they can be, bring out the best in people. In the same way the toughest and most uncomfortable places tend to produce the happiest missions. Of course families, like the diplomats themselves, often yearn for the comforts and pleasures of great cities and enjoy them when they are there. But they can be frustrating and alienating environments for the wives unless they have jobs to do. And for those who have to lead a busy social life, formal societies like Paris and Washington are very demanding. Standards are high and the demands are heavy, and in addition to providing the entertainment or accepting it graciously, one must look good and offend nobody. Without being boring one must swallow one's private political opinions and say loyal things about the government of the day.

Many of the problems of being married to a diplomat are compounded if you happen to come from a culture different from his. No one knows how many foreign-born spouses are attached to the Office, though the British Diplomatic Spouses Association are trying to compile statistics. Even in the 1970s the figure was estimated at around 30 per cent, and that was at a time when a foreign-born spouse was required to give up his or her nationality and become a British citizen. It was a rule that did not change until 1975, and which bore particularly harshly on wives from cultures like the Japanese which regarded the giving up of their nationality as an act of treachery.

Frequently then, the foreign wife finds herself jobless in a country she has never been to before, and married to a man who inhabits a tightly-knit community from yet another foreign culture. If he is a rising star in a representational grade she has to cook and entertain on behalf of a country she does not know. For many of them there is a difficult and painful adaptation to a bewildering world. Some try to be more British than the British; others give up trying to represent Britain and make a major issue of their own nationality. The most successful are those who have a clear sense of their own identity and do not try to become what they never can be. If confident enough, they can bring to the British diplomatic round a whiff of the exotic and a welcome cross-fertilisation. Three of the seven most senior Foreign Office diplomats – Sir David Gillmore, Sir Christopher Mallaby and Sir Robin Renwick – have foreign wives, all of whom have managed to do just that.

But the problems of the non-English speaking wife are of course compounded by language difficulties. Many a foreign wife will have been courted by a gifted linguist with a first-class grasp of her language and indeed often of her culture. But if she is going to function as a spouse in his world, she, who may perhaps be without much linguistic aptitude, has to tangle with an extremely difficult and sophisticated language and move among people whose grasp of its nuances are exceptionally subtle. The cultural references, the sense of humour and even the sporting metaphors will be alien.

The parsimony of the system can also cause a lot of distress, especially in the days of youth and poverty. Travel allowances take no account of where a spouse comes from and so if you and your Malaysian wife are posted to Paris and one of her parents dies at home, she will be given a compassionate travel grant of only enough to take her from Paris to London. Persuading the Treasury to be more generous on such an issue can take years.

FOREIGN SPOUSES

The fact that they marry foreigners adds to the suspicion with which British diplomats are viewed at home, but it should hardly cause any surprise. Young Foreign Office diplomats are sent forth to strange countries in their early twenties when the sap is rising and often they are at their most lonely and vulnerable. Courtship or cohabitation gives way swiftly to marriage when a diplomat has to move to a new post and the beloved makes the choice to give up career, family and culture and follow him.

The British Diplomatic Spouses Association recently identified seventy-two different states or regions from which spouses originate.

I AFRICA Algeria, Egypt, Tunisia, Kenya, Madagascar, Mauritius, Mozambique, Nigeria, South Africa, Zimbabwe.

II AMERICAS Canada, United States; the Caribbean; Costa Rica, Guatemala, Honduras, Mexico, Panama; Argentina, Bolivia, Brazil, Chile, Colombia, Ecuador, Guyana, Paraguay, Peru.

III ASIA Afghanistan, India, Nepal, Pakistan, Sri Lanka, Burma, China, Hong Kong, Japan, Korea, Laos, Malaysia, Philippines, Singapore, Taiwan, Thailand, Vietnam.

IV AUSTRALASIA AND PACIFIC Australia, Fiji, New Zealand.

V EUROPE Austria, Belgium, Czechoslovakia, Denmark, Finland, France, Germany, Greece, Iceland, Ireland, Italy, Malta, Netherlands, Norway, Portugal, Spain, Sweden, Switzerland, Yugoslavia.

VI MIDDLE EAST AND MEDITERRANEAN Armenia, Cyprus, Iran, Israel, Lebanon, Turkey.

An American-born spouse wrote in the *BDSA Magazine*:

I knew I had embarked on a linguistic adventure when I married a British diplomat. Witness the telegram my husband's brother sent to congratulate us on our wedding. Purporting to come from the FCO it said: 'ERROR IN PREVIOUS INSTRUCTION STOP FOR IMPROVE RELATIONS WITH AMERICANS PLEASE READ ARMENIANS STOP WE HOPE THIS HAS NOT CAUSED ANY INCONVENIENCE.'

And yet in other respects the British Diplomatic Service is infinitely more liberal than most other foreign services in its treatment of foreign spouses. For a start, there is no racial, religious or nationalist prejudice; nor is there any observable paranoia. In some foreign services – the American, for instance – a diplomat who marries a foreign diplomat has to give up his or her job and will be unable to work with an American Embassy even on a locally-engaged basis. But the Foreign Office, like some of its European equivalents, has instances of officers married to foreign diplomats who manage to run a tandem career.

One British diplomat and his Danish wife were simultaneously chargés d'affaires for their respective countries.

Women's assumption that they will work throughout their lives is set to have a drastic effect on the Foreign Office. When Sir David Gillmore was high commissioner in Malaysia, he and his wife used to rise together and work every day from 8 am to midnight at their different diplomacy-related tasks. Although French, Lucile Gillmore has few of the problems of foreign spouses, having studied English at the Sorbonne and then been a Fulbright scholar in America. Like most senior diplomatic wives these days, she believes that spouses abroad should be as free as possible to decide how involved they wish to be. Like her husband, she encouraged an egalitarian atmosphere in Kuala Lumpur. The grand residence with its swimming pool and tennis courts was almost always available to all their staff, which prevented her from feeling isolated and, was, she felt, a great leveller.

Susan Fenn sees herself as fortunate because her husband, Sir Nicholas, now high commissioner in India, had always seen his career as theirs; she has never been an adjunct, but half of a team. Such was her commitment that she has acquired a language everywhere she has been. She even learned Irish (an extremely hard language) when in Dublin – to a level far ahead of most of the population: in Delhi she is learning Urdu. She is fully briefed on the local politics and is therefore an ancillary diplomat and an extremely useful one. For of course one of the ironies of formal diplomatic entertaining is that the ambassador's wife is usually between the two most important male guests, while the ambassador sits between their wives. It is obviously a tremendous advantage if the wife knows what she is about.

Lucile Gillmore and Susan Fenn know that few of their successors will be prepared to be full-time, unpaid, ancillary diplomats. Their husbands – and many others of their generation – wonder how their successors – male or female – will be able to function properly without that kind of support. What such able, dedicated women provided was first, a means of enhancing the man's performance by protecting him from practical stresses and strains, second, a sensitivity which improved human relationships at post and third, by going into parts of the community that the husbands could not reach, they added a depth and breadth to the embassy's performance. In Saudi Arabia, for instance, Mary Gore-Booth has access to the women, whom David will not even be allowed to meet.

Looking back, however, many of the wives of that generation have mixed feelings. There is some resentment that younger wives can get away without sacrificing themselves in the same way. And while glad to have supported their husbands, the lack of recognition from the Office has caused great pain over the years. They have received neither official expressions of gratitude, nor decorations, nor financial acknowledgements.

Financial considerations loom ever larger. The ambassador who fell in love with a young woman towards the end of his career and married her on his retirement, by divorcing his self-sacrificing wife along the way, left her to a certain impoverished old age, for the pension is entirely with the husband, and that generation of wives facing divorce were too well-bred and diffident to fight for their financial rights. Not that they have to be divorced to face financial problems; when their husbands die, they receive only half of his pension.

There is a long struggle going on for some kind of financial recognition of the sacrifice involved in a lifetime of hard work and enforced economic dependency. The British Diplomatic Spouses Association wants pensions in their own right for those members, who because they could not work, have no occupational pension. (The Treasury has so far succeeded in remaining obdurate, seeing this as the Trojan Horse; once they give in on Foreign Office wives, military wives will follow.) Other foreign services face the same problems and some have been more generous. Since 1991, for instance, the German Government has compensated spouses at posts abroad at the rate of 5 per cent of the officer's salary for lost career opportunities and as a recognition of work at post. That case was much assisted in 1989 when the television cameras showed German Embassy wives in Eastern Europe caring, under extraordinary conditions, for tens of thousands of refugees from East Germany.

The Foreign Office itself, always hard up and with the Treasury calling the shots on how it can spend its money, can do little enough on the financial front, but it has made efforts to help spouses in practical ways, including helping them to get jobs abroad. Ironically, while the British allow the spouses of any foreign diplomat to work in Britain, only a small number of foreign countries reciprocate.

Increasingly, pressurised by the British Diplomatic Spouses Association, senior diplomats, ambassadors and ministers take up this particular cause with their foreign counterparts, but it is a long and rocky road. For instance, in cultures where women are regarded as second-class citizens, the issue seems to the locals to be one of startling irrelevance. And sometimes in countries where women are permitted to work, the language often causes a huge barrier. Even in Holland, it is extremely difficult to get a job without speaking Dutch.

The answer for many is to get a job as a locally-engaged member of staff at the British Embassy. Enlightened ambassadors have always encouraged this. Even unenlightened ambassadors are now leaned on heavily by London to welcome spouses and partners into the workforce. Up to a few years ago there was no such pressure. Ambassadors could not only discourage wives from working; they could ban them from doing so. Nowadays an ambassador who forbids a spouse to work has to explain himself to headquarters.

But locally-engaged jobs are relatively low-grade; the financial rewards depend completely on the market rate in a particular country. Thus in a European capital you will do reasonably well, but in a Third World country you will be paid peanuts. Nor are the jobs that are available for the locally-engaged likely to hold much attraction for doctors or lawyers. There is, too, a finite limit on the number available.

The Office has helped there also, squeezing out some money for training spouses in highly marketable and portable skills. Their most popular courses are in teaching English as a foreign language and in computer and secretarial skills, but grants have been made available for the acquisition of such relatively exotic skills as aromatherapy and reflexology.

In 1992 the Spouse Sponsorship Scheme provided 132 spouses with a maximum grant of £775 for courses which included Business Studies, Building and Counselling.

Ideally a spouse should be an artist or a writer of fiction for whom constant upheaval and changing environments might provide invaluable inspiration. Interpreters too, are in an excellent position. Maria Fairweather and Mary Gore-Booth, respectively ambassadresses in Italy and Saudi Arabia, are interpreters who keep their part-time careers going successfully and value being able to get away from post for some weeks at a time to work at an international conference. As Maria Fairweather says, 'To be an interpreter is about the most perfect job you can have being married to a diplomat.' After a period in Jedda in Saudi Arabia in the early 1980s, Mary Gore-Booth swore never again to be trapped, so she worked towards independence. 'I'm quite lucky,' she says. 'I have a profession that allows me to be available sometimes and not others. I love what I do professionally so I'm only too delighted when people offer me work. I jump at the chance.' And her work as ambassadress 'has got to be fitted around it'.

But in practice the career women among the spouses inevitably tend to have inconvenient professions which normally can only suffer through disruption. A determined wife may succeed in getting jobs abroad but they will normally be at the same level so there will be no career progression. 'I will almost certainly be leaving the FCO,' observed one second secretary, 'because I cannot imagine marrying the kind of woman who would be prepared to give up her career.' The Australian and Canadian foreign services are concerned about an increasing trend for women not to accompany their spouses abroad, first for career reasons and second because they do not want to be parted from their children. Although it is unusual, it is beginning to happen in the British Foreign Office too, and no one is happy with that.

For a male spouse the situation is both easier and harder. On the plus side, he is regarded with awe for being so self-sacrificing as to forego his prospects for his wife. There were incidents in the past when a horrified head of chancery tried to block the appointment of a woman with an accompanying male spouse, a notion which he obviously saw as a shocking interference with the natural order.

Nowadays these men are accepted, and they have the huge advantage that they are not expected to be unpaid hostesses. A woman who accompanies her husband on official duties is doing what is expected of her, a man is a dog walking on hind legs, his very presence still a source of amazement.

Alex Sutherland, whose wife Veronica was ambassador to the Ivory Coast, wrote with humour in the *BDSA Magazine* about his experiences as 'male ambassadress'. During a visit to one particular village, when the elders refused to permit her to come to the political discussion – the palaver – she had to nominate him to stand in for her. But he has the self-confidence to be (normally) in second place. He took early retirement from a high-powered job and now freelances. Indeed, the older, retired male spouse is often best suited of all to the job of consort. One such joined the wives' sewing circle in Maputo, much to their disbelief, and persuaded them to change it into a unit for making and selling items for charity. But for younger, less confident men, it is harder. There is inevitably – especially in male chauvinist societies – some contempt for a man so lacking in macho virtues as to give precedence to his wife's career.

Then of course there are the children. 'People sometimes say to me that the life of a child from a diplomatic background is a life of sophisticated cosmopolitanism,' observed one scarred adult product of the Irish Foreign Service. 'It is not. It's quite often a life of painful transit. *And anybody, anybody* in the diplomatic world will tell you that.'

The life tends to throw up quite a lot of disturbed children; there is even a disproportionately high incidence of suicide. Essentially, they have two kinds of life. Either they travel round with their parents, moving from international school to international school, with all the upheavals and cultural confusion that that involves, leaving friends behind wherever they go; or from an early stage, to protect them from disruption, they are sent to boarding school in the UK.

'How has being a diplomat's child affected you?' I asked a twenty-year-old who was spending a few weeks on vacation from university in the UK with her parents in Washington. 'I don't know where I come from,' she said simply. 'When someone asks you where you come from it's very embarrassing not to know what to say.' She was passionately determined to buy a house in the most English of English countryside and never move from it again. One mother described how, after the children had lived in two or three countries, the family went back to England on leave to buy a base to go home to in the future. They were contemplating a cottage they thought might be a possible choice, when the children disappeared, returning with a notice, which said: 'THIS COTAGE [sic] IS NEVER EVER TO BE SOLD'. Like many other parents, they get seized by guilt at such memories.

Other children become so acclimatised to travel that they can never settle down to living permanently in one country. Diplomats' children often become diplomats: although he felt distant from his permanent under secretary father, David Gore-Booth joined the family firm. One young woman wrote in the *BDSA Magazine*:

I don't belong and therefore need to move all the time. [However] the advantages are quite plain: discovery, knowledge, widening of scope and ideas and the satisfaction it brings. Insecurity and non-closeness to parents is the price. But very few have everything in life, and I wouldn't have missed the experience.

'The worst thing', wrote another,

is boarding a plane for England, especially as one grows older and appreciates parents' support more. If one of us started crying (I travelled with my two sisters) the other two would have difficulty in refraining from doing so. We never upset our parents by crying in their presence, we waited until we were out of sight.

A seven-year-old boy in Tokyo had the clearest view.

I think it is not necessary for Mum to go out all the time! I don't like babysitters. There shouldn't be so many parties in a year or even a week. I like it when Daddy takes me on the Bullet train.

COMPOUND LIVING

The embassy compound is a small village which a few nosy neighbours can make threatening and claustrophobic. The junior staff, particularly the young single women, are conscious that to arrive home at 1 am is to invite a question in the morning as to where you have been. Idle gossip invents romances where none exist and frightens off some that might otherwise have been possible. In the average compound the standardised flats have thin walls and you can't reach your front door from the lift without a high possibility of running into a neighbour.

There are a few nosy gossiping women in every compound, but they rarely number more than a few and they tend to be women who, back home, would have their time occupied with running their houses, looking after their children, and perhaps doing a part-time job of a not particularly taxing kind. To come abroad, with your children at boarding school, servants available at a pittance, no work available because the local authorities ban foreigners from working and there are no more jobs left in the embassy, induces laziness in some people, particularly those whose husbands are not in representational grades and who therefore have to do no more than social entertaining. Artistic wives in those circumstances produce their watercolours, their embroidery, their pottery and their sculpture; they study local art forms, and adapt their skills to it. The public spirited – those bred to the concept of *noblesse oblige* – will hurl themselves into charitable works. Others seize the opportunity to travel as widely as possible. But there will often be some ordinary women, nervous of foreigners, and without ambition, artistic skills or intellectual interests, who simply have nothing to do, so they while away their time in mindless gossip and the deepening of the sun-tan.

There are positive aspects to the compounds. In some countries they are vital to the well-being of the staff, particularly the youngsters in their first postings. A twenty-one-year-old registry clerk posted to Delhi, however much he enjoys dipping his toe into the exotic East, will be relieved that he is doing this from a secure vantage-point. For the young singles, a bolt hole, pre-furnished and maintained by the embassy staff, a servant passed on by your predecessor, a club where you can play darts and meet people your own age, and even some comforting grown-ups around, is normally a tremendous plus, and worth the sacrifice of a measure of adventure and privacy.

For more senior staff it can be a frightful constriction on freedom. Even twenty-five-year-old second secretaries take apartments outside the compound if they are permitted to do so. But in some countries, for security or financial reasons, compound living is compulsory.

For senior staff one of the difficulties is that the compound house goes with the post, not with the needs of the individual, so a Grade 4 with no children occupies a house with four bedrooms, because Grades 4 are assumed to have three children, while a Grade 6 with four children occupies a house with half that space. They cannot swap because the Grade 4 cannot give away the right of his or her successor to a spacious establishment.

On some compounds single or divorced staff, who would like to live outside in small apartments, rattle about in over-large accommodation which they can never fill up with enough possessions to call home, while UK visitors click their tongues at the waste of space and the profligacy of the Foreign Office. It is an intractable problem: so the compounds, with their Number One house, Number Two house, Number Three house, Number Four house, Number Five house, like all other diplomatic compounds, continue to reflect status rather than need and propriety rather than convenience.

The ethos of the Foreign Office led to the assumption that children would go to boarding school from an early age, and there are substantial allowances towards boarding school fees. This, some disaffected members of the Office have bitterly observed, serves to bind staff to the Service. It is only those who could command large salaries outside who can, with equanimity, consider taking on the full fees, so a parent who wants to leave, knows that to do so will mean removing his children from the only stable environment they have known. The system was loaded against those wanting their children to be become day pupils – even in their boarding school – while the family is based in the UK. The system has now changed and there are allowances for day-school fees.

Until recently boarding school was the norm. Most senior diplomats had themselves been sent away from home and regarded it as a perfectly normal way of dealing with children. Young parents today often see it differently and many foreign wives are absolutely appalled at the very notion.

Conditions have improved since the time when parents who were expensively far away from the UK, said goodbye to their children in September knowing that it would be impossible to see them before July. It caused tremendous rifts in families. I have come across grown-up children who went through their childhood with a sense of betrayal and met their parents as virtual strangers every year. Even now, with three return tickets per annum (usually on an APEX fare basis) and two tickets for over eighteens still undergoing full-time education, much hand-wringing goes on. Where, fret the parents, can their children be sent for the ten days of half-term? If they stay at the school it underlines their isolation. Yet only close relatives or friends are likely to welcome such a responsibility, and of course diplomats, because of the transient nature of their lives, tend not to have close friendships.

The difficulties for children are compounded by the exceptionally long hours so many diplomats work. Many of them refer to their wives as running single-parent families. Men with little understanding of what constitutes a normal family life have made the rules for the Diplomatic Service, and men whose only criteria were financial determined the allowances. The fight to get a decent deal for families has been led by the BDSA. 'God bless the BDSA,' observed one frustrated, overworked and exploited male Grade 10. 'They are the only ones with the balls to stand up to the Office.'

Left to the serving diplomats there would have been few improvements in conditions; chaps have more important things to address than family values. So it has been a fascinating aspect of Foreign Office life that ambitious men, who never challenge those at the top of the pyramid up which they are climbing, have wives who politely but bluntly – in person and in writing – criticise heartlessness and stupidity where they find it, spell out problems and demand some compensation for their contribution to the Office's work. Most important of all, the BDSA has brought the wives closer together and has encouraged them to be frank about the realities of life 'as a piece of accompanying baggage'.

Pets also qualify as 'accompanying baggage'. 'Of course it might sound silly' said a man whose job had just been abolished by the Foreign Office Inspectorate, 'but what my wife and I are most upset about is the cat.' For the cat in question was fourteen years old and instead of being likely to die peacefully during what was supposed to be a four-year period abroad, it would now have to be put down or go into quarantine for six months.

The British diplomat is doubly penalised. Not only is a love of animals built into his culture, but he has to pay the price for savage quarantine restrictions. Every day a British diplomatic family is agonising somewhere over decisions about animals. Do you refuse your children the normal childhood experience of a pet in order to preserve them from inevitable heartache? And if you decide for a pet, how do you cope with the expense? The cost of transporting an animal across the world and then keeping it in quarantine for six months can run into thousands of pounds.

Jane Ewart-Biggs's memoirs give a classic account of the difficulties that beset a Foreign Office dog. Having successfully coped with different climates, peoples, foods and even with being kidnapped, Konrad, their cocker spaniel, was then faced with quarantine. She decided to visit regularly in order to retain Konrad's affections.

The circumstances of these weekly visits were rather bizarre, and only to be encountered in Britain. On the arrival of the owner, the kennel maid went to fetch the dog from his personal kennel and put him in an exercise pen measuring about six yards by four. . . . The owner was then ushered into the pen, given a chair to sit on and unceremoniously locked in. This was to prevent a demented owner making a dash for it with his dog. To begin with, feeling foolish, I used to stay only for about fifteen minutes, ample time for a quick word, a bit of brushing and combing and presentation of chocolate drops. However, the kennel maid, entirely concerned for Konrad's wellbeing, said that these short visits upset Konrad, who would then bellow for hours after my departure and upset all the other inmates. I must stay a minimum of half an hour, she said. It was important not to reflect too closely on the sight one presented on these visits; for, after all, most of us want to keep

RIGHT Kevin Fuller with his son leaving the embassy compound in Bangkok.

what reputation we can for a semblance of sanity. The sight of a seemingly conventional human being sitting under lock and key talking to his or her pet – and on a rainy day doing it all under an umbrella – was surely beyond the limits of credibility. I was never sure whether the fact that the same charade was going on in the neighbouring pen made it better or worse.

I even came across a family who chose the quarantine kennels first and then bought a house nearby.

Quarantine restrictions also operate on some UK territories abroad. I saw a senior diplomat, a glittering star at the top of the tree, who was unfazed by danger or political crisis, burying his head in his hands because he had to respond negatively to a letter from an eight-year old, begging him to permit her rabbit into the embassy compound in this rabies-ridden country. The child and her mother daily visited the rabbit in its lodgings down the road.

Families with children have particular problems, but many single people cannot bear to be without an animal in their lives. Maeve Fort is driven through Beirut in her armoured Range Rover accompanied by Chloe, a long-haired white terrier who had proved irresistible when spotted in a shop window in South Africa and whose feisty personality enslaves the bodyguards. In Tokyo the political counsellor's labrador is looked after during the day by the ambassador's wife.

Animals abounded almost everywhere I went. The ambassador in Damascus was plagued by – but resigned to – an unattractive cat which had moved into his residence, and which sported a rasping purr that was so loud sometimes as to distract people from conversation. In Tel Aviv, since the ambassador's house was being fumigated, he had no option but to bring his enormous sociable dog to his morning meeting. The dog gambolled happily around the room throughout, sniffing all the participants.

In Delhi, Sir Nicholas Fenn, like many other diplomats, has inherited a dog from his predecessor, for quite frequently animals become attached to residences and posts rather than to people. Scud the budgie, for instance, lives in the registry in the office of the UK permanent representative to the European Community. A young second secretary in Cyprus, who had not wanted an animal, had proved too soft-hearted to leave a small kitten in the road beside its dead mother; he shrugged and said his successor 'will just have to lump it.' Janet Douglas's cat Dominic lived with her for almost four years in Ankara and now lives with her successor.

Even back in London there are tales of animals. In the days when the Foreign Office building sported an army of self-confident and extrovert mice on the third floor, the housekeeper had a cat to keep them in their place.

So animals are not just deliberately acquired, they are adopted, they are inherited, or they impose themselves. It is another aspect of the British that continues to baffle foreigners.

The key campfollowers, however, are the wives. Although some have become deeply resentful, and have thankfully divorced their husbands and the Foreign Office, or feel very bitter about neglect and exploitation, there are many – particularly among those whose

Delivering a pizza at the embassy compound in Bangkok.

husbands have done well – who would hate the image of their lives to be negative. The woman who had put in 1000 hours a year cooking for Britain in Ulan Bator wrote at the end of her substantial complaint about idiotic regulations:

Finally, I would like to take up something that one wife wrote some time ago: 'I owe the Foreign Office nothing.' I imagine that we all feel like that at times – at the end of a long stint in the kitchen or after a particularly tedious East European reception, for example. But against the loss of so much of my children's youth (if that *can* be weighed) and of my career, against the work, the sudden and inconvenient moves, the occasional boredom and the invasion of my privacy, I must, in all honesty, set the following things (which are only the first to occur to me): ten days all together at Angkor Wat; my first sight of the East of Colombo; four years of sailing and spear fishing in the Gulf of Thailand; an amateur production of *Twelfth Night* in Bangkok; a long leave in Italy and Greece;

trips from here through the Gobi to Peking to the Wall, the Ming Tombs and the Forbidden City; our return from leave to Ulan Bator via Samarkhand, Bokhara, Tashkent and Alma Ata; the Armoury and Pushkin museums in Moscow; three years of Vienna with its Breughels and music and surrounding country, not to mention trips to and from home via Munich, Brussels and Bruges; over three years in Berlin, which I remember in the flowering hills of Mongolia; [and], above all, the great network of friends from Ulan Bator whose visits will be, we hope, one of the delights of Brussels when we go there in September (the ambience and cuisine of Brussels will clearly figure in my later lists). I do not know whether the Office owes me more than I owe it, but I suspect that the account just about balances.

There will be no revolution, but the process of gradual reform advances remorselessly and there are few men or women at the top of the Foreign Office who are not now sympathetic to the needs of spouses. What will happen in the future will reflect changes in society and in women's expectations. Now that the principle has been accepted that spouses are free to lead their own lives, most of them would be happy to be voluntarily supportive. Few spouses I have met object to playing a positive role: it is the feeling of being exploited mercilessly and without recognition that causes most resentment. A modest amount of money would make a considerable difference. If the terror of penury in old age could be removed through decent pension arrangements for non-working spouses, if more grants were available for training for portable careers, for transporting children, for visiting aged parents and for keeping in touch with the home-base by telephone, and if there were enough diplomats to do the jobs that have to be done without working impossible hours, some of the strains would be lessened. The Foreign Office has moved a long way to recognise spouses's changing expectations. But the Treasury controls the money, so financial concessions will be too few and usually too late.

· 14 ·
CUTTING IT

Cheeseparing

Bureaucracies are always subject to idiotic and petty rules about expenditure. When a bureaucracy controls members of its staff living abroad and doing a great deal of entertaining, the desire to ensure that there is no misuse of public funds, coupled with the great British preoccupation with fairness, can lead to a miasma of financial regulations, the ludicrousness of which was neatly encapsulated by this announcement from the chief clerk in his Newsletter in 1985: 'The mythical eight-year old child – "Horace" – will go, and staff will be paid for the children that they really have.'

When living abroad, in addition to free accommodation and utilities, diplomats are given various allowances of great complexity which usually leave them substantially better off than when at home. Most diplomats rely on periods overseas to pay off their debts and save enough to be able to afford to survive London on low salaries. It has been a great blow to both fast streamers and Grade 10s that latterly they have been required to spend much more time in London than had been predicted when they joined. Fixed 'kitting-out' allowances, which include 'transfer grants, outfit allowances and climatic clothing additions' are made available when an officer is posted. Then they undergo what is darkly described as 'The COLA Process', in which fact and fiction merge in a frequently highly comic attempt to crack the fiendishly difficult problem of how to measure accurately constantly-changing worldwide standards of living.

COLA, the 'Cost of Living Addition', is intended to ensure that officers can live at overseas posts at the same standard of living as they could expect at home. The standard comparison used is 'Bromley Man', a mythical beast who is thought to represent an average man in an average household in an average place. There is a shopping basket of goods which the Bromleys are thought to purchase; these goods are priced abroad and the cost of living allowance is adjusted appropriately. 'It's supposed to be an average shopping basket at your average Sainsbury's or Tesco's in Bromley,' said David Walters, the vice consul in Atlanta, as he hunted round the shelves of his local supermarket for Pledge furniture polish. 'Everything's based on averages nowadays, the average Civil

Servant's average shopping basket. We're not filling our shopping baskets with pâté de foie gras or champagne, just general everyday household things [that] the man in Bromley [needs].' Bottled water, for instance, can be put in as an addition to COLA only if, after boiling and filtering the available water, it is certified as undrinkable. 'The tap water in Washington isn't going to poison anybody,' said Nick Browne, the press counsellor in Washington, defending his expenditure on bottled water. 'It's just that the people we live among don't drink it.' But it is not enough that tapwater tastes unpleasant: bottled water was disallowed.

The COLA process involves, among other elements, a monthly update from the management officer at each post reporting changes in the prices of specific items from lavatory cleaner to Bird's Instant Whip, which the Bromleys are thought still to wish to eat in Bangkok or Minsk. Throw in a system of costing 'using, as appropriate, local currency, fixed sterling and optional sterling elements' and it becomes really challenging. The regulations are reassuring: 'COLA will change only if, as a result of the COLR [Cost of Living Return] – and any changes in the standard sterling elements or salary contribution – the new total budget provision (TBP) exceeds the existing TBP by plus/minus 5 per cent.'

Then there are allowances like the IRS (Indirect Representational Supplement), AIRS (Accountable Indirect Representational Supplement), RA (Representational Addition, which includes a provision for 'representational' flowers, or, where local flowers 'are prohibitively expensive, the cost of good quality artificial arrangements may be allowed') and many many more.

Most interesting to an outsider is the DPA (Difficult Post Allowance), not to speak of the SDPA (Supplement to Difficult Post Allowance). The literature on the subject is admirably unemotional.

DPA is paid to any officer who serves on Diplomatic Service terms, at posts where conditions are classified as 'difficult', (commonly known as hardship posts). A DPA review committee meets annually to agree the Posts which qualify for DPA. The committee takes account of comment by Posts, DS [diplomatic staff] and security inspectors and the Medical and Welfare Unit. Posts not receiving DPA who wish to be considered by the committee must complete the living conditions questionnaire at post.

Then comes

Supplement to Difficult Post Allowances (SDPA I and II)

SDPA I [£1778] is paid at a few exceptionally difficult and dangerous Posts (Beirut, Bogota, Guatemala City, Khartoum, Lima, Luanda [Angola], Port Moresby [Papua New Guinea].
SDPA II [£889] is paid at Posts which suffer from extremes of squalor and deprivation (Bombay, Calcutta, Freetown, Georgetown, Hanoi, Ho Chi Minh, Kampala, Maputo, Ulan Bator).

It is heartening for the taxpayer to know that the Treasury caps DPA; so only 100 posts qualify. If a new post qualifies, another post has to drop out – even if conditions there have not improved. For single people, the four categories of payment extend from £370 to

A Pox on Accountants

This despatch from the Duke of Wellington pithily sums up how British ambassadors feel these days about the extent to which they have to justify everything they do.

MESSAGE FROM THE DUKE OF WELLINGTON to the British Foreign Office in London (written from Central Spain, August 1812)

Gentlemen,

Whilst marching from Portugal to a position which commands the approach to Madrid and the French forces, my officers have been diligently complying with your requests which have been sent by HM ship from London to Lisbon and thence by dispatch rider to our headquarters.

We have enumerated our saddles, bridles, tents and tent poles, and all manner of sundry items for which His Majesty's Government holds me accountable. I have dispatched reports on the character, wits and spleen of every officer. Each item and every farthing has been accounted for, with two regrettable exceptions for which I beg your indulgence.

Unfortunately the sum of one shilling and ninepence remains unaccounted for in one infantry battalion's petty cash and there has been a hideous confusion as to the number of jars of raspberry jam issued to one cavalry regiment during a sandstorm in western Spain. This reprehensible carelessness may be related to the pressure of circumstance, since we are at war with France, a fact which may come as a bit of a surprise to you gentlemen in Whitehall.

This brings me to my present purpose, which is to request elucidation of my instructions from His Majesty's Government so that I may better understand why I am dragging an army over these barren plains. I construe that perforce it must be one of two alternative duties as given below. I shall pursue either one with the best of my ability but I cannot do both:

1. To train an army of uniformed British clerks in Spain for the benefit of the accountants and copyboys in London or, perchance,
2. To see to it that the forces of Napoleon are driven out of Spain.

Your most obedient servant
Wellington

£1185. Tirana, Albania, for instance, earns a DPA of £3556 for a married couple. I met the first incumbent at that post, John Duncan, who had lived with his wife in an appalling hotel where water was only available between three o'clock and six o'clock in the morning; he kept stores of water in old Evian bottles so that he could wash and shave before going out about his representational business.

The form assessing levels of hardship is a monument to the adaptability of a bureaucracy. Marks from zero to 100 in total are given by the post and then checked by inspectors according to how bad things are on the following fronts compared with

Bromley: Diseases; Medical Facilities; Sanitation; Housing; Absence of Normal Amenities; Restriction on Movement; Isolation; Possibilities for local leave; Security; Climate; Tour length.

Examples of the assessment given to various situations include:

	SCORE
Serious problems from flies, cockroaches, rats, etc.	0.6
Virtual absence of cultural facilities (cinema, theatre, libraries, radio, TV, concerts, etc.)	1
Movement seriously restricted for females due to pestering, which sometimes verges on molestation	1.3
Complete breakdown of law and order with the constant need to take utmost precautions against personal violence	10
Serious threat from HIS (Hostile Intelligence Services) in the form of compromise attempts, recruitment attempts and deliberate harassment	4
The British Diplomatic or Consular Mission has been invaded, attacked or burnt down in the last twelve months or is virtually a battlefield	10

And all that together amounts to only 26.9 out of a possible 100.

Maybe there should be a special bonus – other than his MBE – for David Hawkes, who had a series of such posts: his first child's first word (in Moscow) was a mangled attempt at 'cockroach'; his second child's was 'raeli', used when he gazed at the skies over Beirut and tried to spot the planes that carried the bombs. Number one child, then aged eight, would often arrive home within an hour of setting off for school because people in one village or another had stopped the car: he would wearily identify the culprit of the day: 'Moslem', 'Druze', 'Hizbollah' or 'Maronite'.

The Hawkes family had bullets coming into their house in Beirut, were held hostage for one afternoon and evening by PLO guerrillas searching for spying equipment and he himself has been stripped at an airport by secret police, and robbed twice. It is only fair to add that he loved the cameraderie of hardship posts and never wanted to live anywhere civilised. Perhaps it is the children who should be given the bonus.

No diplomat can refuse to be posted abroad except in exceptional circumstances; his conditions of service require him to be mobile and he receives, when overseas, a Diplomatic Service Allowance (7.6 per cent of the mean salary of the officer's grade) to compensate for the obligation to move around the world as required. Until recently Personnel took the decisions and it was felt to be bad for one's career to jib at being sent to even the most godforsaken places, but nowadays people bid for particular jobs, so they can usually avoid places they actually detest. There is still an element of compulsion. It would not do to be seen to be unreasonably picky.

The fact that Foreign Office people are prepared to take rough postings is one of the strong arguments for maintaining a large group of career diplomats rather than relying on outsiders brought in on short-term contracts. Fortunately for the peace of mind of the

Foreign Office, people's tastes differ. I met one young woman in the plum posting of Brussels who thought the work there very boring and suitable only for ambitious males. She longed to be back in Africa. Single people, like Maeve Fort, are happy to volunteer for dangerous postings that most families would prefer to avoid. And a posting to the UN is welcomed by the ambitious and feared by the family-minded. David Hawkes graphically described the joy people in hardship posts found in overcoming problems together. He remembers, in Baghdad during the Iran/Iraq war, the huge excitement occasioned by the arrival of a colleague with a box of matches which he had miraculously found in the souk [market], thus enabling both of them to have candlelight. Another example was when he followed a meat lorry until it stopped to unload and he was able to buy half a frozen lamb carcass. Having chopped it up and shared it out, the Embassy had a celebratory party. Still, there are not many people queueing up to serve in Kinshasha in Zaire, where the sewage system has collapsed, water and electricity supplies are unreliable, famine is looming, leprosy and sleeping sickness are on the increase, riots and death squads abound and ethnic hatred is raging. Another £1000 or so a year when the DPA Committee catches up with current events is not a great sweetener.

Allowances are reviewed and recalculated every time the inspectors come to call. These come from both Treasury and the Diplomatic Service and they arrive at posts every three to five years. The Treasury concern themselves only with the material aspects of life; the Diplomatic Service inspectors are in effect also itinerant management consultants, though, being recruited from within the Service themselves, they are amateurs. No other Civil Service department has such an institution. Its stated purpose is 'to ensure that both its [the Foreign Office's] structure and its resources are matched to its needs and priorities. The inspectors scrutinise every aspect of the post's operation and produce reports full of recommendations like: 'Regrade LEIII Visa Clerk/Receptionist post at LEIV', 'Delete DS7M Second Secretary (Management) post', 'Fax modem interface with UNIX to be provided if possible' and 'Urgently consider how to provide an acceptable room for Embassy drivers.'

The inspectorate is staffed by volunteers from the middle ranks who are attracted to the job mainly because it gives extraordinary variety and a unique overview of how the Foreign Office operates. They all know something of what the job entails, for since all posts are visited at least every five years, all have, in the course of their careers, almost certainly been inspected themselves two or three times, and they are given training. Being an inspector counts as a home posting and after two or three years they return to normal

OVERLEAF Members of the Overseas Inspectorate led by the chief inspector Richard Muir on their way to a meeting with the permanent under secretary at the end of the USA inspection tour. From left to right: Muir, Kit Burdess, Fraser Wilson, Peter Harborne, Marian Binnington, Mike Tobin and David Pearey.
PAGES 234–5 Sir David Gillmore discusses the cuts suggested by the inspectors after the US inspection tour.

diplomatic life. They undertake inspection tours of two to three months at a time, three times a year, so they are apart from their families more often during this tour of duty than at any other stage of their career.

A senior inspector, Peter Harborne, explained the principles of the job:

What we're trying to do is to ensure that there's a match between the tasks that are laid upon the Mission and the resources at their disposal. If there's a mismatch, we try and find out why and offer solutions to bring the two together. There's, in a sense, nothing special about it. This is a process that's been going on for thirty or forty years; it's fundamentally a way of getting money out of the Treasury. Because we are first and foremost a people organisation – an organisation about which a lot of other people have misconceptions, we need to be able to demonstrate to the Treasury and to Parliament and to public opinion that we actually do a job of work and that we take seriously the business of getting value for money.

Inspectors do save the Foreign Office about four times their annual cost, and they have a tough job, needing both physical and moral courage. While David Pearey and Mike Tobin, for instance, were inspecting the New York British Consulate-General in late 1992, Mike Tobin gave an example of the outside pressures of the job during the tour they had both just completed in West Africa.

We progressed from Ghana to Cameroon to Zaire where the local political pressures were mounting and getting greater in each country as we left or as we arrived. And David very nicely put in the report of one of the countries we were leaving: 'The tension is mounting as we prepare to leave.' But of course it was mounting there but it was worse in the next place, and in fact we were supposed to go on to Angola and we had to abort that because of the civil war that broke out again.

Moral courage is called for when it is necessary to explain – often to senior colleagues – that their operation could be better run, that perhaps they are doing work more suitable to a grade beneath them or that the work which they have been doing devotedly is not particularly valuable compared to other priorities of the Foreign Office. Staff often fear the inspectors. They are referred to as 'the Spanish Inquisition' or 'the ogres' and in advance of an inspection, staff put a great deal of thought into how to defend their posts.

For busy people the amount of time inspectors take up is often irritating. When I visited Saudi Arabia, for example, they were fed up after an inspection that had lasted five weeks, greatly disrupted the work of the Mission and led to – among others – a prolonged dispute over David Gore-Booth's Rolls Royce which they wished to jettison for a saving of £1500 per annum. Saudi Arabia, like other Gulf States, is a lucrative market for Rolls Royces. 'Can it possibly be true,' asked a young American diplomat when I was there, 'that the Brits are getting rid of the Rolls? They must be crazy.'

RIGHT Sir Robin Renwick, British ambassador in Washington, entering one of the embassy's Jaguars en route to a meeting on Capitol Hill.

(Many ambassadors used to drive round proudly in Rolls Royces, which were instantly recognisable and famous throughout the world for style and durability – a symbol of Britain that in most countries could only do it good. But ministers became jealous because they were Roller-less and objected to officials having what they did not. Press and parliamentarians complained about extravagance and the beleaguered Foreign Office caved in. Only the four senior posts – Bonn, Paris, Tokyo and Washington – are now authorised to run Rolls Royces.)

The theory behind inspections is that there should be no clashes, that with diplomacy and common sense on all sides a deal will be struck without causing pain to anyone. It is the job of inspectors to explain to people that it is their posts, not their performance, that is under scrutiny, but many people do not see it that way and feel humiliated by a decision to abolish the post.

At times when the Foreign Office is not under financial pressure, inspectors can go forth with an open mind and recommend cuts or additions as circumstances dictate. When times are hard – which is usually – although they are slow to admit it, they are sent out to posts as executioners, briefed by the head of administration, the chief clerk, who is often in league with an ambassador who cannot bring himself to cut his own colleagues' posts: butchering does not come easily to the Foreign Office. 'Cut as much as you can and come out alive,' one inspector was instructed by a chief clerk. As Peter Harborne explained, the US inspection in 1992 was particularly important,

because of the tremendous pressure on public resources [which] bears as heavily on the Foreign Office as everybody else. The difference with the Foreign Office is that in Health or Transport, for example, you can stop and postpone huge capital expenditure programmes. We can't do that: the vast majority of our running costs are the costs of the people in the Embassies overseas. So for that reason the premium is on ensuring that we get as many miles to the gallon as we possibly can.

'I'm very familiar', said David Wright, the consul general in Atlanta,

with the sort of pressures that the Treasury are putting on our resources and the ways in which we are manoeuvring to overcome those pressures . . . essentially what's happened is that the Treasury have frozen our base line, the amount of money we receive every year. . . . despite the fact that we are having to open up a large number of posts in all these newly independent states in Eastern Europe. Now we can only man those posts by finding savings elsewhere, so it's not surprising that these inspectors have come out to America to look for one or two savings which can be redeployed somewhere else.

The Treasury's three-year plan was such, he observed, that it was difficult 'to see how we're going to achieve it without some reduction in coverage or diminishing of standards.' And Sir Robin Renwick, ambassador to Washington, assuring the inspectors that he and

RIGHT Jonathan Powell, a first secretary at the British Embassy in Washington,
leaving the Capitol building after a meeting.

his staff would cooperate fully in making sensible economies, sounded a note of warning about any further reductions in the number of consulates in the States, since

we are now very close to the bone. We have to fight our battles very hard with the Americans, [with the] Administration and with Congress on a whole [range] of issues, and particularly on economic and trade issues. And we do need to keep both the Consulates and the Embassy in shape to be able to fight those battles . . . that implies looking very carefully at ways of making savings that do not affect the 'teeth' functions of these operations.

The cuts went deep. Across America 18 per cent of UK-based, ie British, posts were abolished. So it was a sign that matters were desperate at the UK Mission to the UN that the inspectors recommended staff increases which were granted. This was a response to a situation where several chancery staff were working from 8.00 am to midnight every day. 'I've just returned from a few days sick with an ulcer,' said Bob Peirce, a first secretary at UKMIS, 'and my doctor tells me I'm exhausted, so I am to some extent a living example of the way that we try to have an active foreign policy but are not prepared to pay for the resources we need to implement it.'

Overseas, diplomats are required by their conditions of service to work twenty-four hours a day, seven days a week, if required to do so. That is acceptable at times of crisis, but prolonged overwork can be devastating. In many of the posts I visited I found very tired people. In one, the person delegated to look after me in the evening suddenly burst into tears of exhaustion. Resources have been cut without eliminating functions. The 'mustn't-whinge' culture has led to acceptance that what has to be done has to be done, even if it destroys family life. By now, the system gives an impression of having reached breaking-point. The elastic is ready to snap.

· 15 ·

THE END

Ministers Must Decide

The rationalisation of the Civil Service, instigated by Mrs Thatcher, has brought about much change in Whitehall that was valuable. It is not only leaner and more efficient, but as *The Times* pointed out in October 1993, 'Britain is now a global leader in government reform.' The Citizen's Charter made the public service accountable to its customers; under the 'Next Steps' programme over 100 government agencies were becoming semi-independent executive bodies; and market testing was enabling the private sector to take over public services.

Yet *The Times*, like other newspapers and commentators, was slightly uneasy about what might be lost. 'It is unclear how contracting out will affect the constitutional relationship between ministers, officials and the public, and how the traditional civil service ideals of integrity and impartiality will be affected as government becomes more pluralist, decentralised and entrepreneurial.' It is right to be uneasy. The United Kingdom will be much diminished if it loses one of its great assets: an honest and patriotic public service.

The Foreign Office is particularly vulnerable to the negative side of reforms. It is impossible to apply modern management techniques to many of its functions. Much time is wasted in fulfilling government requirements to set quantifiable objectives in completely inappropriate fields. It is right that officials should be clear about their priorities, but it is ridiculous that, for instance, a Foreign Office commercial officer in a Far Eastern country is told his objective is to increase British exports to that country by 5 per cent. More seriously, notions of contracting out work or putting significant numbers of people on short-term contracts threatens to undermine the Service's whole ethos. A foreign service is not an organisation suited to cut-and-thrust competition and rampant entrepreneurialism. Any developments that are liable to encourage venality in diplomats are potentially disastrous for British interests. And the institution's effectiveness is already seriously threatened by merciless financial cuts.

The Foreign Office is bureaucratic, hierarchical, organisationally less than nimble, unduly reverent to its ministers and dominated by old male (as opposed to macho) values.

All institutions are flawed but this one is better than most. As an ex-civil servant I had a vague Whitehall prejudice against the Foreign Office which had in recent years been tempered by some occasional contact with a few impressive diplomats. After spending a great deal of time with them, I must admit to a tremendous admiration and liking for the Foreign Office and most of its people. Their dedication to their jobs, their submerging of their egos in the interests of the team work, their discretion, extreme competence, their loyalty and their simple and rather touching desire to serve their country makes them a group which, as a British taxpayer, I believe should be treasured but which instead is under serious threat.

'The Foreign Office', said Tristan Garel-Jones in one of his interviews for the BBC series,

which . . . is about the best fighting machine of its kind that any country has – is hanging on by its fingernails. And I think one of the big decisions that this government's got to take is whether Britain is going to continue to sit at the top table. At the moment, here we are. We're a tiny little island, fifty or something million people. We're on the Security Council of the United Nations. We're members of the G7. We're a leading country in the Commonwealth, a leading country in the European Community. There is hardly a major international organisation which Britain doesn't appear to influence way beyond its size, way beyond its apparent importance. I think it's demonstrably the case that that is good for Britain, not just good in terms of producing jobs and investment and exports for Britain but good in terms of exercising an influence for the sort of values that British people generally believe in. Now if you want to go on sitting at the top table it carries a price, and I think it's going to be not far down the line when a British government is going to have to decide whether we have the confidence in ourselves as a nation, I mean [in] our ability to play an influential role in the world and whether we're prepared to pay for it.

We do not pay much for it. In a speech in May 1993, in an attempt to win some public support for the Foreign Office, Douglas Hurd put the figures in context.

We estimate we spent about £60 billion on Social Security last financial year, £30 billion on Health, £24 billion on Defence, and £1.36 billion on the diplomatic part of our overseas effort as run by the Foreign Office.

And the actual amount spent on diplomacy itself is only 61 per cent of the total:

Per cent	£	
20	270m	Peacekeeping and subscriptions to international organisations, eg, the UN and the OECD
12	166m	BBC World Service
7	92m	The British Council
61	832m	Running diplomatic posts overseas and offices in the UK
100	**1.36bn**	

In common with all the other Whitehall Departments, the Foreign Office has rightly been expected to make economies, but there comes a time when no further economies can be effected without causing severe damage. The Treasury has the simple and destructive approach to public expenditure known as salami-slicing: every Department must takes its punishment like a man. In the 1970s the cuts were tolerable. The difficulty today is that the Foreign Office is being cut at a time when the demands on it have risen to unprecedented levels. Yet it is a very small spender in Whitehall terms: its managers refer bitterly to its running costs as being equivalent to the small change in the pocket of the Department of Social Security. At the end of 1992, discussing budget strategy with senior colleagues, Sir David Gillmore drove home the point that the cavalry were unlikely to be coming over the hill.

We can't plan on the assumption that we might get further funding in future years. The fact of the matter is we're not going to get increased funding in future years. [We must seek] to establish . . . the consequences of a shortfall of something like £10 million in year three and make [them] clear to ministers.

There is no reduction in the demand from British business for an effective commercial service or from the British public for consular support. Cuts made in contributions to international organisations are already damaging the UK's influence and image internationally. (A prime example was the negative publicity accorded the Foreign Office's withdrawal of the £2.4 million grant in Autumn 1993 on which the highly-esteemed, and symbolically important, Commonwealth Institute in London survived.) Further cuts would hurt even more. 'If ministers are prepared to accept,' Gillmore told his colleagues,

that when they go to one of your posts, there is only one UK-based person there, and all the rest is done by locals; that the residence is not a very grand place and . . . that the offices are small – fine. . . . But at the moment I think the expectation of ministers is that there will be instant communications with London . . . [and] a sufficiently strong team to give them good support and plug them in immediately to whomever they need to be plugged into.

The Foreign Office is getting tougher. Recent options proposed to ministers include the abolition of one ministerial post and sending the unfortunate foreign secretary around the world on commercial flights instead of in the Flying Foreign Office. But such savings would still be tiny.

Every time defence cuts are mooted, there is a tremendous outcry. No one ever gets excited when the Foreign Office is squeezed. The public have no idea what diplomats do, but they can identify with 'our brave lads'; they can bleed for the families of the squaddie killed in Northern Ireland; they can revel in the Falklands operation; they can burst with pride at the sight of brave Brits in blue berets bringing humanitarian relief to Bosnia. They have no idea that their diplomatic service is a great national asset envied by almost every country in the world.

What would be sensible would be for the financial implications of the UK's relationship with the outside world to be considered as a whole. A balance has to be struck between expenditure on the armed forces, on weaponry – conventional or nuclear – and on spies and on diplomats. It seems logical that with the collapse of Communism we need fewer spies and fewer nuclear weapons, but perhaps we need more swiftly mobile conventional forces as well as a diplomatic service at peak fighting efficiency. At the simplest level, it should be taken into account that wars occur when diplomacy fails.

Just one day of Desert Storm cost as much as the whole of the UN peacekeeping budget for 1991. The total estimated cost of the Falklands War, which lasted just over two months, is £3 billion, more than double the Foreign Office's 1991–2 budget. 'Peacekeeping is therefore cheaper than war-making', Gillmore told the Foreign Affairs Committee in March 1993.

For example, we made a strenuous effort during our Presidency [of the European Community] to ensure that quarrels between the then Czechoslovakia and Hungary over the Gabcikovo Dam on the Danube did not degrade into outright argument, and that seemed to me a thoroughly worthwhile exercise. We continue, through the Community, to try to bring the two sides to a sensible conclusion. Perhaps small beer, perhaps there was no risk of confrontation, but the fact is that it has cost us, relatively, nothing. To have to send in a force to keep the peace in that area would be much more expensive; a force to fight would be even more expensive.

The Treasury is notorious throughout Whitehall for its narrowness of vision. Its clever people conscientiously do their job of stopping the UK from spending more than it can afford, but in a dismayingly blinkered fashion: it is impossible to interest them in the notion that spending a modest sum today may save a vast expenditure tomorrow. In the present frighteningly unpredictable world, like other responsible countries, we need to marshal our best resources and put them in the front line of preventative diplomacy. In a world where there are huge new business opportunities opening up in the former Soviet Union and in Asia, we need to step up our commercial service. If we can get the newly-opened-up parts of the world speaking British English and admiring the World Service, immense political and financial rewards must follow. Yet crazy short-termism cuts back both on them as well as all the other functions of the Foreign Office.

Our competitors are mystified by this approach. The US hurls money and people at its Embassies all over the world. Our major European partners and rivals are expanding. Already the UK has fewer posts abroad than have France, Germany or Italy (214, 291, 230 and 236 respectively) and the ratio becomes worse by the year. Since the Soviet Union expired, all four countries have opened missions in the Baltic states and in some republics in the former Soviet Union. The average number of staff in each is: France twelve, Germany eight, Italy ten and the UK four. Germany is on its way to open Missions in all fifteen former Soviet republics, France in eleven, but the UK has only eight. That John Everard and his wife should be operating in one room at the back of the fourteen-man German Embassy in Minsk is a stark and humiliating example of how little value is attached by the UK to its British representation abroad. There is nothing wrong with the notion of sharing accommodation and services with friendly nations; what is unseemly is for the UK to do so in the role of poor relation.

More than a hundred diplomatic jobs abroad have been cut in the last few years in addition to the closing of four posts. Improvements in, for instance, communications, have led to staff cuts and considerable savings. The organisation is more innovative than it appears from the outside. 'Things are changing,' said Sir David Gillmore in an interview for the series:

Society changes, people change, customs change, attitudes change and our job changes and we have to be able to change. So I think the greatest challenge to us is actually to change with the times, not to be a stuffy rather died-in-the-wool old organisation against which the tides of history are beating. . . . We should be moving and flexible and changing too.

The ethos of the Foreign Office does not change. The people it recruits and trains have values like integrity, patriotism and a sense of service that can seem rather old-fashioned, and that – allied to their long periods away from home, their inevitably international cast of mind and their distancing diplomatic carapace – makes them rather an alien group in today's Britain. The organisation strives to be flexible, yet its shortage of funds reduces its ability to change swiftly with the times. Thirty years ago the Plowden Committee recommended that staffing levels should have a 10 per cent margin for training, emergencies and so on. As things stand, there is no margin whatsoever. And with the massive and growing need for political diplomacy there is absolutely no possibility of introducing innovations like sending the gifted young to experience consular life. Fixed costs like international subscriptions inexorably increase and the only room for manoeuvre is in staffing levels. The next round of cuts will reduce the machine's efficiency; the ones after that could damage it fundamentally.

'Foreign Policy', observed David Gore-Booth, 'has to be a reflection of what this country thinks of itself and what this country is worth, otherwise you can't sustain it.' Britain has to decide if it wants to capitalise on its considerable historical, political and diplomatic assets. It has been dealt a lucky hand, but the hand has to be played or the cards thrown down. Foreign policy should not be Treasury-driven.

The Foreign Office has tried hard to rationalise its expenditure and eradicate waste and inefficiency. The money the Foreign Office needs to meet its requirements – in Garel-Jones's words –

hardly registers on the Richter scale. . . . Most other departments spend in a week what the Foreign Office spends in a year. It's very good value for money. . . . The values that Britain has sought to defend over the last fifty, sixty, a hundred years are good values, they're right and proper values and it is right and proper that we seek to advance those values throughout the world. So I think there is both an economic and a moral case for Britain continuing to play, as it were, first division football, not be relegated into the second division. But there's [also] a case for . . . dignified retirement into the second division and those who believe in it must put it.

Tristan Garel-Jones resigned as minister of state for foreign affairs in 1993. It is today's ministers who must decide whether they want a first, or a second, division Foreign Office.

APPENDIX

Who's Who and What's What
in the Foreign Office

The role of the modern **Foreign Office** is, quite simply, to promote the interests of the UK abroad. For instance, the British seat on the UN's Security Council is occupied by a member of the Foreign Office; European experts at the Foreign Office advise ministers on the UK's role in the Community and individual Foreign Office experts advise ministers on the UK's global bilateral relations.

The **British Council** is partially funded by the Foreign Office. The **Overseas Development Administration** (ODA) is the aid wing of the Foreign Office.

The modern Foreign Office divides functionally into five main areas:

Political and economic work focuses on long-term objectives within such organisations as the EC, the UN, NATO and the Commonwealth and defence, while pursuing bilateral objectives with major allies.

Commercial work promotes British exports abroad and investment in the UK.

Information work supports political, economic and commercial work and helps promote the UK's standing worldwide.

Consular work provides assistance for British citizens abroad.

Entry clearance work, or visa work, operates immigration controls and is performed by a combination of Foreign Office and Home Office staff.

Ambassadors represent the monarch abroad except in Commonwealth countries which have **high commissioners** who do the same job. **Diplomats** report to the **foreign secretary** who works closely with the **head of the Diplomatic Service,** the **permanent under secretary**.

The ministers

The prime minister appoints a **secretary of state for foreign affairs** (the **foreign secretary**) and as many **ministers of state** as he wishes. The current foreign secretary, Douglas Hurd, has four ministers of state and a parliamentary under secretary of state. The foreign secretary is responsible to Parliament for the work of the Foreign Office. The ministers' work is determined both geographically and functionally so, for instance, the minister for the European Community is also responsible for all internal Foreign Office security issues.

The civil servants

The **permanent under secretary** is head of the Diplomatic Service. He is responsible for running the Foreign Office machine which advises ministers on all aspects of foreign policy, and subsequently implements agreed government policy. The **chief clerk** is the Foreign Office's chief administrator. **Deputy under secretaries of state** and **assistant under secretaries** supervise the individual Foreign Office departments, and advise on foreign policies. The departments are divided both geographically and functionally.

    Private secretaries work directly for ministers in the **Private Office**. They are young high fliers who organise their ministers' lives, attend meetings, take notes, listen in on all official telephone calls and accompany the minister on his travels. Private secretaries do not suggest policies, but they know how their ministers think and are a vital conduit between the Foreign Office and its political masters.

Embassies, High Commissions, Missions and Consulates

The Foreign Office has **Embassies** in foreign countries and **High Commissions** in Commonwealth countries. They are also known as **Missions**. Essentially they do the same job. **Consulates** provide assistance to British subjects overseas and are also responsible for issuing visas and for immigration controls. Depending upon the geographic and/or economic size of a country, consulates will either be located inside an embassy, or on their own premises in a separate part of the country, where the consul general may be expected to devote much of his time to commercial, information and political work.

WHO'S WHO AND WHAT'S WHAT IN THE FOREIGN OFFICE

The table below shows the organisation of a typical large mission.

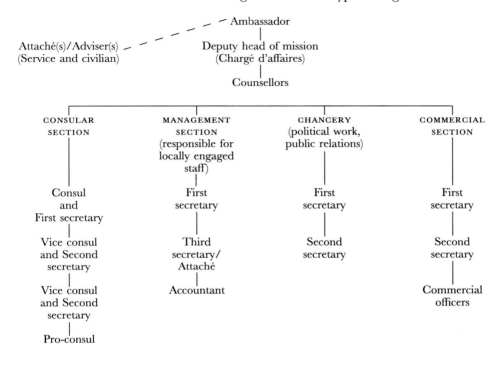

Locally engaged staff work in all sections

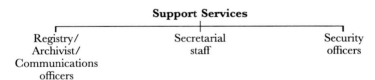

The **deputy head of mission** takes over in the absence of the ambassador or high commissioner. He does not become ambassador, but is known as the **chargé d'affaires**. In some countries where the Foreign Office wishes to have a presence, but not an ambassadorial presence, a chargé d'affaires will be appointed on a permanent basis and will run the mission.

Home-based or UK-based

Home-based Foreign Office employees **never** work overseas. UK-based Foreign Office employees are required by their contracts of employment to be mobile. The UK-based part of the Foreign Office is known as the **Diplomatic Wing**.

Numbers and Streams

The Foreign Office in the UK is staffed by Diplomatic Service personnel, who serve both at home and overseas, and by Home Civil Servants. In January 1994 the Foreign Office employed 6650 staff, some 2500 of whom are employed overseas.

On entering the Foreign Office, employees are **streamed** into either the **fast stream** (which used to be called the **administrative or A stream**), or the **main stream** (which used to be called the **executive or E stream**). The jobs are graded from **Grade 10 (the lowest grade) to Grade 1**, and the **salaries** and **titles** belonging to each grade are listed in the table on page 88.

Men at the Top: the last fifty years

FOREIGN SECRETARIES	DATE OF APPOINTMENT	FOREIGN SECRETARIES	DATE OF APPOINTMENT
Anthony Eden	23 December 1940	Michael Stewart	15 March 1968
Ernest Bevin	28 July 1945	[1]Sir Alec Douglas-Home	20 June 1970
Herbert Morrison	12 March 1951	James Callaghan	5 March 1974
Anthony Eden	27 October 1951	Anthony Crosland	9 April 1976
Selwyn Lloyd	21 December 1955	David Owen	22 February 1977
Lord Home	28 July 1960	Lord Carrington	5 May 1979
R. A. Butler	21 October 1963	Francis Pym	5 April 1982
Patrick Gordon Walker	16 October 1964	Sir Geoffrey Howe	11 June 1983
Michael Stewart	24 January 1965	John Major	25 July 1989
George Brown	12 August 1966	Douglas Hurd	26 October 1989

[1] Lord Home disclaimed his hereditary peerage in 1963 to become Sir Alec Douglas-Home and – briefly – prime minister.

PERMANENT UNDER SECRETARIES	DATE OF APPOINTMENT	PERMANENT UNDER SECRETARIES	DATE OF APPOINTMENT
Sir Alexander Cadogan	1 January 1938	Sir Denis Greenhill	1 February 1969
Sir Orme Sargent	1 February 1946	Sir Thomas Brimelow	8 November 1973
Sir William Strang	1 February 1949	Sir Michael Palliser	22 November 1975
Sir Ivone Kirkpatrick	16 November 1953	Sir Antony Acland	8 April 1982
Sir Frederick Millar	4 February 1957	Sir Patrick Wright	23 June 1986
Sir Harold Caccia	1 January 1962	Sir David Gillmore	28 June 1991
Sir Paul Gore-Booth	10 May 1965		

NOTES ON SOURCES

Unless specified otherwise, quotes from named individuals come either from the books listed in the bibliography or from interviews conducted by Stephen Lambert for the BBC television series. Unattributed quotes are from people I interviewed.

The quotation about George Brown on pages 24–6, 'The reality . . . drove him mad', appears in Peter Paterson's *Tired and Emotional*. The extract on page 26 from Sir Evelyn Shuckburgh's letter to *The Times* is quoted in Lord Gore-Booth's *With Great Truth and Respect*. The quotation by Richard Crossman on page 40, 'the only operation . . . a new patient', appears in Sir Nicholas Henderson's *The Private Office*. The extract by Walter Bagehot on page 86, 'adopted the idea . . . clerk', comes from *The Collected Works of Walter Bagehot* (ed. Norman St John Stevas, 1974).

Quotations from training and other official Foreign Office publications and material are Crown copyright material used by permission.

Jenny Joseph's poem 'Warning' is published in *Selected Poems* by Jenny Joseph, Bloodaxe Books Ltd. (London 1992), © Jenny Joseph 1992.

'England Expects' by Ogden Nash is published in *I Wouldn't Have Missed It: Selected Poems of Ogden Nash*, André Deutsch (London 1983), © Ogden Nash.

'The Diplomatic Platypus' by Patrick Barrington is published in *The Penguin Book of Light Verse* (ed. Gavin Ewart), Penguin Books (London 1981), © United Newspapers.

BIBLIOGRAPHY

I found the following particularly useful:

Sir Douglas Busk, *The Craft of Diplomacy* (Pall Mall Press, London 1967)

Sir James Cable, 'Foreign Policy Making: Planning or Reflex?' in *Diplomacy & Statecraft*, Vol. 3, No. 3 (1992), pp. 357–381

Jules Cambon, *The Diplomatist* (Philip Allan, London 1931)

Marcus Cheke, 'Guidance on foreign usages and ceremony, and other matters, for a Member of His Majesty's Foreign Service on his first appointment to a Post Abroad' (internal Foreign Office document, 1949)

Eric Clark, *Corps Diplomatique* (Allen Lane, London 1973)

Michael Clarke, *British External Policy-Making in the 1990s* (Macmillan, London 1992)

John Dickie, *Inside the Foreign Office* (Chapmans, London 1992)

Lady Ewart-Biggs, *Pay, Pack and Follow* (Weidenfeld & Nicolson, London 1984)

Lord Gore-Booth (ed.), *Satow's Guide to Diplomatic Practice* (Longman, London and New York 1979)

Lord Gore-Booth, *With Great Truth and Respect* (Constable, London 1974)

Sir Nicholas Henderson, *The Private Office* (Weidenfeld & Nicolson, London 1984)

Sir Geoffrey Jackson, *Concorde Diplomacy* (Hamish Hamilton, London 1981)

Simon Jenkins and Anne Sloman, *With Respect, Ambassador* (BBC Books, London 1985)

Alan Judd, *Short of Glory* (Hodder & Stoughton, London 1984)

Grant V. McClanahan, *Diplomatic Immunity* (C. Hurst, London 1989)

Dame Alix Meynell, *Public Servant, Private Woman* (Victor Gollancz, London 1988)

Geoffrey Moorhouse, *The Diplomats: the Foreign Office Today* (Jonathan Cape, London 1977)

Harold Nicolson, *Diplomacy* (Oxford University Press, London 1939)

Harold Nicolson, *The Evolution of the Diplomatic Method* (Constable, London 1954)

Sir Harold Nicolson (ed. Nigel Nicolson), *Diaries and Letters 1939–45 and 1945–62* (Collins, London, 1968)

Sir Anthony Parsons, *They Say the Lion: Britain's Legacy to the Arabs* (Jonathan Cape, London 1986)

Peter Paterson, *Tired and Emotional: The Life of George Brown* (Chatto & Windus, London 1993)

D. C. M. Platt, *The Cinderella Service: British Consuls since 1825* (Longmans, London 1971)

Satow, Sir Ernest, see *Satow's Guide to Diplomatic Practice*, under Gore-Booth, (ed.).

Zara Steiner, *The Times Survey of Foreign Ministries of the World* (Times Books, London 1982)

Charles W. Thayer, *Diplomat* (Michael Joseph, London 1960)

Humphrey Trevelyan, *Diplomatic Channels* (Macmillan, London 1973)

George Walden, *Ethics and Foreign Policy* (Weidenfeld & Nicolson, London 1990)

Adam Watson, *Diplomacy* (Methuen, London 1982)

Martin Wight, *International Theory* (Leicester University Press, London 1991)

INDEX